ONE GUTSY BANK'S STRUGGLE FOR SURVIVAL AND THE MERGER THAT CHANGED BANKING FOREVER

Robert H. Smith
Former Chairman and C.E.O. of Security Pacific Corporation

With Michael K. Crowley

Oakhill Press
Winchester, VA

This publication is designed to provide accurate and authoritative information in regard to the subject matter covered. It is sold with the understanding that the publisher is not engaged in rendering legal, accounting, or other professional service. If legal advice or other expert assistance is required, the services of a competent professional person should be sought. *From a Declaration of Principles jointly adopted by a committee of the American Bar Association and a committee of Publishers.*

10   9   8   7   6   5   4   3   2   1

Library of Congress Cataloging in Publication Data

Smith, Robert H., 1935–
     Dead bank walking: one gutsy bank's struggle for survival and the merger
     that changed banking forever / Robert H. Smith and Michael K. Crowley
          p.   cm.
     Includes index.
     ISBN 1-886939-33-0
     1. Crowley, Michael K., 1960–   . II. Title.
                                                                99-

                                                                          CIP

Dedication

This book and the story it tells are dedicated to the thousands of employees of Security Pacific. These individuals offered consumers and businesses alike, during many years, a level of service and personal attention to individual needs that distinguished our bank from many others. These same employees were also proof that an environment which promotes creative entrepreneurial thinking and individual decision making builds the mind and the spirit of customers and employees as well as the stature and reputation of the organization.

Table of Contents

Part I: Troublebound

Part II: The Merger

Table of Contents

Note to the Reader

This book is a firsthand account of events that took place during my career in banking, and the story relies heavily on my recollection of the times and events, personal notes, date-books, and memoranda, as well as on broadly used and reviewed Security Pacific publications, video- and audio-tapes, annual reports, public filings, and securities analyst reports. The story is also based on independent analysis, archival newspaper articles, consultants' reports, press materials, and public briefing information. In order to confirm some facts and numbers, or in cases where my recollection was foggy, I contacted, where possible, people involved to consult their independent recollection of particular events. In some instances I have relied on secondary sources, including books, magazine articles, on-line databases, and impartial analysis to refresh my knowledge of the broader economic history of the time.

Where dialogue is used, it is accurate in fact and spirit to the best of my recollection. In the case of certain discussions I have referred to notes I often kept of such events. Where appropriate, I have recreated dialogue, relying on notes, and in some instances consolidating conversations and discussions that occurred over time, while remaining as faithful as possible to the information conveyed as well as the intent, flavor, mood, and attitude of the conversation and the verbal style of the people involved.

This book represents my independent views, thoughts, and interpretations of the facts, conversations, people, and individual feelings involved, all of which may or may not necessarily be universally shared by all participants.

To the best of my knowledge and belief, no information or data revealed in this book is considered classified, confidential or secret within the context of the interests of Security Pacific, its subsidiaries, or their successors.

Preface

S urf to the business section of your Internet browser, click
on *business headlines*, and you'll see that many of the top
stories pertain to banking mergers—agreed-to mergers, re-
pelled mergers, ought-to mergers, and prayed-for mergers.
Merger is the buzzword of the day. The dollars and ramifications of these business combinations are ubiquitous; they affect us all, whether we know it or not.

Although the merger of Security Pacific and Bank of
America happened only seven years ago and was—for a number of years—the largest ever, it is no longer included among
the top ten U.S. banking consolidations. That transaction is
today dwarfed in size by the multibillion-dollar deals capped
by the $82 billion merger of Travelers Group and Citicorp. In
April 1998 we learned that Bank of America was going to do
it again, this time in a $67 billion deal with NationsBank.
Wells Fargo Bank also finalized a high-stakes "merger of
equals" with Norwest Bank of Minneapolis. You may remember that a few years ago First Interstate acquiesced to a
hostile takeover bid by Wells Fargo—the paint on the new
signs has barely dried.

Two major players at that time—Bank of America and
Wells Fargo—continue to be the players now and their excit-
ing battle for market dominance continues at a furious pace.
The scores change by the hour.

As Yogi Berra said, "It's déjà vu all over again."

▼

There has never been more emphasis on consolidation. This
is exciting stuff, and it affects us all, whether we bank with

these institutions or not. We will most likely see more mega-mergers in the future, as overcapacity in the banking system is mitigated through acquisitions and mergers that broaden the product mix and create the means to deliver more products cheaper and faster. This is the wave that we anticipated in 1990, and it is currently sweeping the nation like locusts across an Iowa wheatfield on a hot August afternoon.

Observers are usually divided into two camps: Those who sanctify mergers and those who revile them. While mega-mergers are in the shortterm often painful—and many customers and communities don't appreciate this brave new world of banking built around technology, the Internet, and less personal attention—it is my view that any voids left in service, products, or community support will quickly be filled—as they historically have been—by new injections of capital, individual entrepreneurs, and the Community Banking System, which stand ready to pounce on opportunities left open in the wake of consolidation. Perhaps a more balanced view is that mergers are neither good nor bad, are harmful to some, helpful to others, and as inevitable as they are unstoppable. Beneath the Federal Reserve applications and paperwork, mergers are operatic human dramas, steered by the idiosyncrasies of the participants and subject to contradictory truths.

What this story offers is the opportunity to witness—first-hand—what goes on in the deep background and behind the scenes of a major banking combination. You'll see the interplay, wheeling and dealing, travail and intrigue, and understand the enormous stakes and egos involved when top executives, corporate boards, politicians, and government officers collide in a clash of symbols and play high-stakes poker for a dynasty whose future balances on the head of a pin.

While this is specifically the story of our merger, it is more generally the story of every merger. The equation is always the same: companies and people who don't intrinsically belong together attempting to join in an effort to gain market dominance and outdo the competition amid the shower of sparks tossed off by personalities, ambition and greed.

I was the chairman of the board and chief executive officer of Security Pacific at the time of the merger. I'd worked at Security Pacific for thirty years, and soon after I reached the top rung of the ladder, in January 1990, the California economy, and the institution with it, began to sink.

This is my story of the merger and of the chaotic, often comedic events and individuals that populated and fueled a decade always on the verge of spinning out of control. It was a thrilling, exuberant chapter in banking—a fantastic exercise in cause and effect. This is not only my story, but the story of a great institution and lot of very unusual people who collided in a frenetic and surrealistic landscape of opportunity, wealth, and uncertainty.

Finally, I hope my book is a little like working at Security Pacific—creative, intense, unpredictable, and fun.

Acknowledgments

A very special thank you is in order to several persons who were part of Security Pacific and others who were not for their valuable assistance in reviewing, advising, encouraging, and counseling me in the development and editing of *Dead Bank Walking*. This group includes Nick Binkley, George Benter, Arden Flamson, Tom Connaghan, Charlie Delle Donne, Al Silverman, Larry Smith, Don Crowley, Ed Brady, Bill Isaac, Tom Collins, Jack Walston, Matt Thoreson and of course, my wife Loretta and my children, Jeff, Steve, and Sarah. Without their assistance the book would not have become a reality.

Part I

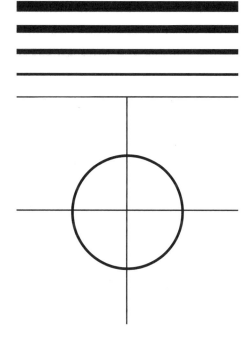

TROUBLEBOUND

*"But I don't think twice
when the sun goes down,
I'm troublebound."*

—The Blasters

1

An Age of Innocence

Enormous consequences are often the result of humble be-
ginnings; a trickle begat the Grand Canyon. And one impromptu meeting between a helpful bank executive and a real
estate developer can set in motion the dynamics of a bank
failure.

The banker was me, and my guest was Charles H. Keating.
It was April 1983, and I had no idea I'd just shaken hands with
a human lightning rod. We sat down for a meeting that, had
it not taken place, or had it ended differently, might have prevented the demise of Security Pacific eight years later and
saved the taxpayers $3.4 billion and the cost of two lengthy
and ultimately unsuccessful criminal trials.

Charles Keating was a customer of ours, and that morning
I'd received a phone call from one of our senior account
officers. "Bob, this guy Keating wants to see you. Our loan

experience with him has been great and he's become a real pioneer in real estate development. Will you talk to him?"

"What does he want?"

"He has expressed to me an interest in buying a California savings and loan."

Because we were one of Keating's primary banking relationships, and we were active real estate lenders, it was only a minor surprise to me that a man who developed real estate in Arizona would express an urgent desire to see us. With $37 billion in assets, Security Pacific was, in Spring 1983, the second largest bank in California—smaller than Bank of America but larger than Wells Fargo and First Interstate banks—with more than 620 domestic and 36 foreign branches.

I thought for a minute, consulted my schedule, and said, "Yeah, send him up."

Keating was an impressive man: charismatic, knowledgeable, even elegant. He was six foot five, with imposing teeth. His physique remained a testament to his youthful passion for swimming. It has been said, appropriately, that he has a "larger than life" quality about him. I offered him a seat.

"Mr. Keating, what is it you have in mind?"

As I expected, Keating was not at a loss for words. "I would like to buy a savings and loan."

I paused for a moment and asked the obvious question. "Why?"

He began by noting, quite rightly, that thrift institutions were having a rough time, and he saw it as an opportunity to buy into the S&L business. S&Ls were lenders to investors in real estate, he observed, and he was a real estate developer; it seemed like a perfect fit. If he could find the right S&L to buy, he saw considerable synergies: it would grow its deposit base and would help finance various real estate projects that his other business interests developed.

While his objective made a certain amount of business sense, I cautioned him: "You know, Mr. Keating, the regulators aren't going to let you run a savings and loan like a captive finance company. They're going to watch that pretty closely."

He knew all that and could deal with it, he said, and asked if I knew of any S&Ls in the West that were currently for sale.

"How much do you want to spend?"

"I'm thinking of maybe a $40 or $50 million investment." This amount was perfect for acquiring the particular thrift I was thinking about.

"Well, as a matter of fact, I do know one institution." I could see Keating straighten up in his chair and begin to rivet his attention on me.

The thrift I had in mind was called Lincoln Savings and Loan. Lincoln had the lowest ratio of delinquent mortgages of any thrift in the area, but like other southern California thrifts, Lincoln was losing money because it was paying increasingly high interest rates to retain short-term deposits while continuing to earn low rates on its long-term fixed-rate home mortgages.

I knew that Lincoln was run by a fellow named Don Crocker, and his number two guy was John Yunker, a good friend of mine. Lincoln was an institution of about $1 billion in assets; this perfectly fit the amount Keating wanted to spend. Recently, John had mentioned that they were uncertain about Lincoln's future.

Keating percolated. "I'm intrigued." He expressed an interest in further exploration of this "opportunity."

"I'd be happy to introduce you. However, we are in the investment banking business, and we have a man named Will Richeson who runs that business for us and we'd like to represent you. I'd be happy to serve as an introduction, but I'd like you to go down and speak to Will." I wanted Security Pacific to represent Keating, but I also wanted Security Pacific to get paid for it.

"No problem," he said. "Set me up!"

Quickly, Keating and Richeson assembled an agreement formally stating that Keating had hired us to represent and introduce him to Lincoln.

Keating was highly intelligent and I could see he wanted to keep his cards close to his vest. He never tipped his hand, in our early conversations, that he might have more ambitious plans for Lincoln.

I stepped into Richard Flamson's office. Dick Flamson was the chairman and chief executive officer of Security Pacific Corporation. An amazing man, he is less often described as eloquent than disarming, and his candid and colorful way of communicating to analysts and shareholders was something that often took them aback.

Born in Los Angeles in 1929, Dick Flamson was a 1951 graduate of Claremont McKenna College, where he majored in economics and business administration. He joined Security Pacific in 1955, was elected president and chief executive officer in October 1978, and assumed the additional role of chairman of the board in January 1981. During his 11-year tenure the corporation grew fourfold, from its 1978 position as the eleventh largest bank holding company in the United States to a rank of fifth largest U.S. bank holding company with assets of nearly $90 billion and stockholders' equity of $4.8 billion.

During his reign at Security Pacific, Flamson was widely recognized as a major participant in civic, educational, cultural, and banking organizations and activities. He sat as a director on several major corporations, including Coca-Cola, Northrop, Santa Fe Southern Pacific, and General Telephone.

From the age of fifty, when he assumed the role of president, until he stepped down in 1990, the strategic trajectory he envisioned for Security Pacific remained one of tempered, but incontestable, innovation. He encouraged it, breathed it, slept it, and dreamt it. He oversaw the conversion of concept to reality.

Under his leadership, we felt we were on a fast ride to the top.

I'd dropped by to ask him about Charlie Keating. "Dick, what could an Arizona real estate developer possibly want with a California savings and loan?"

Flamson shrugged. "He must want the S&L to make loans on the homes he's building."

"Yeah, that's what he implies. It makes sense. That's a very low-risk, easy-access source of funding for the homes. Seems like a lot of effort to go to. And the regulators might not permit some of what he has in mind."

"Well, it sounds like a good deal for us. Hell, maybe this is a trend—that real estate developers will want to own ancillary thrifts to help finance the sale of homes."

In retrospect, that conversation was like our Age of Innocence. We could not at that point possibly conceive of the monkey business that lay in store for Lincoln.

I returned to my office, phoned John Yunker, and made formal arrangements for Keating's introduction at Lincoln. Will Richeson accompanied Keating to the thrift, where they had a productive conversation with Yunker and Crocker. When Keating offered Lincoln $51 million—one and a half times its book value—they struck a deal. Keating signed an agreement to purchase Lincoln Savings and Loan. The application was approved on February 21, 1984. Later, Keating told us he wouldn't pay us our $250,000 fee because we "only" introduced him. We ultimately settled for half.

▼

Seven months after Keating acquired, Lincoln I received a mysterious phone call from John Yunker. "You ought to know, Bob, this guy Keating is not on the same course as everybody else. He's laid waste to top management, and the people Keating hasn't fired are going to walk. He's buying land in foreign countries, he's buying *huge* blocks of land all over Arizona. He's not making real estate loans, he's making land investments and doing all sorts of strange things. So watch out."

John was an intelligent guy, and I took his warning seriously. Keating had obviously recognized the faulty conduits in new legislation—specifically, Garn–St. Germain and California's Nolan Act—which would newly permit him to make

a lot more money building dream resorts than financing homes
for minority families. Avarice had overwhelmed tradition
and common sense. Why build homes and absorb the anguish of a slow return when he could own an S&L and originate all sorts of high-risk, big-return deals?

I immediately hurried down the hall and relayed to Harry
Meily, our chief credit officer, details of my ominous conversation with Yunker. "The word I get is that this guy Keating is going off in all kinds of different directions, and we'd
better watch out. Hopefully, now that he owns a thrift he
won't need us anyway."

Mercifully, we did take Yunker's caution to heart. We
stopped being Keating's principal bank.

▼

Home lending, as we recognized in the months that followed,
was not Keating's objective. In 1984 Lincoln Savings and
Loan granted only eleven home mortgages, four of them to
employees. Keating was, to put it graciously, a man with bigger plans in mind.

While the regulators looked the other way, Keating promptly
embarked Lincoln on a series of "nontraditional" banking
deals, carefully structured to capitalize on the newfound S&L
rules and their liberal powers. These deals eventually triggered
Lincoln's failure and Keating's personal legal entanglement.

▼

Keating was certainly not the only fringe operator of the day.
Michael Milken and other rogues of the period would become household words in the years ahead. When I had occasion to brush elbows with some of these other operators, who
at the time were heralded as icons and celebrities, they often
perplexed and concerned me.

While flying from New York back to Los Angeles I found
myself sitting next to Abraham Spiegel, a man who while a
first-year law student made so much money in the stock mar-

ket that he dropped out and became a stockbroker. His son Thomas was elsewhere on the plane.

Thomas Spiegel was president and CEO of Columbia Savings and Loan and ran that institution with his father. Thomas was compensated with a generous $9 million salary in 1985, and was an enthusiastic buyer of junk bonds and a disciple of Michael Milken. Thomas was said to so idolize Milken that he availed himself of every opportunity to display photographs of himself and Milken posing together at parties and expensive restaurants.

One-third of Columbia's portfolio was in junk bonds, most of them obtained through Milken.

I was actually surprised to find the Spiegels on a plane like this, because it was common knowledge that they, in collaboration with Milken, had recently purchased a Gulfstream private jet.

I introduced myself to Spiegel, who immediately figured he had a sympathetic listener beside him.

Columbia Savings and Loan had just gone public and he began to gripe aloud. "I can't understand why we go public at such a low multiple to earnings. I can't believe we go to market at four multiples."

I finally took the bait. "Well, what kind of real estate loans do you make at Columbia?"

With obvious contempt for the naïveté of my question he said, "We don't do real estate loans. We would never do real estate loans."

"Well, what do you do?"

"We do *deals*."

"What do you mean, you do 'deals'?"

"We do Biltmore Hotel. We do Newporter Hotel. We do takeovers. Real estate loans are for fools. We can make more money doing deals."

That may well have been true, and I let the conversation drop. But there was more going on, of course. Columbia had purchased $3 billion in junk bonds, and when those bonds later went into default the deals became imperiled and the Spiegel dynasty unraveled overnight.

▼

In May 1988 I got a call that chilled me to the bone. Keating said he had to come over and see me. *Holy Christ*, I thought, *What does he want with me?* But I was fairly certain he wanted to borrow more money to shore up certain of his endeavors.

When I revealed this to my account people, they were ecstatic because Keating was viewed on some fronts as a leader in the development of real estate projects.

"Whoa, whoa, whoa, hold on a second," I told them at the time. "This might not be the kind of guy we want to do business with. He is off on another planet. We gently dropped him from our principal customer list some years ago."

"Well, he's back."

As I generally met with anyone who wanted to see me, I set up an early morning appointment for the next day. Keating arrived with his entourage of five, which included his son, Lincoln's chief financial officer and a secretary who was a real head-turner. Even before introductions could be made, the secretary jogged to the conference room phone, spoke for a few moments, rushed urgently to Keating, and whispered in his ear. Then she ran back to the phone, listened, returned to Keating, and whispered some more.

I waited patiently with a couple of my account officers while the antics continued for several moments.

"Bob, what the hell is going on?" an account officer whispered.

He's either doing another deal or about to be indicted, I thought.

Finally, we began the meeting. Everyone took a seat, except for the secretary, who left the room, I supposed in search of more telephones.

"Charles, what brings you back?"

"Well, Bob, we'd like to rebuild our relationship with Security Pacific, and with yourself. After all, I was with you for a long time."

Oh shit, I thought. "To be honest with you, Charlie, I haven't closely tracked all of your—" I almost said "*shenanigans*"—"deals very closely. Tell me a little bit about your S&L. What are you guys up to? Are you making home mortgages?" A stupid question.

"Not so many of those. We're not really originating too many real estate loans. In fact, we don't even have a real-estate loan department to speak of."

"How does Lincoln meet the definition? . . . How do you qualify as a savings and loan?"

"Well, you see, we buy mortgage-backed securities at the end of each quarter."

"Charlie, how then do you invest the deposit funds at Lincoln to earn a return?"

"Well, Bob, we've bought land that we're developing and we work with some of the key leveraged buyout or LBO groups in participating in the junk bonds."

"So you're taking a leveraged company and leveraging it even more by acquiring leveraged instruments?"

"That's a way of looking at it."

Jesus, I thought. "Charlie, I understand you've got a fortune tied up in an Arizona development called the Phoenician Hotel."

"Oh yeah, the Phoenician! It's going to be glorious! We've got $250 million in the Phoenician."

"I thought it cost more like $500 to $600 million."

"Well it did, but I've got a Kuwaiti that's taken about half of it."

"Forgive me if I'm mistaken, but I thought that project was in big trouble."

"No, that silly business is all over with, thanks to the Kuwaitis," he said.

"But from what I understand, it's costing more than $400,000 a room, and that means you're going to have to get about $400 per night at 100% occupancy to make it cash flow. I guess what I'm wondering is don't you think it's going to be somewhat difficult to find people willing to pay $400 a night to stay in Phoenix?"

"Oh, don't worry. The Phoenician is absolutely going to work out fabulously. You come down there sometime and enjoy yourself. It will take your breath away."

His secretary, meanwhile, continued to hop back and forth like a cardinal dipping through a birdbath, in and out of the room, phone to phone, then back to Keating to whisper in his ear. In an attempt to get the meeting back on track, I asked him to give me some more details on the thrift's assets. "What else are you doing, Charlie?"

"Oh, we're part of some of the LBOs with Sir James Goldsmith and some of the other guys. We've got Drexel deals. All the big boys are in the deal with us. Bob, have you heard about Rancho Vistoso?"

"No, I haven't. Fill me in."

"Well my god! Conley Wolfswinkle and I are involved in this stupendous undertaking outside Tucson—a utopian dream community called Rancho Vistoso. We're going to build 11,000 homes on 7,430 acres of land. It's going to be something else. And then we're working on some real surprises."

"That sounds interesting and all, Charlie, but please understand that from our point of view, these types of assets you're discussing are not really very liquid. Arizona is in severe trouble and has been for some time now and your projects are all funded with shorter-term deposits which could not renew if you get into trouble."

"That's an exaggeration. Besides, it doesn't matter so much to us because our investments are geared toward the good partners. We've got good deals."

"Be that as it may, you're creating long-term illiquid assets and not assets that have any liquidation value. Security Pacific would need to know, were we to loan you money, how we would get it back when—or I should say, in the event that—your primary source of repayment fails. For example, the deal stalls or doesn't make it for any reason."

"Bob, you can always trust me. That shouldn't be a concern. My deals are all good deals, and they're going to be mesmerizing when they're finished, not to mention fabulously successful, and we really want to do business with you and your institution. I was with Security for a long, long time. And now you run the Arizona Bank right in my backyard."

"I know, Charlie. Let me think about it. But I doubt if we'll be interested."

After the meeting I conferred with my account officers. "What did I tell you? I wouldn't touch his deals with a ten-foot cattle prod."

Although it was fascinating to watch a man like Keating at work, I felt it would have been financial suicide to once again lend him money.

▼

The problems faced by the S&Ls in the 1980s were the result of intrinsic structural flaws established by Congress over a period of decades. They were also the result of our government's tight monetary policy, implemented by the Federal Reserve to halt double-digit inflation. These faults only proliferated when the banking industry pressed Congress for financial reforms.

The resulting legislation came to be known as Garn–St. Germain. This was the brainchild of Freddy St. Germain, chairman of the House Banking Committee, and Senator Jake Garn of Utah, and authorized thrifts to invest up to 40% of their assets in the direct development of any kind of real estate, a major departure from the financing of home ownership. Moreover, this legislation permitted thrifts for the first time to make consumer loans. The bill also provided for the acceptance by the regulators of "goodwill" as part of capital which in many respects became the ultimate death knell of the industry.

This lunacy was quickly followed by the Nolan Bill, California legislation that authorized California-chartered thrifts to invest in almost anything and everything—to purchase stocks, acquire junk bonds, make commercial loans, do greenmail deals, whatever—with up to a whopping *100% of its deposits if desired*—in any endeavor, no matter how risky, fiscally indefensible, or idiotic. If Garn–St. Germain was an automatic pistol, the Nolan Bill was nothing short of a license to kill. Like news of a gold rush, the Nolan Bill lured marginal operators from all over the world to seek their fortune in California's thrift industry.

Some time after these new pieces of legislation were fully understood, I discussed their implications with Dick Flamson. "These laws are crazy," I said. "They make it possible for individuals to purchase a thrift and operate it with little or no capital and do anything they want with easily accessed, government-backed subsidized funding."

"What do you mean, *no capital?*"

"Essentially anybody can leverage an S&L with nothing but thin air to back it up," I said. "Remember, goodwill can count as capital."

"Why, that's ridiculous. How can we, as a bank, compete with that?"

"I'm not sure we can unless we get some similar legislation. I don't think Congress knows what it just did."

"Bob, this means that anybody with a fountain pen and a lot of guts can buy a thrift and probably whip our ass in the short run."

Notwithstanding the apparent risks to the system and competitive disadvantage the new laws created, we both knew that one upside of legislation like Garn–St. Germain and the Nolan Act was that these greater freedoms to the financial services industry could eventually trickle down to banks. Soon, we imagined, and hoped, Security Pacific would be able to enter the domestic securities business and other heretofore unexploited and conceivably lucrative markets.

▼

In April 1989 federal regulators seized Lincoln Savings and Loan and charged Keating with a number of both state and federal crimes. A series of criminal trials degenerated into cosmic fiascoes and incontrovertible farce as government prosecutors paraded a samba line of the elderly victims Keating was accused of defrauding before an apoplectic jury. Spectators wept as witnesses in their eighties testified that they had lost their life savings.

Prosecutors gleefully portrayed Keating as an avaricious psychopath, the worst of the worst in a barrel of putrefied apples that would cost American taxpayers nearly $350 billion.

Keating served five years. In April 1996, his California conviction was overturned after an appellate court ruled that Judge Lance Ito had issued faulty instructions to the jury. Nine months later a federal judge ruled that Keating's federal trial was tainted and that there was not "overwhelming evidence" of guilt. Keating was freed but still faced $5.2 billion in civil judgments from the 23,000 Lincoln customers who had purchased debenture bonds from Keating's American Continental Building Company through Lincoln Savings. Most of his victims have since recovered about 70 cents on the dollar.

Certainly a primary reason Keating was singled out was because of his close relationship with five U.S. senators whom he had supported in previous, political campaigns. Senators Alan Cranston, Dennis DeConcini, John Glenn, John McCain, and Donald Riegle—the so-called Keating Five—had received about $1.3 million in support from Keating and, in March 1987, when Keating came under pressure from the Federal Savings and Loan Insurance Corporation, (FSLIC), he called an unprecedented two-hour meeting which all but Riegle attended. At this historic gathering, Keating asked the U.S. senators explicitly to get the FSLIC off his back and to discourage the regulatory body's further impedance of his real estate activities.

Keating came to epitomize the worst of the S&L debacle and subsequent deposit insurance bailout. His personal involvement with these five U.S. senators was frowned upon by a nation and legislative body—so much so that by introducing Keating to the S&L industry I later felt like an unwitting accomplice in his misdeeds and the legislative avalanche which followed.

Like Lincoln, Columbia was also seized by the regulators. When Thomas Spiegel was eventually sued by the Office of Thrift Supervision for his mismanagement of Columbia, his assets were frozen; he had difficulty freeing even enough money to hire an attorney.

Thomas Spiegel was ultimately acquitted of all charges. Columbia's failure is believed to have cost taxpayers nearly $1.2 billion.

History has demonstrated that if there is a way to bilk the system—especially a legal way—it will be undertaken with impunity.

▼

Ultimately, Keating became a symbol, an emblem, that epitomized all that was wrong with the S&Ls. Congress probably loved Keating, prayed for a man like Keating, because he had so egregiously abused the system that they could blame him and his ilk for the nationwide calamity rather than shoulder any responsibility for the imbecilic legislation they'd enacted that made the crisis possible.

Congress gleefully panned the klieg light of impropriety across the faces of Keating and others and thereby relinquished any governmental blame for the irresponsible legislation that begot it all.

Lincoln's failure remains the most costly and spectacular S&L failure in history.

But most importantly, the transgressions of Keating served as *the* lightning rod for Congress to enact new legislative changes that were a catalyst for Security Pacific's downward spiral. Although Security Pacific had barely begun its meteoric rise to fifth largest bank in the United States, in many respects its path to destruction was carved the moment Keating walked into my office. If only I'd smelled the cheese of deceit in Keating and sent him packing at that first meeting, our story and the stories of many other banks might have turned out differently.

2

A Well-Oiled Machine

Historically, banks were understood to be essential to the stability and continuity of economic growth. Security Pacific was one of the engines that nourished expansion and growth for the small, middle, and large businesses that came to us for infusions of credit in the operation of their companies.

As new sources of credit and capital became available, markets ballooned through the 1970s and 1980s and banks lost some of their competitive position with corporate America, which turned increasingly to alternative venues and lower-cost, more efficient sources—instruments such as commercial paper and those based on asset securitization—in order to finance its needs. We felt this would be a short-lived phenomenon; we believed it was only a matter of time before Congress would bestow upon us the powers that would permit full-scale participation in the securities markets. Then we could certainly recapture and hold a new and sizable demographic of customer.

Additionally, particular demographic markets—Texas and California, among others—had traditionally been immune to all but transient economic downturns, thrived during good times, and weathered recessionary twinges with minimal scarring. This rugged historicity bred a certain arrogance in the bankers doing business in these markets. Security Pacific, like its three California competitors—Bank of America, First Interstate, and Wells Fargo—believed itself to be, by virtue of its dominance and longevity, beyond any significant setbacks and geographically poised to take unprecedented advantage of this period of opportunity.

However, in this environment of diminishing traditional business, Security Pacific and its competitors had little choice but to pursue riskier, albeit more profitable, avenues for growth—expanding into new geographic and product markets and originating more loans to the developing countries, energy and energy service companies, real estate companies, land developments and, of course, participation in the notorious leveraged buyouts. We believed we could manage these risks through good times and bad and, frankly, had little choice but to try.

Initially, assumption of these risks paid off handsomely. Security Pacific was not the only beneficiary of unique market exploration; large banks all over the United States were soon riding high in what appeared by all financial signals to be an era of global—perhaps mythical—opportunity. Security Pacific found itself in the fast lane with the Big Boys, with capital to burn, and poised to take advantage of thrift failures, burgeoning markets, and new products and services made possible by technological breakthroughs and economies of scale. We anticipated success not only in California, but in other traditionally resilient markets and, eventually, throughout the world.

▼

The enormous and immediate success and self-importance of banking in the 1980s led to demonstrations in queasy excess such as elephantine office buildings—glittering steel and glass towers with vast cobblestone plazas designed to comfortably accommodate forty-foot-high fountains and contemporary sculpture. Every bank wanted to have the biggest edifice in town, the largest worldwide headquarters, the shiniest plaza, the most provocative artwork. Bank of America, Citicorp, and First Interstate each constructed a skyscraper during that period of extravagance. Only Wells Fargo was smart enough to remain in their very modest headquarters in San Francisco.

We'd already erected our 54-floor monolith at 333 South Hope—dead-center Los Angeles—and commissioned an exorbitant Calder sculpture on its plaza. But that wasn't enough: late one afternoon, outside Flamson's office—where, appropriately enough, hung a brazen painting of an Indian warrior—Flamson, myself, and John Kooken, our chief financial officer, discussed the efficacy of purchasing what amounted to a small airforce.

"Other banks have Gulfstream jets," Flamson argued. "And I'm not talking about just one or two institutions—everybody who is anybody has a jet. We need to be able to keep pace in a quickly evolving industry. We must not allow ourselves to fall behind the prestige curve."

The prestige curve. What could I say? "Dick's right," I agreed. "We need the security that private aircraft provide and we have to be able to move rapidly from point A to point B."

"What about the expense?" Kooken asked. John Kooken had a mind like a mainframe computer. He was bright, calm, helpful, on top of nearly every crisis, and flexible in his ability to suggest solutions. He always arrived at work before sunrise. And he always looked like he'd pulled an all-nighter. If I interrupted him while he was deep in thought, watching him "come to" was like seeing a zombie stir to life under the impulse of electrostatic implants. He had a memory—

and an office to boot—that should have been donated to the Smithsonian Institute. His fatigued, bleary-eyed, almost robotic countenance and deadpan delivery of financial results, *John Kooken Reports*, had become a staple of Security Pacific's quarterly video report to shareholders, who looked forward to it with the anticipation of soap opera addicts. The dark pouches beneath his eyes—like his unruly and cluttered office—were testaments to the long nights he spent crunching our numbers. "Can we afford to put this much money into airplanes?"

Flamson was adamant. "We can't be hamstrung by airline schedules and taxi cabs—all that mundane nonsense. We should on a moment's notice be able to fly to New York or London to seek out an opportunity and to be 'fresh' for the meeting, go in, do the job, and cut the deal."

One result of this meeting was a $12 million Gulfstream III. This awesome plane seated twelve and was spacious enough to accommodate a table, couch, galley, TV, and dual lavatories. A 15 x 15 inch gold-plated Security Pacific logo was mounted just inside the plane's foyer. The GIII could travel 3,000 miles in six and a half hours, and make it to London, Tokyo, or the southernmost tip of Chile with one refueling stop.

▼

Everybody in the bank wanted a piece of the growth. Every division and subsidiary wanted an upgrade, a blank check. John Singleton managed our computers, and the free access to capital was something he wanted a piece of.

Singleton joined Security Pacific in 1982 to renovate the company's technological functions and facilities. Singleton was intense, fast-paced, and proud. His success always seemed to be contingent upon some expensive plan to be executed at a future date. Now John urged us to allocate money for an improved management information system—an MIS. "If I can have the money, we can make things *move*."

"But, John, I thought we already had an MIS."

"We do, but we need a *better* MIS."

"What do we get that we don't have? Tell me so I can understand."

John launched into Singletonese. Like a motivational speaker, he seemed to begin every sentence with *We need to* or *We have not*. "We need to have more information. We have not worked together to leverage our skills and look strategically down the road. We need to be able to track it more and make sure we really get those savings out of technology and operations. We have not channeled our powers into new products. We need to lower costs. We have not learned how to use technology to move market share."

My eyes glazed over as he wrestled with the language. Oh, John had the clichés down pat—he knew how to frown at funerals, grin when earnings were up, and cheer when he saw a yellow ribbon round the ole oak tree—but I didn't understand a syllable. *Whatever*, I thought. "By all means. Go for it. Spend money." Besides, I knew if I didn't hand him the blank check, Flamson or Moody would. "Get us an MIS."

John went dizzy at the prospect of a shopping spree. "By when?"

I looked at my watch. "By seven o'clock tonight," I deadpanned.

At times our goal seemed to be to spend as much money as quickly as possible.

▼

It wasn't always that way.

Security Pacific was founded in 1886, in a pastoral Los Angeles suburb called Monrovia by a twenty-eight-year-old attorney named Joseph Sartori. He was by all accounts a fascinating man with a rare combination of altruism, civic obligation, and entrepreneurial spirit, one who managed with vision and exuded guts in addressing the needs and problems of the community whose growth he fostered.

The son of an impoverished stone mason, Sartori fled Cedar Falls, Iowa, after earning a law degree, discarded his dream of playing professional baseball, and came to Los Angeles in 1887 during a flurry of immigration. Sartori was a diminutive man with wide, flat cheeks and a self-composure that assumes a charmed glow in photographs. He was a man who took enormous risk at a young age, endured long and difficult travel, faced the personal betrayal of business partners, and was separated from his wife and family for long periods of great uncertainty as he labored to assemble a bank.

Sartori had a vision. "You will see a continual stream of people pour into Los Angeles and the surrounding country. The possibilities for this land are almost limitless. No other place will be as densely populated as Los Angeles."

In Sartori's time—he retired in 1933—acquisitions and mergers, from the bank's inception, were synonymous with our history and remained so until the bitter end.

But it was Richard Flamson III who, upon taking over in 1978, really pushed the envelope. Criticized as overzealous by some, hailed as a creative genius by others—sometimes for the very same reasons—Flamson was convinced that Security Pacific was now strong enough to pursue and eventually assume a prominent role on the transcontinental playing field.

Flamson's philosophy was best summed up this way: diversify, grow the company, trust and treat the employees well, honor and reward the shareholders, and give something back to the community. That fundamental strategy, to expand our geographical reach and diversify the mix of financial products we offered to our customers, remained the cornerstone of our success and promoted an acquisition strategy that was among the most aggressive in the country. Flamson envisioned Security Pacific as a prestigious financial supermarket. He was Sartoriesque insofar as his devotion to an ideal often carried more weight with him than even a sound, reason-based argument in opposition. This was a divine gift when Flamson's hunch was correct and a grave weakness when it was wrong. Also like Sartori, Flamson was fearless when it came to predicting and adapting to shifts within the industry. Sometimes he was wrong, sometimes he was a decade ahead of his time, but most often he was *right*. Under his leadership we prepared for—sometimes *bet* on—changes that never came, or arrived five years too late to be of benefit to us.

▼

By the mid-1980s Security Pacific had become a major banking and financial services company determined to satisfy the needs of a broad range of customers—corporate and individual, domestic and international—yet dependent upon an environment we thought would not fluctuate significantly enough to seriously damage our diversified base of business. With over $60 billion in assets, more than 30,000 employees and 1,200 domestic locations and 70 abroad, our bank, the fifth largest in the country, was structured to serve a multiplicity of market segments.

In California, our home base of over 600 banking offices and an equal number of automated teller machines, we were meeting the needs of more than 2.5 million retail banking households. In the Retail Bank we searched out, developed, and offered new products, including discount brokerage, mutual funds, and income tax preparation. Reflecting a strategy of growth and expansion, we actively sought to acquire ownership of other banks in California, the Pacific Northwest, Nevada, and Arizona.

In concert with our desire to become the top financial supermarket, our nonbanking financial services system (FSS) offered a wide variety of innovative products and services such as consumer and commercial finance, leasing, venture capital, insurance, mortgage finance, auto dealer finance, manufactured housing finance, and more. These companies operated from approximately 475 offices in 46 states and eleven foreign countries, including Great Britain, Germany, Japan and Hong Kong.

The securitization and internationalization of traditional domestic and international credit and debt markets was changing the way both providers and users of funds around the world conducted business transactions. Anticipating future trends, as early as 1984 we formed the capital market system—an early prototype of our Merchant Bank—focused on merging activities that augmented our exotic wholesale banking capabilities. Through this organization, traditional, international, and corporate banking functions were consolidated with Security's trading, corporate finance, debt strategy, and securities services.

▼

Dick Flamson's dream had become my own—to turn Security Pacific into a diversified financial services company with a worldwide presence, the monetary equivalent of McDonald's, but with the brand-name prestige of Saks Fifth Avenue. We would cater to the best customers in all markets, and our FSS would handle the overflow of less creditworthy borrowers. Security Pacific would be all things to all people.

We could afford to take reasonable risks not only to remain competitive but because of our escalating stature and because we felt the government would never allow us to get into serious trouble. Government had permitted and even encouraged our participating in enormous loans to foreign countries and, when the loans soured, allowed us to work through the problems. Government *wanted* U.S. banks to succeed. Under no circumstances would they stand idly by and allow the failure of an institution like Security Pacific— it was inconceivable.

▼

Flamson's number two man was George Moody, a man with an uncanny ability to connect with the employees and the community we served. Moody was tall and handsome. He carried himself with unflinching grace, ramrod posture, and considerable distinction. He was an impeccable dresser with ruddy cheeks and a tan complexion. Moody was an enormously charismatic speaker. He could read a list of combination platters off the menu of a Mexican restaurant and still hold us spellbound. He was the closest thing any bank in my memory ever had to an ambassador. There was a halo around George. His strong religious convictions and proud sense of our bank's history were the origin of his devotion to community. He often read the Bible at work and tried to apply its principles to the way we conducted business. When Moody promoted teamwork in our orientation videos, it was not just propaganda but the fervor of pure belief. For Moody, teamwork wasn't just a concept but a vocation, a higher calling. He cherished the notion that Security Pacific was strong enough to extend generosities to our employees, and that in return they would demonstrate loyalty.

Moody was not especially a Man of Vision—innovation was not his strong suit—but he had uncanny harmony with our branch employees, for whom he served the role of surrogate uncle. He communicated effectively with them, gained their support, earned their confidence, and repaid their loyalty with respect and allegiance.

Perhaps one of the most important elements he brought to his work was a fearless ability to voice dissent. While he opposed some moves we made, once Flamson or I decided to go forward, he was generally supportive—until we screwed up. If a strategy he disliked soured, Moody was not at all reticent to remind us of his initial opposition. He was the spokesman for a small but strident faction within Security Pacific that was suspicious of change, abhorred risk, and believed we should focus on basic banking—banking the old-fashioned way, covered-wagon banking. He more often executed than originated strategy. He did not like trouble, and when trouble arose he looked for the person responsible. On occasion, when it came to locating the origin of fault, or the source of a problem, George could be a scalp-hunter. Sometimes, I felt, he took the wrong scalp.

Flamson, combustible, intimidating, and animated; and Moody, dapper, stalwart, nostalgic, and dubious of innovation; they made a unique combination. While Moody clung protectively to his fear of change, Flamson wrestled with his trepidation head on and successfully concealed from analysts and journalists whatever hesitation he had about entering new markets.

▼

During this era of unprecedented opportunity, Security Pacific was able to engage in more acquisitions than any of its competitors. Bank of America was struggling through a near collapse; First Interstate was in trouble with real estate in Texas and Arizona and was constrained in what it could do; Wells Fargo had a policy of focusing on the home front and was not aggressively interested in exploring new products and new markets.

Security Pacific's scope was wide and its appetite insatiable. We had a three-prong strategy. One, augment our California branch network through acquisition, particularly in northern California, where we were weak. Two, expand into the Pacific Northwest—Washington and Oregon—and other Western states like Arizona and Nevada. Three—and most intrepid of all—enter emerging leading-edge markets like the securities business. We felt these goals were best achieved through acquisition.

▼

In 1987, Flamson called me into his office and confided in me that I would most likely be named the president of the California Bank, reporting to both he and Moody. "If you get the job, I want you to grow the company. Take the strategy— the *dream*—and turn it into bricks and mortar."

I was elated, until Flamson suggested that there was the chance that another, senior officer might return to Security Pacific to fill a top-level post. It was a name I had not heard in some time. "What," Dick asked, "would you think about the return to Security Pacific of Frank Cahouet?"

I was deflated and somewhat irritated. By now I was onto Dick's game. This was classic Flamson, dangling the same carrot before two donkeys. Sure, I liked Frank. A graduate of Harvard University, he was also considered an innovator and he had unquestionably planted many seeds here at Security Pacific. But Frank had bailed on Security Pacific for Crocker National, where he'd made a successful run at chairman and CEO. Following Wells Fargo's acquisition of Crocker, he'd now become the president and chief operating officer at the Federal National Mortgage Association.

In a period of minutes I'd shifted from having no fixed aspirations whatever to unbridled resentment.

I voiced my mixed emotions. "Ultimately, if you want Frank, then take him and get rid of me. He's older, he's got more experience, but there's really not room for both of us."

As I heard the words coming out of my mouth I thought, *What if Dick says, "Okay, we'll get rid of you"?* I held my breath and waited for the response.

"Well, I understand. That's the answer I expected," Dick said.

Flamson went with me.

▼

As chairman and chief executive officer, Flamson had his hands full. He had to rely on people like myself to extend the vision, and he had the guts and the belief to take the risks we would undertake jointly. Flamson would set down the criteria of a broad strategic vision and I would break it into realizable components and transfigure those components into actions. Ultimately, Flamson allowed me to attempt many of these innovations.

Flamson also taught me to think on a long-term basis. He often said, "We can't be preoccupied by short-term solutions that will make next year's annual report better than the year before. We have to think longer than that." Thinking on a long-term basis freed us from certain psychological constraints. We weren't paralyzed with fear by how analysts might interpret a given maneuver. We knew it might take years for a new idea to blossom; we might have to wait for some time to see return on value. We felt that if we could be at the leading edge and take advantage of the first wave of competition in a new arena that it could be enormously profitable.

As president of the California Bank I worked with Flamson to particularize and establish an interstate strategy. To maximize the existing base of customers it was essential that we become *the* low-cost provider while remaining competitive and maximizing our margins. We could then begin to add to the customer base by acquisition, both within and beyond California, wherever and whenever it made economic sense to do so.

To lead this initiative, my first and most significant step was to attract new leadership.

Jerry Grundhofer, diminutive and boyish but pugnacious, was initially considered to be an "outsider" when I brought him from Wells to Security Pacific as vice chairman to undertake an extraordinarily difficult renovation of the Retail Bank. The ignition point for his departure from Wells Fargo to Security Pacific had been a comical brain drain that I and a colleague, George Benter, had orchestrated at Annandale Golf Club. George and I wanted to find out what Jerry and his brother, Jack, had done to restructure and consolidate branches at Wells. We took the brothers to play golf and just listened as they began to brag about Wells Fargo and their strategy. Although I took copious notes on cocktail napkins and the back of my hand, I knew the ultimate solution was to bring Jerry into the company so he could work his magic.

With his seemingly incongruous mix of personal affability

and harsh "can do" presentations, Jerry was an extraordinary addition to upper-level management. Anything he said he could do, he did. Sometimes there were casualties in his military campaign to turn "Security Pacific" from a bank name into a brand name.

He was dedicated to shareholder value and could be somewhat of a mercenary in pursuing his idealized concept of relationship banking. He analyzed such concepts as reciprocal interest, mutuality, and relationship strategy: "We must identify all the potential relationships within our customer base. We should literally study the very *life cycles* of our customers—starter household, empty nesters, retirees—and target those segments."

Although Moody was initially apprehensive about Grundhofer—the "outsider"—he wholeheartedly supported domestic expansion: "As we look at deregulation and the opportunities that exist in the marketplace, as we look at legislation going on in the states around us, we really have to capitalize on the things that we know best."

Meanwhile, Flamson began to prepare the investment community for the western banking expansion upon which we were soon to embark.

▼

Given this fundamental long-term objective of augmenting our customer base, we acquired—in rapid succession—a number of large institutions whose geographies made them strategically advantageous to Security Pacific. Among the most important were the Phoenix-based Arizona Bank (purchased September 1986 for $480 million); The Oregon Bank, a Portland-based commercial bank (purchased May 1987 for $49 million); Nevada National Bank, a Reno-based bank (purchased January 1989 for $38 million); and Rainier Bank, a Seattle-based bank whose purchase in November 1987 for $1.15 billion in stock was considered by analysts to be a watershed acquisition.

For every Rainier and Nevada National Bank, there were perhaps five smaller acquisitions, executed with rapacity, renovated in a matter of days, and unveiled under the Security Pacific umbrella by what was now a well-oiled machine. This snowstorm of acquisitions fortified our Retail Bank and cemented our domestic inhabitance. What we needed next was to cultivate inroads for untested, more creative products and services to allow us to amplify growth and perfect performance in a difficult market with many nonbank competitors. One solution was securities.

I felt strongly Security Pacific could be a leader in securities processing, in the same league with Bank of New York and Chemical Bank.

George Moody had a true fear of entering the securities industry. For one thing, he didn't understand the issues involved very well. Second, securities was logistically complex, costly to establish, and our ultimate success would be predicated upon future change in the markets.

"I don't think we should do it," George said. "It's an area we don't know. It's too great a risk."

Flamson was on the fence. "Securities is a higher risk venture that's far more volatile than traditional banking business, and if you're going to get us into it, Bob, you'd damned well better control everything."

Sequor was a partial answer to this quest that virtually fell into my lap. The concept behind Sequor sprung out of my experience running Security Pacific's Trust Department. I didn't feel the Trust Department's future potential for worthwhile earnings lay in probating estates but rather in building a base from which we could establish ourselves as a major, nationwide—perhaps worldwide—provider of securities processing, investment management, and custody services.

Convinced that the traditional trust business had an intrinsically limited ability to generate meaningful earnings, I sought ways to utilize knowledge and techniques to build innovative business activities that relied on our best skills. We brought in new investment management people with better skills and set up the first bank-sponsored, private mutual fund—the Pacific Horizon Funds. We inaugurated a novel discount brokerage operation as well.

Then Sequor happened.

▼

Through an effusive and jovial Security Pacific employee named Tom Connaghan I was put in contact with a contingent of four guys—Michael Caggiano, Sal Ricca, Jimmy Pauline and Peter McKay—whose niche was the clearing and physical processing of municipal bonds. They had all worked at a company called Bradford, but had since left and were searching for a new home port. Tom's unique idea was for Security Pacific to augment its operation with theirs and to offer the basic custody, clearing, and processing of municipal bonds.

Connaghan was tireless and persuasive. Every time we talked, light bulbs went on in my head. We put up $2 million in capital and gave Caggiano and his team 20% of the business, which we later called Sequor. We began with eight customers in a tawdry office on Wall Street across from the New York Stock Exchange.

The Sequor team, whose street-smart autonomy and aggressive know-how initially scared the hell out of everybody, were about to show a commercial bank what it could do in the 1980s. And they took off. Year over year success turned our Rip Van Winkle trust function into an awakened giant.

Growth soon necessitated that we move Sequor's headquarters into what became their sordid building at 127 John Street at Water, two blocks off Wall Street. Unfortunately, the entrance to this building, consisting of strawberry-colored neon tubes extruding along a dim, concrete tunnel to an ominous elevator chamber, resembled nothing short of a flat-out bordello. Whenever I knew one of our California executives—particularly traditionalists such as Moody—was to visit Sequor, the hair on the back of my neck stood up.

Sequor looked and felt like some rogue CIA operation holed up in a whorehouse.

Moody finally did meet the Sequor team; he was impressed by the people, but troubled by the ambiance of the building that housed them. "Like a brothel," he reported. "We are a family organization with a long, conservative history, and we take this image seriously. I would be cautious about who meets these boys, who visits the premises, and under what circumstances."

Right off the blocks, their business segued into the government bond custody business and securities lending. Connaghan pursued foreign markets; the Japanese became big customers of ours.

As the processing business began to flourish, we began to outline a plan to position Sequor as *the* bank to the Wall Street securities business. That was the final destination and would represent the culmination of a strategy.

But out West, I found myself in constant conflict with staff people about what was going on back East. Sequor's executives were imagined to be roughnecks; mysterious, uncontrollable, misunderstood, and exotic.

Needless clashes were aroused even by relatively trivial matters such as the installation of a new vault on the premises. Security Pacific's chief of security, Debbie Jacobs, felt the physical plant raised issues of security and didn't rise to the standard set for branches. She voiced her fears to George Moody, who became agitated and related these concerns to myself and Dick Flamson. "These odd fellows in New York trouble me. It sounds like we may have a pack of desperadoes on our hands."

The mythology surrounding Sequor was definitely getting out of hand. I tried to reassure George. "I'm not sure what it is you imagine these men to be. You've met them; you've seen them with your own eyes. They're businessmen. They wear suits, they have families, they go to church, they drive automobiles, just like us."

"What about the security issue?" Moody persisted.

This dispute over nothing irritated Caggiano. "All we're trying to do is install a goddamn vault. What is Debbie's big problem? She doesn't know shit about our business anyway."

I dropped by Moody's office and assured him the new vault would be virtually impenetrable, watchdogged by a full alarm system and twenty-four-hour armed guards.

"Ms. Jacobs is adamant," George said. "She wants the vault to be risk-free."

"George, *nothing* is risk-free, but our vault is pretty damned close."

"But you're the physical custodian of over $300 million in securities."

"Non-negotiable securities," I reminded him. "Who in his right mind is going to break into Sequor, disable one of the most advanced alarm systems in the world, shoot the watchman in the lobby, go up the elevator, trip the alarms, murder two armed guards in cold blood, and then spend two hours jackhammering through 8 inches of steel-encased concrete in order to steal non-negotiable securities? This would be one of the dumbest crimes in history."

We eventually installed our vault.

I also found myself in contentious discussions with our compensation committee of the board about what the Sequor group was worth. "We want to be in this business," I concluded, "and these are the guys we want, and we are making so much money with them that it would be foolish not to pay them well."

▼

Caggiano and his people were not loose cannons; they were well managed and disciplined. They had auditors, comptrollers, knowledgeable financial analysts, planning sessions, written policies and controls, just like any legitimate banking operation. By now I had seen an indisputable correlation between the success of any given venture and the amount of autonomy and entrepreneurial spirit we fostered in the people who undertook that venture; as a result, I wanted to give them room, space, and leeway. Their success was incontrovertible.

Analysts were slowly persuaded that the autonomy Sequor and our other entrepreneurs enjoyed was what distinguished Security Pacific from other major banks.

Soon Sequor was buying, selling, and managing a variety of securities-related brokering operations. Initially it accessed the brokering business through the acquisition of RMJ Securities, a U.S. securities broker populated by young hotshots, "The Wild Bunch," who served as brokers for undisclosed principals in the purchase of government securities. Anonymity was imperative because in this supply-and-demand market the primary security dealers were all competing with one another; for example, Salomon Brothers didn't want Merrill Lynch to know whether it was selling or buying, and how much. When it was important for an entity selling government bonds to remain anonymous, they utilized the service of a firm like RMJ, one of only four such brokers in the country.

RMJ acted as a broker to the primary security dealers; the amount we received as the broker was a fixed amount. This is a market in which tens of billions of securities trade each *day*. On certain securities we received $75 per million brokered; if we brokered $500 million, our commission would be $37,500. Returns like this made it a very profitable business.

While strong earnings with very little capital were the pluses of the business, there were a number of minuses. The primary security dealers universally felt that the brokers—or "pimps," as they referred to them—were overcompensated for what they were doing. The commissions were too high. Second, the success of these brokers was unofficially contingent upon the ability of individual brokers to have "quality" social contact with the primary dealers—in other words, the ability of RMJ brokers to personally entertain the primary dealers. They had to buddy up with their clients. We had to come up with tickets to hockey and basketball games, limo rides, front row seats at a Broadway show. This atmosphere bred some real Damon Runyan type characters. Our RMJ brokers went by nicknames like "The Rat," "The Mongoose," and "The Aardvark." The chasm between these young tyros and the conservative bankers we were used to seeing at Security Pacific was considerable. RMJ's brokers were typically in their late twenties and early thirties and inhabited a different world—a nocturnal blizzard of neon lights, nightclubs, limousines, wild parties, and God knows what. They were operating at breakneck speed, at burnout pace, earning individually amounts up to $1 million a year and spending lots of dollars on entertainment in the process. Stories began to filter back to headquarters, some of which caused considerable consternation. Most of these guys used the "F" word as if it was an accepted industry substitute for every noun, verb, and adjective. I wanted to be very cautious about the circumstances under which they met our high-profile staff executives. We kept somewhat quiet about RMJ—it was not a stop on the Security Pacific tour bus.

While the monthly $25,000 plus limousine bills caused us some concern, to me the RMJ boys were a perpetual source of fascination and apprehension. This was a side of finance I had not seen before; I was simultaneously repelled and enchanted.

Sequor itself was by no means opposed to entertaining clients in the hope of facilitating business. They, along with RMJ, hosted an annual golf tournament in Pebble Beach to which we flew our best customers on a chartered aircraft at our own expense to play two rounds of golf and feast them at a banquet before flying them home in time for Monday's opening market. Inevitably, our employees returned to New York to find a surge of big orders from the bedazzled clients and the cost of the weekend was rapidly recovered through new business.

For strategic reasons, as well as to mitigate the potential for public embarrassment—and, to a lesser extent, preserve the dignity and image of the company as a family organization—we sold RMJ in 1986, after three years of operation, for $54 million, or $42 million more than it cost. The strategic reason we parted with this profitable subsidiary cannot be discounted: we had nearly finalized assembly of our Merchant Bank and, as planned, we wanted to situate the Merchant Bank as a primary securities dealer. Security Pacific was prohibited by Wall Street from being both a broker and a primary dealer, so bidding *adios* to RMJ with all its warts was not a tough decision.

Convinced that Sequor was in good hands, and animated by the potential of the securities business, I turned my attention to the creation of our Merchant Bank. This had been a dream of mine for some time. Merchant Banking is a hybrid of commercial banking and securities involving elements of investment banking, financing, syndicating, distributing, trading, and holding principal positions in securities, both debt and equity. The prize we had our eyes on, however, was global and ultimately domestic securities—the unbroken sound barrier of banking. And a Merchant Bank would be our vehicle.

Difficult? Yes. Long-term? Probably. Expensive? *Extraordinarily*. But if it worked it would catapult us to the Major Leagues. We would be positioned as few other banks were to seize an opportunity that had eluded U.S. banks since the passage of Glass–Steagall.

Dick Flamson was all for it. He was obsessed with, and spoke often about, our "ability to foresee and manage change." To him this was key.

George Moody, on the other hand, hated the idea of a Merchant Bank. And with reason. "I have a considerable aversion to any exorbitantly expensive endeavor whose ultimate success is based on trying to read the minds of Congress." Furthermore, he felt analysts would find such a grandiose undertaking by a U.S. bank—let alone Security Pacific, a relative newcomer to the list of top five American banks—precipitous and confusing. "The concepts are alien, the ideas are embryonic, and the complexities enormous. The big payoff hinges on a dream."

When I first explained to George that I was moving forward on the purchase of securities firms in the United Kingdom, Canada, and Australia, I thought he would swallow his tongue.

"Good luck," Moody said in his soft, velvet voice, and added, "Are we going global, or buying trouble?"

Flamson was excited. "We're going global. Bob, try not to step on your dick."

▼

Fortunately, some of the groundwork for the Merchant Bank had already been laid by my predecessors and, early in 1987, I brought David Lovejoy into the mix. He would become the chief architect and builder of the Merchant Bank dream.

David Lovejoy was a slender man in his forties who bore a slight resemblance to Senator Bob Kerry of Nebraska. Richard Flamson had brought Lovejoy into the company fifteen years before. Brusque, intense, acerbic, at times off-color, Lovejoy was adept at assembling new products, building new markets, and attracting some of the best talent available. A proficient strategist and extremely bright conceptual builder, Lovejoy was a shrewd judge of lending and had a rational approach to credit extension. He understood the enormous potential of such an operation and was persuasive when he discussed our ability—in fact, our very *need*—to compete in the international marketplace: "These are products that we are committed to and want to deploy to our client base, be it small companies, individuals, or large corporations, which are truly global in nature. You just can't compete effectively or at the top of the heap if you're not global." His feeling: we *will* succeed and we *must* succeed.

And I was on his wavelength, 100 percent.

▼

The analysts who studied bank stocks observed Security Pacific with amazement. They didn't know what to make of our grandiose concepts and couldn't tell if the Merchant Bank was profoundly reckless or shrewd beyond their ability to recognize. We didn't know ourselves. "If Glass–Steagall falls," I told Lovejoy, "they'll call us geniuses. If it doesn't, we may go down in history as fools."

When analysts questioned our moves—be they conservative actions like taking huge reserves on the lesser-developed-countries debt or more unconventional excursions like the construction of a Merchant Bank—Flamson justified the activities by focusing attention on management's purpose and its obligation to growth and long-term performance. His emphasis was weighted toward shareholder value. "What the management is paid for is to deal with all these different interests. There's the short-term interest—some ask us to manage on a ninety-day time frame. And then there's the longer-term interest of our other shareholders and our employees. What we're trying to do is blend our actions so they take into consideration all those interests—our employees, our shareholders, and our customers—both short- and long-term."

Sometimes, Flamson scolded skeptics outright: "You'll just have to get used to the fact that, as long as we're operating in a less inflationary environment than we have operated in for the last ten years, companies not only in our industry but in many other industries are going to have to take unusual risks to have 10% to 15% compounded growth in earnings year in and year out."

▼

Despite a modicum of regulatory resistance and industry skepticism, in 1987 we began to quickly assemble the Merchant Bank, bringing together existing pieces and many new products and geographic venues. We poured our heart and soul into it; the Merchant Bank was a twenty-four-hour-a-day, seven-day-a-week, $25 billion proposition. Our strategy was built around the de novo development or purchase of base organizations in the United States to the degree permitted, the United Kingdom, Australia, and Canada, with nearly one hundred satellite operations worldwide and, particularly, along the Pacific Rim. While the many pieces would initially be disconnected we felt that its ultimate success was dependent on their functioning as a connected whole to achieve common goals.

The global reach of the Merchant Bank would enable Security Pacific to capitalize on the twenty-four-hour-a-day pace of the world markets. These were lofty goals, and many obstacles lay in the path of any commercial bank that sought them. We would be attempting to enter a fickle and competitive industry, subject to the vicissitudes of world economic cycles and restrictions imposed by Glass–Steagall's related legislation and regulation on U.S. commercial banks.

Glass–Steagall was a 1933 act that prohibited banks from providing most securities-related services to its customers within the United States. Specifically, it prohibited banks from underwriting and distributing mutual funds and from underwriting or dealing in corporate equities or debt.

Quickly thereafter we acquired controlling interest in Hoare Govett for $56 million in cash, advancing our ownership of the London-based brokerage dealership to 83%. One year later, in accord with our agreement, we acquired the remaining shares to have 100% ownership. Our total cost in acquiring the company was about $125 million. With its five hundred U.K. employees, and additional one hundred dispersed among its constituent offices in Hong Kong, Korea, and Japan, Hoare Govett was an organization of considerable size and scope.

▼

As the second critical pillar in our global strategy, we acquired a 30% stake for $41 million in a Canadian securities broker called Burns Fry. Burns Fry was a far more sophisticated operation than Hoare Govett and was a leader in Canada with an unexcelled reputation and extremely capable people. At about the same time we acquired control of McIntosh Hampson, a minor but locally significant securities firm in Australia.

Springboarding off these basic operations, combining them with other offshore and permissible U.S.-based securities functions, we stepped up efforts to construct a worldwide Merchant Bank.

Early indications were that the Merchant Bank might succeed. By 1989 our global mergers and acquisitions unit was ranked sixth in the world in number of deals and eleventh in deal value, with 119 transactions. As the combination of Security Pacific, Burns Fry, Macintosh Hampson, and Hoare Govett fell into place, we felt confident the system would be well ahead of the pack in its ability to meet the needs of the 1990s market.

Because ultimate success was predicated upon a continuous freeflow of information between many disparate operations, we implemented a program called Project Alliance, whose purpose was to promote the interconnectedness of all units, especially the three pillars. Thus McIntosh Hampson, Hoare Govett, and Burns Fry were interlocked—so much so that Hoare Govett owned a percentage of McIntosh, and McIntosh installed representatives in Hoare Govett and Burns Fry who would sell Australian securities in the United Kingdom and Canada. Burns Fry also had representatives in several Hoare Govett offices, and vice versa, offering their respective country securities. Each subsidiary had a vested interest in the success of its colleagues. These operations were in turn intertwined and cross-linked with securities and banking operations around the world; swaps, foreign exchange, underwriting, distribution, investment management corporate finance, mergers and acquisitions (M&A), and credit, all up and running in every market. The Merchant Bank was like a snaked multitude of interlaced coils which together we hoped would form an unbreakable rope.

▼

Finally the schematic was complete. The network was in place for worldwide, twenty-four-hour-a-day banking and securities activities.

We felt about the Merchant Bank the way Albert Einstein felt about the Theory of Relativity: "The idea is too beautiful *not* to work." And we expected the operation to blossom with the authority of Quantum Electrodynamic Theory once we were allowed to do domestically what we were doing overseas. It was too intelligent, aesthetically pleasing, and economically tantalizing to fail. There was no other logical way for banking to go in the 1990s—this direction was *inevitable*—and we were going to be there first. There was a perfect symmetry to it. It looked unbeatable on paper, or when charted on a world map.

We felt we were so well positioned, so strong, and utterly prepared—so very close to achieving The Vision. The strategy was pure genius. If Sartori was watching us from On High, he was no doubt rejoicing. Now all we needed was for restrictions to dissolve and for laws to change domestically. Congress had to blast to smithereens that bastard Glass–Steagall once and for all, so that we could do in the United States what we were doing everywhere *but* the United States. After that, marketing to our domestic customers would be easy, and this international corkscrew of acquisitions would pay off.

We had the United States totally surrounded. Now we waited—waited for Glass–Steagall to fall so we could bring it all together. Our question: How long would we have to wait?

▼

Fairly soon, other particular venues began to turn a profit. Lovejoy was rightfully proud of the swaps operation and at management meetings described its success with the effusive reverence art critics reserve for Van Gogh: "This year we'll do about $100 billion in swaps. Ours is arguably the most successful swaps operation in the world. I swear to you, you would not be embarrassed to drag this one out and take it anywhere."

"What about the rest of the Merchant Bank?" Flamson asked.

"M&A is also performing well."

"What about the rest of the Merchant Bank?" Flamson repeated. "What about the global connect? What about all the other activities?"

"We'll hit the jackpot when Glass–Steagall tumbles."

"Until then, what?"

We had waited, and it hadn't happened. What could we do in the meantime? Continue to *get prepared.*

▼

During this time the cockiness of bankers—and Security Pacific in particular—was leviathan in scope, and the queasy extravagance of the time was epitomized by the American Bankers Association conventions, which during that period could attract 10,000 to 15,000 senior bankers and people who wanted to do business with bankers. These were elaborate brag-fests of leisure and self-congratulation—a high-class Mardi Gras for financiers. Queues of shiny black and white limousines, stretched around resort hotels like glittering angels cascading up and down Jacob's ladder, prepared to shepherd executives from golf course to swimming pool and then back again.

Prestige figured powerfully in this equation. It was not only part of our strategy, but tremendous PR, to participate in this megalomaniacal show and tell with an array of congresspeople, senators, lobbyists, deal-makers, and Federal Reserve luminaries. The bank-sponsored parties were often pretentious, as competitors tried to outdo one another. Some banks set up private tours to visit local historical landmarks like Pearl Harbor. Parties were hosted at the five-star hotels or clubs where top-bill entertainment was provided. Such lavish self-indulgence was beyond the pale.

These conventions were routinely held in New York, Chicago, New Orleans, Hawaii, and other major U.S. cities. Naturally, there was intense rivalry among the top banks to see which institution could host the most exorbitant party. Competition was stiff. Security Pacific, once viewed as a respected but Minor League player, was now one of the Big Boys.

▼

It was October 8, 1988.

Dick Flamson, George Moody, and myself stood at the door shaking hands and welcoming people to a grand seaside suite at the Colony Surf Hotel and, later, at a private mansion on Kahala Beach. Snow-capped confections, succulent pastries, ice molds of our logo, and a full bar were all displayed beneath a lighting configuration that would humble Pink Floyd.

When the major players on the guest list were present and accounted for, George Moody—adored by all, the heartthrob of every elderly widow, and the closest thing any bank ever had to an ambassador—would stroll to the microphone, impeccably attired, a spin-master's grin on his face, head tilted just so. He'd glance over his shoulder at the bedazzled crowd and, with the studied casualness of a Dean Martin or Ronald Reagan, begin to speak. "I like to dream about what Security Pacific will be ten years from now. If we are right and if we can demonstrate that we know how to run a multi-bank holding company, then why shouldn't we have a bank in every state? Why shouldn't we be able to transfer our intelligence and technology across state borders wherever there are opportunities? Just think of that customer base: 2.5 million customers. Now expand that—5 million, 10 million. The future is ours. Not just Security Pacific's but all of ours. Enjoy yourselves tonight."

Braggadocio masked idle chatter that would have made Donald Trump's palms sweat. Visions of grandeur danced in our heads as we enthusiastically discussed deals, fantasized the next technological advance, or compared itineraries of upcoming travel. These events were exhilarating with promise and blind to the inevitable eventuality of economic downturn.

As we sat down for dinner, a major corporate chief financial officer at my table asked me what we were up to.

I shrugged as if I hardly knew where to begin. "Now that the Merchant Bank is up and running, we're doing major transactions virtually all over the world. We just made a multimillion-dollar loan to help finance a Major League baseball team, and we're into most of the LBOs and are one of the premier lenders in California real estate. We're also experimenting with Video-Banking. Soon you'll be able to sit down at your home computer and do a face-to-face purchase with a Security Pacific stockbroker or trade bonds or conduct a swap transaction in any currency, twenty-four hours a day."

It was a shameless answer; I was blowing smoke up his ass. But in this rarefied atmosphere, the urge to boast was irresistible.

"Our new MIS is one of the finest in the industry, isn't that right, John?"

Singleton, seated at our table, nodded and spoke with his mouth full. "Unbeatable. We're the Chuck Yeager of technology."

Following the party, I kibitzed with other Security Pacific executives beneath a grand ice sculpture. We bathed in the warm glow of what felt like a very successful evening. Nevertheless, Bob Corteway, our chief credit officer, was beating—as he often did—the Gong of Doom. His voice was monochromatic and his body language heavy with unwelcome prophesy as he spoke of dark clouds on the horizon. "You watch: the conservative Wimps of the Eighties will become the Giants of the Nineties."

Corteway was a serious, intense man. I was relieved he'd waited until the guests were gone to hold forth on how deluded we might be about our strength and bright future. Flamson wanted none of it. "Oh brother," he said. "Have a drink, Corteway."

I, for one, was interested in hearing what he had to say.

Corteway gestured to the jolly wreckage we'd left in the Kahala Beach mansion. "The market share of the top-rated banks' commercial loans has shrunk from 35% to roughly 20%, so while we slap ourselves on the back so enjoyably, believing we are important, it may ultimately turn out that we are not all that important because what happens is that there is always a better mousetrap invented. Someone will find a better and cheaper way to provide a form of financing to people who need it. In this process, we're taking on higher risks and supporting ourselves with less and less capital."

"But Corteway," I responded, "capital is always available; it's just a matter of what the price, terms, and conditions are, and how they affect the ultimate purpose and use of that capital. If you assume a little more risk, with a little more leverage, you'll just pay a little more for your capital."

Corteway remained unconvinced and stoic. "We'll see. Because of our victories and good results I sense a certain conceit; we've forgotten the rudimentary importance of a strong capital base. We are highly leveraged, believe we are too big to fail and will always be able to attract capital. One of the weaknesses in this strategy is that we've become less concerned about the basics—capital and funding."

"We don't have to be concerned with that right now," I commented. "That's the beauty of this phase. We can always get capital and we can always get funded."

"It appears that way now. But our day will come, and that day may not be so very far off."

Flamson piped up. "Bullshit. If we want to do something, we do it. Build the deals, and the capital will come."

Corteway frowned. "It's rather natural that when things are going well and everyone is comfortable there is a tendency for an individual, an institution, even an entire industry, to become somewhat self-pleased."

Flamson challenged Corteway. "You're forgetting that time and again the banking industry has weathered dire economic storms and now, in the 1980s, we have emerged like some Darwinian wet-dream. This is a unique period in the United States and we are at the top of our game."

Corteway cocked an eyebrow. "If I'm not mistaken, the founder of Security Pacific, Joseph Sartori said, 'Every large city is filled with persons who in order to support the appearance of wealth constantly live beyond their incomes.' That is the state of big U.S. banks right now," he said, "living beyond our means, in obstinate denial that there could possibly be a day when the bill comes due."

▼

Although we didn't want to believe it, Bob Corteway was correct—in fact, he was dead on. The wimps of the 1980s were about to become the giants of the 1990s; the market leaders, the top of the heap. Their prudence and restraint during this period of excess positioned them for success in what would be the greatest consolidation and highest market valuation era in banking history.

Flamson warned us frequently never to "bet the bank," but we were already betting the bank. We had been betting the bank for years, sometimes on a daily basis. We were betting the bank on global securities and California real estate. And four years later, the headquarters building we were so proud of would sit vacant, and not a soul from the Security Pacific of 1988 would participate in the Hawaiian ABA convention five years hence, when our bank would be a memory—a quaint pageant of Security Pacific signs in a junkyard, a roster of empty offices, and several hundred ReadyTeller machines covered in bubble plastic and locked away in a deserted warehouse.

3

Building the
House of Cards

I'd smirked when Abraham Spiegel told me that he did not
run a bank in any conventional sense of the word: "We do
deals."

Flamson and I thought many of these guys were unconventional operators. Meanwhile, we got deeply involved with
our own menagerie of unconventional operators and, at the
time, didn't make the connection. We thought if we made the
right loans, did business with some big names—got a piece
of the action—we could make a lot of money. Like Spiegel,
we were building a house of cards.

A contortion of emotions overtook Security Pacific in the
late 1980s. We had grown and had become a broadly recognized bank worldwide. Only four banks in the United States
could claim more total assets. We wanted to take advantage
of our prominence and narrow the Prestige Gap between
ourselves and our more powerful competitors.

The Merchant Bank remained in a holding pattern as we, like Citicorp, actively sought broad markets and pushed products to the edge of permissibility. We lobbied vigorously to exterminate restrictions imposed on U.S. banks by Glass–Steagall, which prohibited banks from underwriting and trading equity securities or engaging in certain investments classified by Congress as "nonbank" activities.

But this would require time and considerable effort.

In the meantime, we decided that a key strategy of the Merchant Bank should be participation in leveraged buyout financing and the trading of corporate debt. The leveraged buyout—a.k.a. the LBO or highly leveraged transaction—was an old technique that had recently been given a new twist in an accelerated market fueled by Michael Milken's creation of the junk bond. Companies now financed growth or purchased companies outright at a price that greatly exceeded the value indicated in the trading of the acquired company's stock.

In a typical transaction sequence, the more junk bonds that could be sold, the greater the leverage, the more bank loans that could be obtained and deployed in acquisition, the greater the value available to the equity holders of an acquired company. As a consequence, more deals could be done. This carnivorous cycle produced more and more leverage and encouraged riskier transactions whose potential profitability made the LBO arena a virtual feeding pool for sharks.

Dick Flamson was not shy about doing business with these operators. "We are struggling to find ways to deploy our capital, to grow, to increase our earnings. We've put together a Merchant Bank and we might as well climb in the pool. We can avoid the pitfalls because I think we're smarter than the rest."

Although these deals were thrilling—not only would we raise the prominence of the Security Pacific name by participating, but we might have some real adventures along the way—I thought we had to be careful.

Lovejoy believed we couldn't afford *not* to play our hand at this exciting new game. "We must evolve or perish. Our credit quality safeguards should protect us from any dumb deals. We have good credit control processes and good credit discipline."

"Commercial banks are no longer relationship financiers," Flamson conceded. "We have to become deal-makers to compete. Let's roll up our sleeves and play. Find deals."

The company message: go forward, but don't fuck up. We imposed an informal house limit on loans that would not involve us in any LBO that required Security Pacific's held share to exceed $50 million. We could, however, underwrite amounts as great as $200 to $300 million, but only if we felt we were able to sell down our position to the $50 million level. This rule would theoretically limit our exposure in the event a deal blew up in our face.

Soon we were an active participant, on the debt side, in most of the major corporate and real estate leveraged transactions of that era. Unfortunately for Security Pacific, success exposed us to charismatic figures against whose considerable powers of persuasion we'd not been vaccinated.

▼

Bob Campeau was a famous Canadian real estate developer who'd engineered a transaction to take over Federated Department Stores in a highly leveraged transaction of mammoth proportions. We had been involved in his first financing and had declined to participate in his second refinancing with additional funds to purchase new pieces for what one might call a psychedelic jigsaw puzzle. Now he wanted more money for more pieces, and he wanted it from Security Pacific.

If we agreed to do business with Campeau, our objective would be to take a major piece of his action—anywhere between $100 and $300 million—and sell it off to smaller banks. We ran a subsidiary whose exclusive purpose was to sell down our corporate debt underwritings within our house limits.

David Lovejoy met with Campeau in New York and listened patiently to Campeau's litany of proposals. Lovejoy returned to Los Angeles aboard Campeau's private jet, which he described as equipped with ultraviolet track lighting, plush velvet seats, and discotheque sensibilities.

Lovejoy shared with me his confidential reservations. "He's a bizarre guy. The way he structures his deals is very risky, maybe even dangerous."

I assured David I would proceed with caution.

When Campeau entered my office to discuss a complex and expensive deal he wanted Security Pacific to take a piece of, I felt I was in the presence of the village jester.

He clambered in, his face a crimson red, introduced himself, sat down, and opened his briefcase on the hardwood floor of my office. His briefcase was cluttered with bits of papers, souvenir sugar packets, pen caps, and stray crackers. "Here's what I'm talking about." He snapped up a torn shred of yellow legal paper and a dull pencil and began to outline for me the phases of this complicated multibillion-dollar transaction.

"Now bear with me, Bob. We put four hundred million junk bonds here, shoot five hundred million mezzanine there, and we need six hundred more there—that's your *first* infusion."

My throat tightened. "Six hundred *million?*"

"Now, now, bear with me. And now here, razzle dazzle, out pops Security Pacific's money."

I thought, *What is this guy?* I'd have expected more professionalism from a fellow trying to borrow on his car.

"And I got this other piece of financing I need over here. You guys slide in here, and plop this second amount down here—the second piece of the pie. Now over here's where—" He reached for his briefcase and involuntarily kicked it upside down; hundreds of memos, pencils, and crackers scattered across the floor. He didn't apologize or make a joke about it. "Now bear with me." He scuttled through the debris, surfing his way across what was now a dustbin of cracker crumbs, pencil nubs, and paper clips, to my side of the desk. He found the greasy sheet of paper he was feverishly looking for, picked it up, returned to his seat, and continued to explain his mega-deal. "And the payoff is big-time and it comes out the hind end—right here. Slam dunk!" He shoved the scrap of paper under my nose. "Behold! You understand how the deal works?"

I couldn't understand a word he was saying. Distracted but entertained by the three-ring circus the meeting had become, I politely interrupted him. "Bob, let me pause your show for one second and ask you: Is there any *real money* at all in this deal?"

"Real money. You mean equity?"

"Exactly."

"No—but it doesn't matter. This is the genius of my transaction. But first let me continue with part two of my demonstration before I lose my train of thought."

I didn't perceive much thought, but I did let him continue with his train. He scrambled, he gestured, he leapt—it was like a Bob Fosse musical. And had there been more hours in a day, I might have let him run on forever and happily marveled at his peculiarities. But my schedule was tight and when he concluded his pitch, I quietly said we would think about it, showed him to the door, and opened it as wide as it would go.

After the meeting I convened with Lovejoy.

David glanced at his watch. "That meeting didn't last long."

"Of course not. I tried to get him out as quickly as possible."

"I won't ask how it went."

"He inhabits a surreal landscape of imaginary money. There's no goddamn way we're going to do business with this guy."

"Was it his presentation or the substance?"

"Both. You're talking about a billion-and-a-half-dollar deal, of which he wants us to chip in $600 million, and he came into my office with no proposal, no reports, no numbers. He doodled on a piece of scrap paper. Then for an encore he kicked his shit all over the place. A guy with a yellow tablet and a crayon tried for fifteen minutes to explain to me how we were all going to go home in limos from being part of his deal. There was no substance. His deal is built on quicksand."

More and more I was finding myself in these types of meetings, where flashy eccentrics wanted to borrow gigantic sums of money to leverage fantastic deals or build extravagant resorts and breathtaking entertainment empires. But the financial reality behind the concepts was as chimerical as a movie set on the backlot of Universal Studios. I felt Campeau was a prime example of an operator whose reach exceeded his grasp, and in 1989, when his junk bonds went into default, Campeau's circus unraveled virtually overnight.

▼

Another market Security Pacific fixated on was real estate development. Our debates on whether to do so were theoretical and sometimes contentious.

Flamson would say, "I know it's risky, but we know the market. It's California, our own backyard. Real estate has good returns, somewhat higher risk, but we can't possibly make the mistakes the S&Ls did. Not only do we have failsafes, but, frankly, we're smarter than they are. They're a bunch of dumb shits. What could possibly go wrong? Bob, tell us what you think."

"I think it's out best, safest opportunity. We know all the developers well. We have existing relationships, and I think we can get a lot more of their business."

"Absolutely. The few remaining thrifts as well as Wells Fargo are our only meaningful competitors. The dipshit regulators just looked the other way while the assholes in the savings and loans did any damned crazy deal they pleased.

Why shouldn't we take advantage of their problems and lock up as much of the good development business as we can?"

Real estate had been the nuclear core of our corporate philosophy for nearly a century, and we knew we could do it better than the thrifts. My intent was to find safe, high-profile deals that would capitalize on this ability and get us involved.

▼

Donald Trump was, by now, a known commodity among lenders and investors. Everyone understood that Trump had a casino fetish. He had labored to revitalize the appeal of Atlantic City following its progressive dilapidation into a virtual slum in the 1960s, 1970s, and early 1980s. He'd also developed skyscrapers in New York City.

When I first met with Trump he had already been heralded as a genius and seemed to be at the leading edge of everything.

Earlier that year he'd made an appointment to see me through some of my people who had been overwhelmed by him. They thought he was enigmatic, luminous, absolutely charming.

I didn't know what he had in mind for Security Pacific, but when he stepped into my office, I greeted him with high hopes.

Trump had a Clintonesque aura around him, the effervescent divinity of a studied deal-maker, and a categorical ability to communicate and inspire the belief of others in his personal vision. He could no doubt have been an evangelist.

Unfortunately, by now it was pretty well established among the investment community that, charismatic though he was, Trump was building a house of cards. I was optimistic but cautious.

"What's on your mind, Donald?"

His dimples flashing, waving a finger at me, he said, "I want you—I want Security Pacific. I need Security Pacific."

"Why us?" I said, trying to screw up my face into a picture of wonder.

"Something big." With the sincerity of the Sages he told me, "The reason I want Security Pacific is that I want a real, true, honest to God West Coast bank to lead the charge."

What he wanted was more money.

"How much?"

"$50 million will get us started."

$50 million was the high end of our "house" limit. It was almost as if he could read our minds. And if we would lend it, he would build it—whatever it was. And he still had not told me what it was. "Donald," I said, wonder completely erased from me now, "What exactly do you have up your sleeve?"

"The idea is to revitalize the Ambassador Hotel area. You know, where Bobby Kennedy was assassinated."

We knew all right.

"Now," Trump continued, "I know that area is not in exactly tip-top shape, but all that's going to change as I put my expertise to it. When this baby is in, there's no telling how much of a draw it's going to be to a more desirable community."

"There's no telling," I echoed as Trump unrolled a map.

"You see? It's right smack on the edge of the business district."

"Well, it *used* to be."

"And it will again—when my project is complete."

I listened, stopping short of drawing any conclusions on this deal, but I expressed my reservations. I didn't tell him there was something faintly morbid about the entire enterprise. But I did discuss the demographic uncertainties. "Donald, my sense of it is that Security Pacific would not be overly anxious to participate in the financing of that particular development in that depressed area."

"Depressed now—sure," he said with some exasperation. "That's exactly why the deal makes sense. I can buy the land cheap. Isn't that the idea behind renovation? You take something that is maybe not so good and work it, build it, and make it great. There's something special about the Ambassador Hotel."

I didn't think it was such a good idea. "Not to pop your balloon, but that precinct is a miserable, terrible, decaying area. Every respectable retail establishment has shut down, the commercial businesses have moved out, and it's being settled predominantly by only the lowest-income immigrants from Central America and Asia. I have nothing against immigrants but, honest to God, I feel it's not a very good idea. We would most likely not put our money into a project of that kind."

Trump was disheartened, maybe even a little surprised.

▼

My colleagues seemed shell-shocked when I told them.

"You said no to Donald Trump?"

"No, I didn't say 'No' to Donald Trump, but I certainly hope the account officer gets the message." I told them I did not think the loan was a good idea. "I just don't think that's the sort of deal we want to do. I don't like the project, I don't like the location, and Trump is leveraged with everybody."

"Yeah, but he's Donald Trump. And he's come to Security Pacific—*he* wants *us*."

"Well, we can't be too naïve. He's probably approached a dozen banks, including Wells and Bank of America, and told all of them that they're special. That's how they swing these deals, they try to play us off against one another. They create curiosity, friction, and envy. The more he can finance at a lower price, the more value there is in the equity of the transaction."

"But he's Donald Trump," the account officer whined.

"So?" I said. "This fever to be a part of prestigious deal—to be able to say, 'I'm with Trump'—is a salient factor in his strategy and has unhinged many a bank." This starstruck gullibility was the downside of the entrepreneurial spirit we encouraged at Security Pacific.

The account officer was heartbroken and implored me to reconsider. "Bob, deals like this—if they succeed—will catapult us up the ladder. Everybody will want to bring their deal to us."

"It's like playing the lotto," I told them. "This project is a $50 million spin of the Donald Trump Wheel of Fortune. And that's just for starters—that barely pays for the development plans."

"But when a guy like Trump gets into trouble, he can refinance to pay us back."

Oh, I thought, *that was a fool's trap.* "When a guy like Trump gets into trouble, he can no longer borrow, because no institution will lend to him."

Trump succeeded in part because of charisma. He was passionate, and professional, presented convincing scenarios, and was able to compel and dazzle entire board rooms with the ardor of a True Believer. Trump would never dare to diagram a billion-dollar deal on a Stick-It notepad. But he would borrow a lot of money that he might not be able to repay.

As a lender, no matter how glamorous the person on the other side of the table is, you look to the borrower to have both primary and alternate sources of repayment. And, while Trump presented a financial statement with many million dollars of net worth, the ability for him to bail even this one project out was limited—because it was leveraged on an illiquid base of questionable value.

Four months later I was flabbergasted to see a credit report that indicated our officers had lent $10 million to something called Taj Mahal Enterprises.

"What's this for?" I asked Bob Corteway, our chief credit officer.

"Oh, that's Don Trump's empire."

I raised holy hell. "What in the hell was going through those guys' minds? Why didn't someone tell me about this before we committed?"

"It's for part of an initial study on the feasibility of restoring the Ambassador Hotel."

"I don't need $10 million to tell you the feasibility of that: it's *zero*. Didn't they listen to a word I said?"

Two years later we wrote the whole thing off. It was a loss. And sure enough, a decade later, the Ambassador Hotel remains a ghastly eyesore.

▼

Chris Hemmeter was another real estate developer to whom it was difficult to say *No*. Chris was the preeminent hotel developer in Hawaii at the time, and had an uncanny ability to talk banks into virtually anything. He was one of the creators of the Destination Resort. You take your family and everything you ever dreamed or fantasized is right smack on the premises; golf courses, waterfalls, swimming pools, gift shops—fountains of gold and Perrier-filled saunas. Tall and suave, Hemmeter had enthusiasm that was contagious and his dreams were enormously appealing. Unfortunately, he had to use a lot of the bankers' money to make them come true. And, as with Trump, there was no escape hatch for creditors if the dream collapsed.

Around this time Chris dazzled Flamson and I with yet another in his parade of major hotel opportunities in the Hawaiian Islands. He pushed us hard for a loan to finance the construction of a Westin resort on Kauai. His presentation was laid-back, self-assured, and engaging.

His preferred method of persuasion was to hijack our imaginations: "*Irresistible* is the word. Cascading waterfalls in an open-air courtyard featuring one of the biggest trees you've ever seen, sitting majestically on a small island in the middle of a pond full of ducks and koi fish—and this is only where you register. That's the lobby! We haven't even talked about the Action Core."

Chris was a conceptual genius who'd put considerable time and money into devising plans, schematics, renderings, and proposals that were scintillating to the eye. Flamson pondered Hemmeter's vision, and I could tell from the way he bounced around on his seat that he was falling under Hemmeter's spell. And so was I.

"Natural saunas, cobblestone walkways lined with Euca-lyptus trees and luminarias." Chris knew Flamson and I loved golf, and was careful to emphasize the two golf courses. "These aren't your ordinary resort-type golf courses; they are PGA quality and very challenging. We are going to construct a network of man-made waterways—*canals*—that weave throughout the complex. Boats will ferry entire families along these canals, taking them to either one of the most unique restaurants in all of Hawaii or a small, very special zoo featuring exotics."

Oh boy, I thought, *Chris is going to make it very difficult to say no.*

Chris continued. "Every weekday at dusk, our staff will re-define the Hawaiian luau. This Kauai resort will be a feast for the senses, a tropical oasis situated between those two *eighteen-hole golf courses*," he repeated. "Our swimming pools will have *themes*. And some of our pools are special, because they are not for people. No, not *these* pools—they will be home to an array of the most exotic fish you've ever seen. Sip a Mai Tai and watch the pretty fish. The beauty will be *humbling*."

The numbers were humbling. Chris wanted a loan in the nine figures. I felt confident we could probably sell it down to our $50 million house limit.

"The resort will have an Asian theme. We are going to pur-chase and showcase a lot of art from the Orient. Vases, ta-pestries, Buddhas—that type of thing."

I wondered if this would make it easier to sell the resort to the Japanese if things didn't work out. At this time, the Japanese were buying many hotels in Hawaii. There was an inflating market—entrepreneurs would intentionally create these fantastic properties and then sell them quickly to Japanese investors at enormous profits. (In a couple of years, the Japanese would own all but two major hotels in Hawaii.)

"Anything the customer wants will be provided for," Hem-meter continued, "including a full array of swimwear, sports equipment, hell—even sunburn remedies. Purchase or rent it on the spot and sign it to the room."

Sign it to Security Pacific, I thought.

While his personality was commanding, the amount of dollars the banks were lending relative to the fundamentals of credit in order to fund his projects was excessive.

Chris somberly admitted that the cost of the project and financing requirements were a lot to ask for. "I know it's a lot of money," Hemmeter said frankly, "but look at the plan. It's all here—the only thing left to do is *build* the damn thing."

With some reluctance I was pretty well sold on what was a breathtaking concept. *Besides*, I thought—tumbling into another credit trap—*we can always sell off the portion of this transaction we don't want to hold.*

With some trepidation, we ultimately took part in the financing of Hemmeter's project. The rudiments of credit were increasingly compromised by our line lenders as we ventured into these *multi-hundred-million-dollar* loans; they'd become so transaction-oriented. This fervor to be part of every prestigious transaction, no matter how seductive the vision, was as compelling as it was unhealthy for an institution like Security Pacific.

▼

Why did Hemmeter get through where Trump and others didn't?

Hemmeter didn't quite get through by traditional avenues. Not only was he lucky in terms of his timing—Chris hit us before we were "grounded" by recession and regulatory warnings, and before credit worries stanched our origination of supernova-sized loans—but another, eminently human factor came into play. Chris Hemmeter was a close friend of Dick Flamson's and Dick chose, as a friend of Chris's, to be part of those transactions. One managerial difference between Dick and I was that Dick felt that the CEO should be the leader and primary authority in the credit decision process. I felt this was a suicidal mistake and that credit decisions should ultimately be the domain of the Credit Department and the chief credit cfficer—people with objectivity.

We couldn't do these projects alone—no bank could—but we could do them in combination with other banks, and there was some comfort in the fact we had partners in these risky tropical adventures.

We did well with Hemmeter and actually got our money back, albeit at the last minute and with a little pain. Chris managed to sell the twin golf courses at the Westin Kauai, but there remained a $50 million portion of the loan secured by the hotel, which Security Pacific held. In time, the hotel was sold separately to Japanese investors and the loan, after an extended period with no interest, was eventually repaid.

▼

But perhaps our single biggest disaster—Security Pacific's *Heaven's Gate*—was the brainchild of Peter Ueberroth, whose spectacular orchestration of the 1984 Olympics had held me spellbound even as the countries whose flags flew so proudly continued to default on billions of dollars' worth of Security Pacific loans.

Peter Ueberroth became an Orange County icon following his successful management of the Los Angeles Olympics, and after he'd successfully built and sold a travel business. He went on to serve as Baseball Commissioner and, in the mid-1980s, started his own venture capital business. At this point he contacted Security Pacific and urged us to participate in an enterprise he would divulge to us only in person.

Flamson, David Lovejoy, and I met with Ueberroth at his Orange County office. Ueberroth was a handsome man with short-cropped hair and an adolescent's contagious grin. His manner was credible and confidant, but his attention occasionally wandered, as if he'd become engrossed in contemplation.

We sat down and the impeccably dressed Ueberroth boldly revealed his proposal: if Security Pacific would finance about $80 million on his transaction, he and his investors were prepared to contribute $20 million in capital to fully fund an absolute first-class deal he'd structured.

"This is a sure bet," he added. Peter's silence lingered like an animal trap.

"Well, I'll bite," said Flamson. "Tell us about it."

For reasons that mystified me, Peter had become infatuated with Hawaiian Airlines. His concept was to purchase the airlines and build a strategic alliance with a major like American Airlines or United; Hawaiian would become the major's primary short-haul provider. Peter felt that Hawaiian Airlines's performance would theoretically skyrocket, become very profitable, and most likely be resold for a substantial gain in three to five years. It was the classic LBO story but the formula hinged on greater bank leverage than most others, and because of the logistics involved, it sounded to me like an uphill climb.

Ueberroth gave Flamson, Lovejoy, and myself a few private minutes to mull over the idea. Flamson asked us what we thought.

"An atrocious idea," I said. Lovejoy agreed. If we were to participate, we could potentially find ourselves part-owner of something we could not possibly sell.

But Flamson wanted to do it and his rationale was convincing: "We need high-profile individuals like Ueberroth to lure deals to Security Pacific and his stature as Orange County's wonderboy could spark financial activity for us." Orange County was one of several affluent cornerstones of southern California and Ueberroth was regarded as a prince of finance, an alchemist that turned nearly every deal he touched into gold.

Ueberroth returned.

Flamson asked for more details. "You know, Peter, we have a house rule—we don't like to bet the company or put more than $50 million into any single LBO transaction. We prefer to diversify. We would rather do four $20 million deals than one $80 million deal."

"I appreciate that, but my idea is a little different," Peter explained, "because it is so good. This idea is so clean and much better than anything else I've seen, and I would be behind it 100%. I don't even think it'll be that much work. I'm pretty sure that the name alone—Peter Ueberroth—can pull the deal through with one of the major airlines. That's the key."

I asked, "Of the $20 or $25 million in capital, what, if you don't mind my asking, would be your personal stake?" This would tell me how much Peter believed in the deal.

"A few million. See: I'm essentially the promoter, and I've got the perfect man—Bob Talbot—to run the intricacies of the operation."

"Who," I asked, "is Bob Talbot?"

"Bob Talbot ran part of United Airlines. And my brother will be over on the islands to personally keep a close eye on things and maintain copacetic relations with the union."

"What will *your* involvement be?" I asked.

"Maximum overdrive. Total immersion. After all, this is a Peter Ueberroth deal. I will involve myself in this thing to the hilt."

▼

Back at headquarters, Flamson said, "I'm inclined to grant Peter's loan. Ueberroth is exactly the kind of guy we want to do business with, even though from a credit perspective it may be too much money."

Lovejoy just shook his head. "$80 million is a hell of a lot of money for this genre of deal. We won't be able to sell it down or sell it off initially—maybe after two or three quarters of performance, but not now."

I had to agree. "Dick, who on earth is going to buy pieces and parts of an overleveraged deal on a decrepit airline, even if Peter Ueberroth is involved?"

"You heard what Peter said. This is his baby. He's hungry. He's got everything riding on this deal."

"No, he's only got a few million of his own riding on it," I reminded Dick.

"I doubt Peter will fail. Anyway, some risks are worth taking."

The way Dick saw it, Security Pacific was paying a premium to be linked to the Ueberroth name, and there was a potential windfall from such a prestigious involvement.

We made the Hawaiian Airlines loan in spite of the fact Lovejoy and Corteway both felt this was far too much credit for this transaction. Even our loan traders felt the credit wasn't good enough to sell down to any level. In other words, the deal structure was below our standards. But it was Peter Ueberroth, and he was a big name.

For Peter Ueberroth we had made an exception, and it was an error.

▼

From day one, Hawaiian Airlines never performed up to expectations. Shortly after we granted the loan, financials and reports began to trickle in that were nowhere near as optimistic as Peter's plan. To find out what the hell was going on, I drove to Orange County for an early morning meeting with Ueberroth. He informed me that he might need more money to pull off his sensation.

"It's not a *problem*," he assured me. "But we do need more seed money."

"Peter, there *is* a problem. The whole deal is becoming a problem."

"Where's the problem? I don't see any problems. I see a *cash need*, but I don't see a problem."

I was holding evidence of the problem in my hand. "Peter, I'm staring at the financials. Not only are you not making money, but you've indicated all these unanticipated expenses. Can you give me some kind of explanation, or at least an update?"

"Things," he said, "are proceeding."

This wasn't very helpful. I needed specifics. "How is the airport sale going?"

Ueberroth had intended to sell the West Maui Airport as part of the deal. Not only was it supposed to happen, but it was supposed to happen fairly quickly and was vital to the success of the vision.

"Unfortunately, that's been delayed."

"What happened, Peter?"

"The local City Council doesn't like the idea."

"Do you think it's going to materialize?"

"That's not entirely clear."

"How about the airline? Is the operation going well?"

"Well, the condition of the airplanes is worse than we were led to believe."

I took a deep breath. What I imagined wasn't very pretty: rundown airplanes coughing across the runway in an urgent effort to become airborne while nervous travelers watched in dismay from the terminal window.

Peter continued. "We really miscalculated. We had no idea how much money it was going to take to get these planes in a workable condition. The fix-up costs have been substantial. And, I don't know, ridership isn't exactly what we hoped."

These revelations lodged in my throat like a chicken bone.

"But don't worry, Bob. I'll take care of Security Pacific."

"Have you approached American Airlines?" Like the sale of the airport, this was indispensable to the success of the venture.

"I haven't quite pulled that off yet. I'm doing my best. I'm on the front line."

But Peter wasn't on the front line; he was here in Orange County. "Peter, are you setting up meetings? Are you trying to *sell* the West Maui Airport?"

"Not to worry. My brother and Bob Talbot are working on it."

"But Peter, with all due respect to your brother, it's a lot harder to say no to Peter Ueberroth than it is to say no to your brother." I felt in my gut that if Peter was in Hawaii these things would get done.

"But I'm too visible."

"That's the whole point, Peter. Your visibility is mandatory. It's your charisma and conviction that will help get these things done. They most likely won't get done without you. I think you should go over to Hawaii."

"I can't do that because it wouldn't be . . . what's the word I'm searching for?"

"Easy?"

"No. It wouldn't be *seemly*."

This didn't sound like the confident pronouncement of a savant. It sounded like Peter was backing away. I drove back to Los Angeles in dismay.

▼

In the months ahead we advanced additional money to meet their cashflow shortfall, but the Hawaiian Airlines deal lingered in uncertainty. By Winter, I felt the writing was on the wall. I convened with Flamson.

"Peter wants to build Stonehenge but he doesn't want to touch rocks."

"He was initially so eager," said Dick.

"Maybe he's one of those guys that's always eager when a deal is just starting up. The problem I'm having is to keep him eager."

Even Flamson's patience had dwindled. "Tell him to get off his ass."

"I've told him. He won't budge. He won't set foot on Hawaii."

"Why not?"

"My sense is that he thinks his image is too precious. Bottom line: I don't sense he's giving enough attention to Hawaiian Airlines."

Flamson was dumbfounded. "Son of a bitch."

▼

Hawaiian Airlines continued to struggle and eventually—as were our loans—sold for cents on the dollar.

I'm sure that Peter was well intended, and so were most of the deal-promoters who sought to maximize leverage and the ultimate return on their deals. Sadly, Ueberroth failed us by not living up to his commitment of personal involvement in the execution of the deal. What the Hawaiian Airlines deal needed was exactly what Flamson, Lovejoy, and I had bought into in the first place—the Peter Ueberroth name; the charisma, the stature, the pizzazz. Without that *ooomph*, all we had was a bunch of empty airplanes.

But in a way, we had failed him too.

Where Security Pacific failed Peter Ueberroth, Donald Trump, Chris Hemmeter, and others like them—as well as our shareholders—was in not holding tight to the credit and lending principles that had served us so well in the past. We thought we could break the rules. We also failed Peter by not telling him that his deal was far too leveraged and was contingent upon too many uncertainties, notwithstanding his personal charisma. We were caught up in ourselves and the times. We were cattle, running hard to get to the feed bin, to be first, to be a pioneering leader—to build our bank as a world-class operation lauded for its world-class deals.

4

A Bad Case
of Firrea

*"When Congress implemented FIRREA, the man
they most had in mind was Charles Keating."*

—Daniel Fischel, *Payback*

In the wake of the Charles Keating disaster and meltdown
of the S&Ls, the relationship between politicians and
bankers became strained and precarious. Bankers were now
personae non grata on Capitol Hill. Senators and congresspeople did not want to be seen within a mile of a banker. And
to prove that they meant it, in late 1989 they passed a draconian law called FIRREA—the Financial Institutions Reform, Recovery, and Enforcement Act. Genteelly described
as "a call for prompt corrective action," it was in truth a law
whose secret determination was to make sure that nothing
like Keating's savings and loan flop ever recurred.

FIRREA was a lengthy and complex set of provisions whose full impact on banking and Security Pacific in particular we had yet to entirely discern. All we knew was that FIRREA mandated sweeping changes in the examination, supervision, and disposal of insolvent thrifts. Incredibly, our early misperception was that FIRREA would help banks.

This distortion was based on tunnel vision: our attention to particularities within FIRREA to the exclusion of the larger picture. By accelerating the seizure and liquidation of ailing S&Ls, FIRREA did remove some competition and make it easy for banks to acquire defunct thrifts. Among the reasons for doing so was to "rescue" (i.e., hijack) an existing customer base and assume the deposits it represented. This was a rapid way to augment regional presence or solve a short-term funding problem.

Shortly after the passage of FIRREA, we acquired Gibraltar Savings and Loan for just such a reason. But we didn't just buy Gibraltar, we bought it with impunity. And we gave the credit to FIRREA.

"Thank God for FIRREA," I told Flamson. "FIRREA made this possible."

The Resolution Trust Corporation (RTC), a federal agency established under FIRREA, seized the failed Gibraltar with an intention to auction it to the highest bidder. At the close of the sale, the RTC would pay the acquiring bank to assume full responsibility for deposit liabilities by writing a check for the full value of the deposits net of the acquisition cost. They'd removed the assets, which were the loans, and planned to later sell them to cover some of the difference. The government would absorb the shortfall.

When I saw that Gibraltar was up for sale, I concluded that we *had* to purchase it in order to remedy a very unusual funding situation. Security Pacific utilized short-term borrowing instruments to fund its bank and holding company subsidiaries. We had significantly overborrowed short-term to lend longer term. This tactic was somewhat risky but advantageous to our bank so long as we were considered among the nation's premier financial institutions. I felt, however, that overuse of the technique had put us in a tenuous position; the ratio of such funding when compared to the size of our institution given the overall market for short-term funds exposed us to danger. At this moment, we had over $14 billion worth of short funding, comprised of about $7 billion of commercial paper in the holding company and another $7 billion of fed funds in the bank. I wanted badly to do something about this.

In emergency meetings I suggested we pursue Gibraltar; the only quick and certain way to correct the shortfall without compromising our short-term earnings was to purchase deposits. "Gibraltar," I pointed out, "is such a disaster that the RTC is selling it without any assets." I also mentioned that it was somewhat unusual to purchase a defunct thrift to access its deposits.

Dick thought Gibraltar was a can-do and a must-do. "Let's bid on it when it comes to the market."

We qualified and submitted our proposal. The bid: $144 million in cash, about 3.5% of deposits. And we won it.

Although we knew Gibraltar was a local S&L competitor with branch offices scattered in various parts of our market, we essentially bought Gibraltar sight unseen, with the carefree tenacity of a child screaming for a particular toy at a garage sale.

We celebrated our acquisition. "The first thing we ought to do is send a telegram to Congress and thank them for FIRREA," I said, expressing for that law an appreciation I would soon revise.

Flamson said he believed FIRREA was the direct result of Keating. "You did it, Bob. You set up Keating and he screwed up and got us FIRREA. You put a crash-test dummy in a Lincoln, and we can thank Charlie for FIRREA and we can thank you, Bob, for Charlie. FIRREA will finally shape up the S&Ls, and help the banks. We finally have a level playing field."

▼

The regulators now found their backs to the wall as, in hearing after hearing, Congress bludgeoned them with allegations of having looked the other way. Congress was embarrassed and passed FIRREA to prevent this from ever happening again, and the bank examiners were determined to broadly interpret and utilize its powers with the full force of their authority. The regulators had endured enough. Their implicit chant: "Heads will roll, you can believe that. Heads will roll until the banking industry looks like a bowling alley during tournament week."

When FIRREA became law, the American Bankers Association was also enormously pleased and regarded it as insightful legislation that, if too long in coming, was a triumph. FIRREA, as they understood it, focused aggressively on S&Ls, would curb the competitive threat they posed to banks, and appeared more or less to leave banks alone.

But, as we were soon to learn, it wasn't only the thrifts who were to be affected by FIRREA.

When FIRREA was published in its entirety and made available to banks, it was hundreds of pages in length. When I examined an abridgment of FIRREA's key points, I was initially enthusiastic. It required S&Ls to adopt new capital standards. It transferred regulatory powers previously held by the Federal Home Loan Bank Board to a new agency called the Office of Thrift Supervision (OTS), under the auspices of the U.S. Treasury Department, and it abolished the defunct Federal Savings and Loan Insurance Corporation. But there were more obscure points I didn't understand. I puzzled over it with Dick Flamson and our chief legal counsel, Russ Freeman.

"FIRREA? What does it do?" we asked.

Freeman's eyes crinkled behind his glasses. "Its stated intention is clearly to reform the regulatory system and tighten restrictions on thrifts and banks. As you can see, the act is very compendious. I haven't read the entire thing. I know it comes down very, very hard on the S&Ls."

Russ had been with Security Pacific for nearly thirty years. He was a man of supreme integrity. Unfortunately, he was also an unrelenting and chronic chain-smoker, so much so that in 1990 he had to have a leg amputated because there was so much cardiovascular blockage. Even after that dire turn of events, Russ was unwilling or unable to kick the habit. Security Pacific had a *No Smoking* policy for everyone, or almost everyone: I'd modified it slightly, to read *Absolutely No Smoking Anywhere Except for Russ Freeman's Office*. He was a spectacularly bright and comprehensible attorney. If he couldn't solve a problem directly he knew how to get it solved.

Flamson was impatient and pressed him. "But isn't it a good law?"

"Well," Freeman said, "it's—I think it's a good law. It's enormously complex. I need to read it closely and sit down with our loan people in order to discern if and how it directly impacts banks."

Flamson sat forward. "It facilitated our purchase of Gibraltar, didn't it?"

Freeman was noncommittal.

Flamson shrugged his shoulders and tried to get Freeman to disgorge whatever reservations might be in his mind. "Russ, it looks extremely thorough to me, for something created by Congress. Anything that cracks down on thrifts is good for us. Who can argue with the fundamental sanity of this law?"

"We'll see. Because of the bill's density and obscurity, it could take some time—perhaps months—to fully recognize its implications."

Freeman hobbled back to his office for a cigarette.

▼

Our ignorance and bliss about FIRREA was enjoyable while
it lasted. When the reversal came, it was the shock of our
lives—a direct hit, a missile fired directly up the bank's
fanny. As I began to review new valuation reports on criticized real estate loans, I saw that something was dramatically different about the way in which these properties were
being valued, particularly by the regulators.

"You've got to figure this out," I told John Kooken. "I
mean, Holy Christ, I'm looking at a loan we made for $24
million that was secured by a piece of property worth $30
million a few months ago that this report says is now worth
$18 million. We're going to have to write this loan down an-
other $8 million because we can't carry loans at values that
exceed the underlying collateral."

"I understand that's a bunch of baloney. I'll get right on it,"
John said.

If it had only been a single write-down of $8 million on
one particular loan—an aberration—that would have been a
tolerable inconvenience. But something was very wrong:
every new appraisal on these loans reflected extreme reductions in valuation. And Security Pacific had billions of dollars of such loans—many of them scheduled for reevaluation
or reappraisal in the next twelve months.

A week later, a flurry of new reports arrived. I read the new
appraisal on a commercial land development that we had financed in Tampa, Florida. Good developer, good location,
good project, perhaps a bit ahead of its time; but we still believed in the ability of this project to succeed. But for some
reason the appraiser had assumed that it would require eighteen years for the project to be completely finished and oc-
cupied, and had discounted this slow build-out at a 15% annual rate, resulting in an $8 million current valuation on a de-
velopment that cost $22 million and was appraised at $26
million just two years before!

I pressed harder and harder for answers. "This is unbelievable. What the hell is going on here?"

Bob Corteway was doing everything he could to track
down the problem. "Bob, we're trying to get our hands
around this thing. I'll get back to you as soon as I find out."

I popped into John Kooken's office.

Kooken's lair was a monument to one brilliant man's pro-
ductivity, and he often labored into the late night, only to
emerge from the office after arriving at dawn with a precious
menagerie of financial updates and the befuddled countenance of Tor Johnson wandering through a graveyard in *Plan
9 From Outer Space*. Hopelessly cluttered, his office looked
like World's End.

Kooken, a man who was mesmerized by numbers, inhabited stacks of paper like a recluse spider and had no idea how
to organize a legitimate executive office.

I had difficulty finding him amid the stacks. In fact, the office was such an aesthetic catastrophe that we had to film
Kooken's portion of the quarterly video report to shareholders in a specially devised "set" designed to look like a respectable CFO's office.

Russ Freeman and Bob Corteway were also searching for
Kooken. Russ was pacing and smoking, and Corteway was
speaking into two phones at once. Although I couldn't see
John, like the Wizard of Oz I knew he was sequestered behind the stacks of papers. "Say, guys, what exactly is going
on with the appraisals? Something is fluky."

I heard Kooken's disembodied voice. "I know, this is
awful. We're scrambling to find out."

New reports now inundated me; the situation was serious,
it was out of control.

There was a $30 million property being developed by a
large California developer that had been revalued at $24 mil-
lion. Security Pacific had pumped $54 million into a project
called Dove Canyon. Its prior valuation at $70 million had
been reappraised to $44 million. A $215 million property had

been valued at 60% of its previous value. The Sir Francis Drake Hotel, whose value we believed to be $46 million, had been downgraded to $33 million. The Northtown Mall, which we'd appraised at $128 million, had been reappraised at $98 million. A hotel operation in Philadelphia formerly valued at $21 million was now worth $7.8 million. In every instance Security Pacific faced the imminent write-off of millions of dollars. It just went on and on, without explanation.

"Bob, we've found out what's going on!" Russ, along with Bob and John, rushed into my office. Russ looked a bit ashen as he put out a cigarette with one hand while in his other hand was a xerox copy of a legal document. "Corteway found it! In order to get a handle on this you've got to understand an innocuous provision of the law. Buckle your seatbelt."

"I'm buckled," I said, bracing myself.

"I'm looking at it right here," Freeman announced in exacting, lawyer-like enunciation. "12CFR34, subsection C, Appraisal, Title 11 of FIRREA directs us to appraise our real estate collateral down to the value of a cash sale solely on the basis of what we can sell it for today."

"That's bullshit," I said.

"No, it's true. It no longer matters what we think land *could* be worth. Any real estate land development or mini-perm loan we have made that is in any trouble, even a slight variation in its timing, lease terms, or use, will have to be reappraised at current value. Essentially a fire sale!"

"No fucking way. Some of these properties, we know, will always be worth a great deal."

Corteway sadly shook his head. "It doesn't matter what we anticipate for the property; it must be appraised on the basis of what it is worth today. In other words, if we have even small problems with a real estate loan, we have to deal on an 'as is' valuation. No long-term solution. All valuations must be made forthwith, based on what a whole property would fetch from a single buyer within twelve months."

"But, but—" I stammered. "We made loans based on what land would be worth over time if developed in a stabilized economy."

"That's the nut of the problem, Bob," said Russ. "And the figures that trouble you reflect that disparity."

"But we're talking about millions—perhaps billions—of dollars."

"I suspect we are talking about *billions* of dollars," said Corteway, who had turned stone white. "It's not a good thing for us."

This was an understatement. Our bank was dependent on real-estate to a degree that was frightening and had been since 1932 when our predecessors christened a new Real Estate Division. Despite the Great Depression, real estate was considered a necessary and prudent investment for a bank that proclaimed its economic roots to be the California land itself. We were committed to the land, and we never looked back. The notion that loans on real estate might become the weak link in our balance sheet, in light of no historical antecedents whatsoever, was *unthinkable*. It never occurred to us that there could be a prolonged and very serious economic downturn in our home state of California, or that legislation as ghastly as FIRREA—seemingly *engineered* to sink our bank—would come our way.

Our Age of Innocence promptly gave way to the Age of Panic.

Flamson did not take the epiphany well. In fact, he was severely shaken. "What are they trying to do to us? The regulators don't know what the hell they're doing. Just because the S&Ls attracted a bunch of crooks doesn't mean they have to penalize the commercial banks. Bob, this is no small thing!" His voice cracked. "Security Pacific is somewhat unusual in that we have more money in real estate development than most other banks, particularly here in California, and our economy is showing some signs of worsening."

"We're into it up to our necks."

Flamson's voice withered; he was distraught. "As a consequence of this provision, our real estate portfolio is going to be very, very hard hit. And if we suffer *any* further economic downturn, we are not as well prepared as a lot of other banks to handle it; we are in very serious trouble. This is no joke. Jesus, Bob, the bank could *fail* over this crap."

I knew it, and I was worried.

The news of subsection C spread like wildfire among top management.

Executives throughout the company aware of a sudden pall on the fifty-fourth floor dropped by my office to ascertain its cause.

"What's going on?" asked John Singleton. "You can hear a pin drop."

"It's FIRREA," I replied.

"FIRREA hurts us? I thought FIRREA was a victory. The ABA called it a triumph."

"FIRREA is no triumph. It's a piece of shit. Absolutely killer legislation."

"I'd like to read it myself."

"It's buried in here." I showed Singleton the provision.

He read it slowly. "What does this mean for Security Pacific?"

"It means we're in the shitter—that's what it means. If the loan gets into trouble or the terms aren't met we have to write it down—now."

Flamson was fit to be tied. "The government got us into this mess and they should help get us out."

No, I thought. That was always the hope, but seldom the reality. What the government excelled at was getting banks in trouble and leaving them to twist in the wind. "All that will be left is the crumbs off the king's table."

"How much exposure do we have out there?" Flamson demanded. "How much do we have in California?"

"We have $13.5 billion worth of real estate land and development loans, of which $12.1 billion are in the United States and $7 billion were originated here in California. We also have about $4 billion of unfunded real estate commitments and standby letters of credit, of which $2.8 billion are in California," Corteway explained.

"Oh man. If these numbers are right, that's over 20% of our total loan portfolio. That's $17.5 billion of fucking exposure subject to this new valuation methodology." I looked at Singleton. "*That's* why FIRREA could be a disaster for us."

Flamson paced. "This is ugly. Congress has just handed us a pistol in which every chamber is loaded, told us to put it to our head and take our chances by pulling the trigger."

I jotted some calculations on a pad. "If these appraisals continue to reflect the trend of about a 30% valuation discount, we would have to eat over $5 billion—and that is more than our capital. We would lose everything, goddammit. Am I overstating it, or are we screwed?"

"No," Corteway said, "I agree that's an accurate analysis."

"Well, then, we have got to halt any new real estate lending right now," I said.

The fact of the matter was that FIRREA was a catastrophe, and its malignant effect on our real estate portfolio could not possibly be overstated. Worse, if it was true that the legislators who penned FIRREA did so with Keating specifically in mind, I was now fully cognizant of the fact that I was the unwitting accomplice and co-author of the pernicious law that would cripple our bank irrevocably.

It was incumbent upon us to confront the regulatory authorities, quickly. We theorized it was possible that the regulatory agencies didn't fully realize the implications of that particular provision and that, perhaps, once they did, they might seek a softer landing either through appeals to Congress or in a softer interpretation.

After George Moody retired from the day-to-day management, I was appointed to serve the remainder of his term on the board of the American Bankers Association. At the ABA I had participated in a number of animated discussions about the new regulatory environment in general, and FIRREA in particular. Passions had been stirred. Naturally, the loudest voices in opposition to the valuation provision came from banks with large real estate development portfolios. We concluded that we should address our concerns to the regulators in person.

We convened an emergency meeting of the ABA in Orlando, Florida, and requested and received a private meeting of the ABA board with Bill Seidman, the head of the Federal Deposit Insurance Corporation, Bob Clarke, the comptroller of the currency, and Alan Greenspan, chairman of the Federal Reserve.

For whatever reason, perhaps because I appeared to feel exceedingly passionate about these issues—and for good reason—I was elected to be the spokesperson to vocalize our concerns.

I didn't know how much sway I held with the regulators, and was concerned that perhaps I'd intensified their antipathy toward Security Pacific by delivering speeches in which I made comments like:

"Our government response to recent problems has been to de-fang the banks, leaving us on a diet of soft food and pabulum. The first so-called corrective measure was the Financial Institutions Recovery and Reform Act of 1989, commonly called FIRREA. Because much of the S&L problem was the result of aggressive real estate lending, this law, as promulgated, requires outside appraisals to support real estate loans. That sounds like a very logical move. But it also mandates that the appraisals must be on an 'as is' basis. In other words, what a single buyer would pay for the entire project within a twelve-month period. This in effect required that real estate be marked to market, a new concept in banking that ignores the historical valuation process which looked at periodic economic downturns as only a temporary impairment to value."

In short, discrediting FIRREA had become my obsession, my crusade, my raison d'être.

▼

Approximately forty members of the ABA board attended the session, which was held in the auxiliary conference room of a convention hall in Orlando.

The tone of the meeting was very civilized. Fed chair Alan Greenspan looked attentive. After introductions and salutations, I was permitted to lay the foundation of our case.

"I will be as concise as possible. Our concern is with the new emerging regulatory environment and in particular the appraisal valuation provisions set forth in FIRREA. In the past decade, hand in hand with the assistance of the government, banks have weathered a triad of considerable crises. I speak of course of the agricultural crisis, the energy crisis, and the LDC crisis. Now we face a fourth: the simultaneous deterioration of worldwide economies and the toll this is expected to take on the real estate industry and the portfolios of large banks that specialize in real estate lending. The application of FIRREA, its passage into law, and subsequent impact of particular of its provisions—specifically Subsection C, Appraisal—was not something that we foresaw and its ramifications are both tremendous and severe.

"The government, and we applaud them for it, did not, however, deal so drastically with our prior crises, worked with the banks, and in each case these problems resolved themselves over time.

"More recently, in the early 1980s, when weather anomalies adversely affected the value of farm loans and seriously impaired the agricultural market, government successfully converted what appeared to be an imminent crisis into a long-term solution. Had those who drafted FIRREA taken the same approach to the agricultural crisis, small banks all over the Midwest would have had to write off all their loans and it would have destroyed perhaps five thousand banks. But government handled it with care and foresight: you allowed us to ride it out, recalibrate the loans on a long-term basis, and the values ultimately rekindled as the economy rebounded. In the mid-1980s, when the lesser developed countries were unable to repay huge sums of debt, government, with foresight and care, converted what appeared to be imminent crisis into a long-term solution. Had analogous restrictions been imposed on banks during the LDC crisis—had FIRREA been applied in this circumstance—that we had to write these loans down to twelve-month liquidation value—we would have witnessed the failure of a majority of the top ten banks in this country.

"It seems to us that government today should be just as interested in the survival of the banks—the engines of our economy—as they were during other difficult times in the 1980s.

"The thesis I am setting forth is that, unlike in prior crises, the regulators seem to be, for want of a better expression, off on a destructive mission rather than a constructive mission, and that they are causing the annihilation of our ability to continue to advance credit to many of the industries such as real estate and others who've we traditionally supported. Banks are having to pull in their reins in terms of their lending standards and policies because of the new fear engendered by regulators in their aggressive examination of portfolios under FIRREA.

"I ask you to consider the ramifications to the economy of this provision.

"While we are absolutely aware of the theory behind FIRREA's stipulation that real estate be valued and assets be valued for collateral purposes on a twelve-month liquidation basis, if regulators rigidly maintain this as a precept for examination, it is going to basically destroy the real estate industry, and lubricate the further deterioration of the U.S. economy. And I don't believe this to be an overstatement. FIRREA casts a dark shadow over all the banks in the United States. While we understand that its purpose is to facilitate the clean-up of the savings and loan debacle, its unintended effect will be to cripple banks across this country!

"Because lending is the engine of economic growth, it logically follows that once this engine shuts off, the economy will slow more and more. Fewer customers will be able to obtain a loan; no longer will our customers be able to readily purchase machinery, build a business, or develop property. Jobs will be lost, and the middle market will be the hardest hit.

"While we fully recognize that we are in weakened economic times, we suggest that we be permitted to deal with the current crisis like we dealt with the LDC crisis, and that you allow us to pursue a long-term solution to a severe problem, rather than impose upon banks a short-term solution. We propose that you allow us to carry real estate loans at a value that anticipates a return to a stronger economy and the value-enhancement that development provides. This approach will be a change to a valuation process whose result is to reduce bank capital and could have a very deep bottom. We believe it is premature, drastic, and Draconian to write these properties and loans down as is now being prescribed. Thank you for your time and attention."

I sat down.

Alan Greenspan didn't take long to compose his response. "We certainly understand what you are saying, and we are sympathetic to your view. And we are aware that this is a very serious difficulty, and has formidable ramifications.

However, the fact remains, FIRREA is a mandate of Congress and it is our job to enforce it."

"Do you believe that Congress fully comprehends the inevitable and anticipated consequences of that provision, and its detrimental effect not only on banks but on the ability of banks to continue lending?" I asked.

Greenspan replied, "That I can't say with absolute certainty. One would hope that Congress would extrapolate the potential consequence of any legislation as far-reaching as that set forth in FIRREA. What I can say with a measure of certainty is that FIRREA was passed into law, and that it cannot be unpassed. FIRREA is a congressional expression of dismay and impatience."

"Regardless of the harm it may cause to banks?"

"Regardless or in spite of the harm it may cause. And FIRREA, they feel, is the way to handle it."

As Greenspan replied, I could see every ABA eye in the room glaze over, not in boredom but anguish.

"Mr. Clarke," I asked the comptroller of the currency, "do you think it is possible for the regulators to exercise some latitude with regard to the rigidity with which they demand banks enact that provision? May they be empowered to use their own good judgment?" What I was asking was, Could regulators be made to use the gift of common sense that God gave them when deciding whether a bank should write down real estate loans whose outlook is strong notwithstanding a harsh appraisal?

"We feel the regulators were rebuked with a rather firm hand for what happened to the thrift industry, and it is our job to make sure it never happens again and to see that the mandate of Congress is *executed*. This is what Congress does, this is what Congress wants, and it is our job to enforce the will of Congress."

"Very well. And you realize what this will do to banks?"

"We, as a government, are going to have to accept whatever fallout is the side-effect of this act."

"So you're saying, if I hear you correctly, this is the way it's going to be, and you guys had better get used to it."

"I'm afraid that's about the size of it."

When the forty directors of the ABA filed out of that conference room, we were dazed. There would be no recourse, no escape hatch. We were stuck.

I walked away shaking my head. Banks had a very serious problem and Security Pacific in particular was facing a chasm. Things had changed. Government was not going to help us this time. Congress saw banks as the enemy. And regulators, I feared, would no longer be mere annoyances but would become avenging angels. We were no longer "too big to fail."

▼

Flamson leapt up when I entered his office. "How did it go?"

"The meeting was a disaster." I gave him the blow-by-blow. "It's no longer a collective We. It's Us and Them. It's every bank for itself."

I'd never seen Dick look so somber, so ashen. "Oh shit. That's a prime-time, top-flight screwup."

"And my estimation of the regulators leads me to believe there is no leeway for further discourse on this subject. FIRREA is written in stone. It's the Eleventh Commandment."

"Bob," Dick persisted, "we don't have a 'problem,' we have a 'catastrophe.' If they force us to write down our real estate portfolio, we'll be goners. Security Pacific has a tremendous cash flow from the rest of its business, almost $2 billion a year pre-tax, isn't it? But if we have to write off $4 or $5 billion or more over the next year or two, we're dead ducks. The future of Security Pacific has been etched in quick-dry concrete."

Concrete, we knew, that had dried around our feet.

5

This Baton Has a Fuse

"I'll even go along with the fact that you ask many of us to kiss your ring. That's okay. But I just wish you'd take the ring out of your back pocket."

—Richard Flamson

If bankers were the personalities—the well-loved athletes and class presidents in the 1950s and 1960s who completed grad school and went on to significant personal achievement—the regulators were the less glamorous students, the *nerds*, no less capable, yet seeking less ambitious and more idealistic careers as the Guardians of America, its people and its original principles. Yet in their capacity as financial traffic cops these obscure protectors of the system had been dumped on by their banker friends and Congress once too often. Their hearts, once full of admiration and compassion, had turned to stone. They were pissed and they wanted their stature back. They were about to embark on a crusade.

Unfortunately, Security Pacific had provoked them.

Throughout the 1980s regulators barely frowned as madcaps like Keating hurdled one legal loophole after another to twist the intentions of poorly conceived regulatory legislation. Why had the regulators ignored the exigencies that had arisen in savings and loans across the country until it was too late—until it was so late that they had to be dragged before Congress by force and spanked as a nation watched on in approbation and despair?

The bank and thrift regulatory system consists of four federal agencies and some one hundred state agencies—the Federal Reserve, Comptroller of the Currency, Federal Deposit Insurance Corporation, and the Office of Thrift Supervision. Then comes state regulators for commercial banks and thrift institutions within each of the fifty states—each duplicating the function of the others, but for a different purpose and subject to the stricture of a disparate set of laws and edicts. The examinations were overlapping and frequently redundant, and because different agencies observed different policies of examination, the results were sometimes confusing or contradictory.

Depending on the circumstances of their oversight, these fellows could promote either desirable improvements and full rehabilitation, or impose a straitjacket of detailed bureaucratic meddling that doubled everyone's workload and contributed to an environment of considerable anarchy.

Security Pacific was a national bank with a holding company and, therefore, accountable to three agencies. The bank was under the principal jurisdiction of the Office of the Comptroller of the Currency—or OCC—although it was insured by and also reported to the FDIC; the holding company was scrutinized primarily by the Federal Reserve and its local regulator.

We were soon to be beset on all sides; then something even worse occurred that shook Security Pacific to its very foundation. Dick Flamson had been diagnosed with a very serious, potentially fatal, blood disorder. His bone marrow produced too many of one type of blood cell and not enough of another. This malady would soon culminate in full-blown leukemia. While I'd known Dick had some kind of problem—he kept frequent medical appointments—his consistent display of passion, enthusiasm, and outgoing manner gave me no reason to suspect just how serious the ailment was. It disturbed me greatly to see him so fatigued, but I never saw his determination flag.

Dick was my mentor and a very crucial influence on my life. Dick and I had clicked from very early on. We shared a similar view of the world and a peculiar sense of humor. His entrepreneurial spirit and fearless curiosity about attempting untested strategies motivated me to a adopt a similar vision of corporate life. The news of his disease was, to those of us who loved Dick, heartbreaking. But the courage, grace, and bravery with which he endured his illness while contending with the difficulties at Security Pacific was remarkable and inspiring.

As he became increasingly ill, he had to have frequent blood transfusions. Dick so badly wanted to be on top of things and alert at important summits and board meetings that he would often undergo a blood transfusion the day before these events so he could be as energetic and alert as possible.

Despite his ailment, Dick Flamson had an exuberant spirit and, like me, a generally comic view of the world. He moved like a metcor shower, filling the space around him with the effusive light of wit and passion. He had an opinion about everything, and trying to change it was challenging and difficult. Some employees found his certitude intimidating rather than as the sporting invitation for debate I thought it often was. He inspired loyalty and fear in equal measures, but he had a good heart, a sharp wit, and a moral composure that was beyond reproach. His genius was strategy. He was farsighted, irascible, and playful at a time when bank presidents generally were encouraged by an unwritten doctrine of etiquette to be myopic, agreeable, and somber.

Once as I entertained prestigious and fairly humorless Japanese businessmen in our largest conference room, I was aghast to see Flamson secreted behind a potted plant. He stuck his head through the branches and, visible only to me, made monkey faces in a frantic attempt to rattle my composure before our serious guests.

But most of the time, his mind was fixed on work. His very countenance delivered the message: "I'm in charge." He moved rapidly, sat on desks, gestured with wide arms. He looked you right in the eye, he studied you, he tested you. He'd pit you against your colleague and watch the drama unfold.

His challenges either alienated or brought out the best in employees. I enjoyed sparring with Flamson and attempting to hurdle the nearly impossible obstacle of changing his mind.

"Bob, now you can do better than that. Any fool knows. . . ."

The better I got to know Dick the harder it was to keep the two straight—the banker and the boy—because I'd see flickers of the child everywhere. The comments that people took so seriously I began to see as playful expressions, thinly wrapped in the veneer of intimidation. It was almost as if Dick took joy in watching the Life Force provoked by confrontation. I sometimes thought he said shocking things just to watch our jaws drop, or to delight in our struggle to convince him he was wrong.

Flamson was the antithesis of stuffy—a walking rebuke *against* the caricature of banker as stifled, repressed, and stagnant. At weekend managerial conferences he dressed casually, sometimes in those awful striped shirts. He watered the plants in the office. He ridiculed some of the modern art masterpieces in the mezzanine. He played games with the elevators and on the phone. He hid coffee cups. He concealed himself beneath desks. Once you became attuned to his wavelength, it was impossible not to respect and love the guy.

To Flamson the regulators were *clowns*, ineptitude made manifest.

Even when Security Pacific was strong and robust, and the regulatory bodies were largely uncritical of our performance, Flamson thrilled to a new opportunity to ridicule and belittle the bank examiners. He never did anything terrible, but to Flamson the regulators were an immense source of comedy that fueled his effervescent, occasionally wicked, sense of humor.

When interrogated by analysts about Security Pacific's increasing diversification and entrepreneurial endeavors, Dick would counter skepticism with measured reason and disarming candor: "We *are* a conservative institution. We've always been a conservative institution. But I don't see conservatism and innovation as mutually exclusive. If conservative means we want this bank to succeed in the modern era, we are going to have to be innovative. If Security Pacific doesn't explore new avenues for revenue, new technologies, and new markets—and do it as creatively as possible—the other banks will."

But if Flamson had to answer to a regulator, or found himself occupying the same room with one, a fever overtook him. He simply could not repress the urge to needle, prod, or vex the poor bastard, especially if he disagreed with a regulator's verdict on a loan or a voiced doubt about our future strategy. Although I saw regulators as a necessary and tolerable annoyance to be endured, Flamson saw them as the unrelenting and incompetent long arm of the government, troublesome and sullen bureaucrats brandishing legal pads who were to be placated during audits and ostracized afterward, and whose multiplicity of examinations were superfluous ordeals to be mocked.

He loved to antagonize the examiners. He looked down his nose at them and, unfortunately for the future of Security

Pacific, he conveyed that feeling *about* them *to* them. And this, I felt, was a major strategic miscalculation.

"Bank examiners are gumshoes, and nothing but," he liked to say. "And we are one of the strongest institutions in the country! Why do they pester us? Don't they know it doesn't matter one iota what they think about Security Pacific?"

Regulators would deliver carefully detailed and painstaking presentations to the board of directors. "We continue to urge the management of Security Pacific to be very cautious in entering the securities markets, and we have some perfunctory concerns over your investments in the United Kingdom. . . ."

Even though this was long before we ran into trouble, the mere fact that they stood in judgment provoked Flamson's wit—he would goad, question their sophistication, and openly criticize their intelligence. Flamson would punctuate regulatory presentations with glib commentary: "Well, I appreciate your warning, but we know what we're doing."

After a pause, the examiner continued. "It's very important that Security Pacific be mindful of limitations set forth in Glass-Steagall and the desired objectives with regard to building and maintaining adequate capital."

I caught Flamson mid-yawn. Then he picked up the examination report and began to fan his face with it.

The regulator coughed, then quickly concluded his review. "But otherwise, your ranking as a strong institution, and your rating as a healthy institution, remain intact."

"Thank you," Flamson said sarcastically, "for that thought-provoking, richly engaging, and tantalizing dissertation. It was very reassuring."

One afternoon a regulator dared to question our Merchant Bank. "What you are proposing to engage in is a highly complex endeavor that has not really been tested before. Our advice is that you proceed with caution."

Flamson's response was direct and immediate: "We certainly appreciate your concern. But if we as an institution accede to the rigid strictures of what institutions are supposed to do, and scuttle from a new opportunity because a particular strategy is too complex for some people to understand, we would be paralyzed with fear and never pursue one single innovation."

Those of us who knew Dick knew these comments were made with some measure of self-parody. But the regulators didn't find the acerbity all that hilarious.

As the regulators vacated the room, Flamson stood up. "Ah, same old crap. That's his point of view. We know damn well what we have in Security Pacific and we know what we're doing with it. Anything these fellows say has to be taken with a grain of salt. If they were any good they'd have real jobs," he said, "and not just be regulators."

Flamson was an equal-opportunity satirist whose irreverence was by no means limited to the regulators. Around this time he disrupted a caravan ushering the British Royals across the Outback. Dick and I were visiting Melbourne, Australia, on one of our Asian tours. Present on the trip were Dick and Dick's wife, Arden, and my wife, Loretta, and I. It was a Sunday and we had been invited by the Security Pacific's resident manager in Australia, who was our host, to visit and observe a charity polo match, in which Prince Charles of England was to participate, and which Diana, Princess of Wales, would attend.

Following the after-game reception, where we chatted with the royal couple, we returned to our limousine. We idled at the driveway exit as the prince and princess's entourage of fifteen white Mercedes limos preceded ours in a dignified queue out of the parking area; they pulled out from a road on our right.

Flamson watched the cumbersome entourage with dismay. "What a lot of razzle dazzle. Who needs it? We'll be here all day."

As the last Mercedes merged onto the road we pulled out, following directly behind the entourage. Because our car was a dead ringer for the others, we naturally resembled part of the royal procession.

People had gathered in excited clusters at the sides of the road for a glimpse of the prince and princess as they passed. The onlookers waved, unfurled banners, blew kisses, and shouted messages of strident support and love.

I can only suppose that Flamson thought this was a perfect opportunity to thwart protocol, to kill time, and to bring out the "boy." He knelt on the limo seat, slid open the rooftop, and grabbed and donned his wife's white hat. He then stood up with his upper body extending 3 feet out of the sunroof and began to smile and wave to the crowds.

His waves were slow-motion and gracious; his grin was wide and sincere.

The looks on the people's faces was a thing to behold. They would be waving and as Flamson passed, looking like some strange, plump queen, the waves would slow down and their eyes would crinkle and their jaws would drop. Movement would cease; the onlookers would freeze in a tableau of dismay. Others pointed at Flamson, aghast, mouthing, "Who in the hell is that?" Then broad smiles would replace bewilderment, followed by a robust volley of laughter in recognition of the friendly lampoon.

We followed the royal entourage like this for about 10 miles. I was rolling on the floor laughing.

▼

Unlike the Aussies, the regulators had no sense of humor.

Beneath all this posturing and banter, both we and the regulators knew they were there because they had to be. Despite rumors to the contrary, I knew they were human beings—citizens of the Family of Man—struggling to perform an unpleasant yet indispensable task: they were the financial industry's policemen.

Like the menial laborer who walks the roller coaster track before dawn looking for signs of metal fatigue and loose bolts, regulators pore over documentation and loan portfolios looking for the hairline fractures that precede credit failure or, in the case of crooked institutions, the telltale residue of negligence and impropriety. Their job is not to deliver good news. For a troubled institution, a report from the bank examiner is like an knock on the door by the county coroner.

Flamson, goading the regulators, even if it was in the spirit of play, eventually incited a most undesirable side-effect: regulatory authorities perceived us as a haughty, overweening, arrogant, overbearing, and egotistical organization. To them, Security Pacific made no effort to work together with the fiduciary inspectors of the U.S. government; we'd drawn a line in the sand and ordered them not to cross it.

The truth of the matter was that there were times when we were too cocksure for our own good, and the regulators—with their industry overview, hundred-million-dollar databases, and batteries of consultants—had important insights that we lacked. They also had the memories of elephants and lots and lots of patience. To treat them with this degree of disrespect was not only an indiscretion but a grievous mistake for the future of Security Pacific, because regulators—individually and collectively—remembered every slight, every instance in which Flamson gave them "lip." I was worried they would someday return the favor.

Unfortunately, Flamson was not the only executive who dissed the regulators. I listened in horror one afternoon as David Lovejoy became embroiled in conflict with a regulator from the Office of the Comptroller of the Currency. I wasn't following the thread of the conversation, but my heart skipped a beat when I overheard Lovejoy refer to the bank examiner, a woman, as a "bitch." While I later reproached him for the epithet, the damage was done and the offense would resurface years later.

Because Dick Flamson involved himself intimately in Security Pacific's issuance of credit, he took it as a personal affront when a classification was challenged by the regulators.

On one occasion—whose fallout would prove nearly lethal at a later date—Dick became embrangled in an acrimonious exchange with a regulator whose arbitrary reclassification of several key loans had provoked Flamson's deepest passions.

Flamson's cavernous voice could be heard in offices on the opposite side of the building. "There you go again! Trying to tell us how to run our goddamn business! It's a wonder you nudniks can tie your damn shoelaces! You know nothing about the circumstances of this loan and you have neither the wisdom nor the authority to instruct us how to classify it."

The examiner's voice was a fractured whisper. "I've carefully deciphered the complete history of that loan."

"I don't care if you've deciphered the Dead Sea Scrolls! These loans are nowhere close to being downgraded."

"It's patently obvious the quality of these loans is in decline."

"Your intelligence is in decline! You let us do our own classifications."

The regulator's face turned the color of steak tartare as he gathered up his paperwork, shoved it into a crammed briefcase and made a bee-line for the elevator.

"Bye-bye, jackass!" Flamson shouted after he'd departed.

The interpersonal dynamics alone were unfortunate. We had not exactly presented our best face to the regulators. But matters were exacerbated tenfold when Flamson refused to let bygones be bygones.

The following week Dick phoned the OCC and complained about this particular regulator. "He's inept! He couldn't find the sun with an astrolabe at high noon. I don't want to see his face in our bank again, and I'm not kidding around. Why don't you give the guy a transfer to, say, the Aleutian Islands?"

The OCC removed the regulator from assignment to Security Pacific and had him transferred to another bank. This was to my knowledge *unprecedented*. The event transcended mere discourtesy—it was a grave miscalculation with dire consequences. Bank examiners were bureaucrats with long memories, and this memory, particularly, lodged in the craw of the regulatory community—it appeared to circulate throughout the industry like the rumor of a wildfire—and was remembered years later.

▼

In the wake of congressional hearings surrounding the passage of FIRREA, the bank examination process was drastically restructured and a diligent and aggressive new posture was assumed by regulators. A crack team of examiners was sent head-first into Texas, where S&L and bank failures were prominent and severe. Regulators were inflexible and went in like vigilantes and stood toe-to-toe with bankers wearing diamond-studded Rolex watches.

We heard again and again: "The regulators are really a bunch of assholes, and they have become inflexible, rigid, and fixed in their views, and destructive in their actions."

In this highly charged atmosphere, the stakes were high. We received constant reports of verbal and legal battles between S&L and bank management and the regulators, and boards and the regulators. The examiners were adamant and, in a fit of righteous indignation, hardened their position. They couldn't, and they wouldn't, take any more shit. As regulators had promised Congress, heads began to roll.

There were rumors of incredible rows and screaming matches, and caught up in this environmental fury regulators began to file lawsuits against S&L and bank management and boards of directors alleging incompetence and egregious misconduct.

The power was shifting. Radically.

Washington, with the American public breathing down its neck, expressed its full support for the regulators.

"This is the way it's going to be now," regulators had told me in Orlando, and now made clear to all bankers. "We are not going to allow what happened to the savings and loans to happen again, ever, especially not in the banking industry. So you boys had better learn the score."

Regulators began to suggest to the boards of a troubled bank, sometimes emphatically, that they replace the sitting management with new leadership because they believed the current leadership to be inept. And if management wasn't changed, board members could be held personally liable on the basis of their negligence. If a bank's capital fell too low, the regulators could place a bank under a *Prompt Corrective Action Directive*. And if the bank continued to perform badly and ignored regulatory advisories, the regulators could obtain a *Cease and Desist* order and force the board to make changes. If these "friendly" approaches failed, regulators could seize the bank outright and sell it. They not only had the power of persuasion, but the sanction of strengthened laws and the tacit approval of Congress.

▼

In late 1989, Flamson's illness worsened. He came to the Los Angeles office less frequently. He set up an office in Orange County for days he was too tired to make the trip to Los Angeles. He was required to have blood transfusions routinely and by the time he began ongoing treatment at the Hoag Cancer Center he had received nearly three hundred such transfusions.

The realization that Dick was living on borrowed time cast a pall over the bank.

▼

Late in 1989 Dick decided to give up his role as CEO and that I would take over.

If, in hindsight, there was a hint that Flamson considered me as a potential heir-apparent, it was in the later 1980s, when Flamson began to pit me against George Moody. In classic Flamson style, Dick would go out of his way to create various challenges and confrontations, some of them illusory. If there was something nasty to be said to George, he would have me go down and tell him, and vice versa. I soon realized he was testing both of us, sizing us up, watching us like a couple of rats in a Skinner Box. He was also challenging George to be more enthusiastic, more visionary, and more involved in the creative side of banking.

By creating the illusion that Moody and I were opponents, Flamson created a palpable tension. People began to take sides and exaggerate our differences. I suddenly had a reputation as a staff-hater; George was the innovation-squasher. I was the wild-ass risk-taker; George the pious sentimentalist who wept every time he saw a Security Pacific commercial on TV and practically trembled with reverence whenever he invoked the name of Joseph Sartori.

As a result of these confrontations, Flamson realized I was more his kind of guy; I had the enthusiasm, energy, and attitude for which he was searching. I wanted badly to build something bigger, better, and stronger.

Like many of my predecessors at Security Pacific, I was a native of southern California, born in Glendale in 1935. I married my college sweetheart, Loretta Gesell, who was at the time nineteen. She was always a guiding force and light in my life; to some degree my conscience. There was a time when I thought I could potentially have become something very different than I became—undisciplined, unfocused, and unruly. Her graciousness, kindness, and virtue rubbed off on me immediately and early; she was a mirror in which I saw the things I wanted to change and picked out the characteristics I wanted to develop. She was a crucial force in my personal evolution.

I'd majored in public administration, intent on becoming a policeman—by that I don't mean a regulator, just a cop. I flunked out of UCLA, made up my grades, reapplied at USC, where through perseverance and long hours I finally achieved straight A's as a senior and graduated with a bachelor of science degree in 1957.

Then in 1958 I went into the Navy. I was stationed on a remote island in the Pacific called Kwajalein, where I also worked part-time as a clerk/proof operator for the Bank of Hawaii facility. At that time I had two sons and a third on the way. My back was against the wall. The bills mounted. Soon I would be out of the Navy. It was 1961. John F. Kennedy was president, and time was moving at the speed of light.

I'd come to the conclusion that I didn't really want to be a policeman. To help find a job from the remote, barren island, I sent home for a copy of the Los Angeles Yellow Pages and each night let my fingers do the walking through the pages until I found something I thought I could do: branch banking. For reasons I can't recall, I picked out Security Pacific. I sent my resume to their Personnel Department, obtained an interview, and was accepted into their management development training program. Not a sophisticated approach, but it seemed to work at the time.

I had no intrinsic desire to work at a bank. I was not born with a passion for banking. But I thrived in the atmosphere, liked the people attracted to banking, enjoyed the competition, felt I understood it, and didn't mind working hard to understand it better. And the more I understood banking, the more fascinated I became with trying to take it to the next level. Part of the fun was to guess where the next opportunities would arise.

▼

Flamson, seeking to offer guidance for the upcoming decade, met with me to discuss my new role and related personnel issues. After roughly an hour, the topic of conversation finally came around to John Singleton, a man who I felt didn't belong on Security Pacific's roster.

Singleton was something of a cryptogram—at least to me. Like David Lovejoy, whose expertise was the Merchant Bank, Singleton had carved out a niche for himself. But whereas Lovejoy's role was clear and of uncontestable importance to the bank, Singleton's purpose was enigmatic, ephemeral, and spooky.

Be that as it may—and for reasons that mystify me even to this day—Flamson and Moody shared a stellar regard for Singleton. They thought he was great—the best. I was aware of this, but unprepared for the tiny thermonuclear device Flamson now dropped in my lap. "I envision Singleton as your right-hand man, your chief operating officer."

I was thoughtful for a moment. I wanted to at least give this man, for whom I had such reverence, the courtesy of a considered response. But no matter how I spun the dynamic of a Smith–Singleton duo in my mind, it came up lemons on the slot machine.

"It ain't gonna happen," I blurted.

"John's great," gushed Flamson.

I tried gently to place the burden of proof on him. "Maybe you can enlighten me—what is it that so enchants you about Singleton?"

"Besides his technical savvy, he's a guy you can trust."

Unfortunately, I questioned the validity of this assumption. So far, Flamson had struck out. "Anything else?" I asked.

"Well, isn't that enough? You need a man like that at your side. Think about this angle: John can do for you what George has done for me."

"John Singleton?" I asked. Were we talking about the same fellow?

Then Flamson put it on the line: "I absolutely envision John Singleton as your George Moody. I can't get this image out of my mind."

I swallowed hard. *Singleton? My George Moody?* Moody had integrity, was credible and well-loved by shareholders, and had been blessed with the dual gifts of oratory transcendence and extraordinary conviviality. Singleton was circumspect, ineloquent, and impossible for me to understand. Whereas Moody could animate and inspire a crowd, Singleton would only put an audience to sleep. "Dick, I don't see it. I can't even imagine it."

"Is it that you don't think he can do it?" Dick persisted.

"I honestly don't know what John *can* or *can't* do, because I'm not really sure what he *does* do." Singleton was sort of a computer guy, but not really. I felt he was certainly no banker.

"You'll see what he can do," Flamson added, "when we put John on the board of directors."

"Put him on the board?" I gasped. This was indeed a joke. "You want me to promote Singleton and install him on the board of directors? You've got to be kidding. Dick, this is no time to be funny."

Flamson said, "I've already made a commitment to John."

Well uncommit, I felt like shouting. "I hear your enthusiasm, Dick, but my bottom line is I don't want John as my COO." The notion made me physically ill.

Flamson was visibly disappointed. "You honestly feel that way about John?"

"I can't get away from him fast enough. I go out of my way to avoid him."

"Hmmm. Do you believe John senses you don't like him all that much?"

"Oh, he *has* to."

After more back-and-forth, Flamson realized I was inflexible. "You won't change your mind, will you?"

I shook my head. "Sorry, Dick. Ain't gonna happen. You can't do that to me. You'd be starting me out on an uphill marathon with one broken leg. I have many ideas about how to run this company, and they don't include John Singleton. But I will keep him on the team and try to determine if he can handle more than technology."

▼

I needed people close to me that I trusted. Now that I was Dick's successor, I made sure that a team was in place who could take us through the 1990s. I knew that without such a team I could achieve little no matter how much enthusiasm I brought to the job.

My executive management team initially was comprised essentially of four individuals; Nick Binkley, Jerry Grundhofer, David Lovejoy, and John Singleton.

Nicholas B. Binkley joined Security Pacific in 1977. He was a slender, articulate executive with a flair for the professional. Nick blossomed while working as the number two officer in the FSS, where in his own way he successfully tested the limits with a number of financial adventures. FSS had its hand in a great many pies, including the financing of businesses of all kinds for a multitude of purposes, and individuals who couldn't qualify for bank credit. The business loans generated by FSS represented a broad range of American industry; cement manufacturers, silver plating companies, radio and television stations, as well as some unusual overseas adventures, including Eurofinance and a fleet of Hong Kong taxi-cabs.

FSS was described by one analyst as a black box that outsiders want to break open to see what makes it work. It was a complex organization that took Nick a good six months to fully understand when he came on board.

Binkley was an all-around character. He liked blue shirts with white collars and loud ties. With his efficiency, economy with the language, and penchant for saying the right thing, he had an almost Zen quality. As history would prove when he later performed and recorded music, Binkley had an artistic streak as well as a gift for business. At meetings, he had a perceptive and colorful way of cutting through the crap and getting to the point.

Binkley was unflappable, a fighter, and unafraid of a potentially acrimonious exchange. It was very difficult to un-
nerve him, and he was adept at balancing the interests of our
primary constituents—customer, shareholder, employee, and
community.

On the staff and technical side, I still depended enormously
on John Kooken, Bob Corteway, and excellent attorneys Russ
Freeman and Maurice DeWolff—our bank's chief legal
counsel—and Kathy Burke, our human resources director.
Flamson and, to a lesser extent, Moody, continued their legacy of guidance. Flamson remained my loyal personal ally
and confidant.

▼

I imagined that, like my predecessors, I would have approximately a decade to run the company. Technology was moving the industry quickly toward some unknown apogee of
transformation and I thought we could take advantage of the
opportunity to capture the New World as never before. I'd be
sixty-five in the year 2000, just past my ten-year anniversary
as CEO. I'd temporarily exorcised my passion for innovation
and my intermediate goals were fairly modest: I wanted to
contribute something—enhance shareholder value, shore up
bank strength—and go out with my flag flying high around
the year 2000.

But the future was going to be very different than I imagined.

6

Honey, I Shrunk the Bank

It was January 1990. I'd just been appointed president and CEO, and for that I was more grateful than not. The *not* part was the source of my anxiety. I was too aware of the propensity for economic deterioration and harsh regulatory oversight to believe the future would be a blissful ride. And although the transition of power had been smooth, there was no time for a honeymoon; I immediately began charting a new course for the 1990s.

My first major undertaking was to convene a high-level, closed-door management summit at the La Quinta desert resort, near Palm Springs. I wanted my team to review and discuss a formidable analysis of Security Pacific conducted at our request by a group called First Manhattan Consulting Group.

We had not yet detected any fatal fractures in Security Pacific's foundation; nevertheless, I was concerned about the immediate financial landscape and what might happen to our real estate loan portfolio if the California economy caved. I was convinced that we had to refocus our strategies and think long term for the coming decade—my decade. Our grasp had exceeded our ability to efficiently integrate and operate our ambitious Merchant Bank. Lobbyists had been unable to lay a hand on Glass–Steagall. The bill remained on the books. We were spread very thin, with a low relative level of capital and overreliance on short-term funding, but maintained a strong cash flow and healthy earnings stream. In this capricious economy, I felt that if we did not redirect our efforts—and quickly—our market value could suffer and, with it, our viability, options, and reputation.

Security Pacific was in a standoff with uncertainty. I'd grown skeptical that foreseeable events would permit us to find any breakthrough technologies, new products, service, or market we needed to in order to accelerate our returns and rate of growth. While our financial muscle and technology had allowed us to penetrate new markets in the 1980s, I had a suspicion that the modern Security Pacific might ultimately have to consolidate with some other bank in the near future and felt strongly that in order for any potential merger to be a merger of equals we would necessarily have to strengthen our corporation and increase our market capitalization.

In private conversations with Dick we had talked about the future outlook for banking. We had broached the subject of a merger.

"There are too damned many banks in this country," Dick said.

"Consolidation is of course the best answer to that dilemma, and I think we'll see a lot more of it in the future."

There were gradations in the desirability of a merger. A merger was not imminently necessary, but was it desirable?

A merger, if possible, could be the watershed event in my tenure as CEO. The value enhancement to our shareholders could be phenomenal and exceed that of any other events or occurrences I could conceive.

▼

La Quinta was my effort to air these ideas, consider our options, and inject Bob Smith into the running of the company. By now Flamson was undeniably ill, and it was unclear how much longer he would remain active at Security Pacific. I had to find my own strategy, my own corporate *voice*, as I charted our course for the 1990s.

Although we were skeptical about consultants—*a consultant is someone who borrows your watch and then tells you what time it is*—Nick Binkley had a high opinion of First Manhattan's Jim McCormick. In November 1989 we'd contracted McCormick to study our company in depth, run our numbers, and give us his perspective. His analysis was complete by January and with equal measures of curiosity and fear, top management rendezvoused in the desert for the results.

Doomsday rumors circulated internally prior and subsequent to the weekend summit, which turned out to be a revelation.

Present were myself, Flamson, Moody, Kooken, Binkley, Grundhofer, Benter, Corteway, Kathy Burke, Singleton, and Lovejoy, as well as First Manhattan's McCormick, and Mont Wilkenson, Jim's managing vice president. McCormick was a likable speaker whose propensity for restating complex analysis in a way simple enough for a common dunce to understand was amusing and condescending in equal parts.

The meeting was a gruesome wake-up call. McCormick had concluded that Security Pacific had a significantly higher risk posture than its competitors. The risk posture damaged the stock price and was directly attributable to the poor performance and higher risk associated with particular business units that, until now, we had been reluctant to abandon. "In short," Jim said, "gotta reduce the risk or the perception of risk of these units or improve their results."

Jim believed that by undertaking the global expansion heralded by the Merchant Bank, we had perplexed Wall Street and inadvertently penalized our primary constituent—the shareholder. He believed that in order to strengthen our institution, in addition to reducing the perception of risk, we had to significantly boost our overall return on equity. "Earnings growth is indicated if return on equity is attractive. Growth is not indicated if ROE is below the hurdle rate. As a result of the weak Merchant Bank, overall returns and generally higher Beta [risk] your growth expectations and stock value will suffer."

"Isn't our asset growth strong though?" I asked.

"Well, it's hard for banks, most banks, to put down ROEs in excess of 16% or 17% to grow assets rapidly in a sustained way and demonstrate a corresponding increase in share price and market capitalization. In fact, as soon as you get to fairly high ROEs coupled with high asset growth the analysts begin to worry about your risk profile. Because they've seen it happen again and again that growing loans too fast can lead to some excessive risk-taking. Now that doesn't have to happen, but analysts worry about that. Here again your valuation by the marketplace is in part hurt by Security Pacific's high assets growth rate and the risk-taking that connotes."

The obvious question, then, was, How did our operating units compare to those of our competitors? McCormick plotted the units on a matrix with our competition.

"You have some very strong activities in your FSS. You have a top-producing Business Banking function. Bravo. Also very strong is what you've been doing in your Retail Bank and your orientation toward acquisitions and gathering low-cost deposits and managing your costs down. In this sphere, you have a very bright future. This is a powerful mix of activities with enormous potential. That helps the stock."

Flamson said, "So what are our competitors doing to get a better ROE? Hell, look at Wells. They are performing in most all of these areas, but so are we. How do we maximize our businesses and get Wells's valuations as a result?"

"Gotta fix your detractors," was McCormick's answer. "Wells Fargo has very few subs that detract from value." I could see where he was going as he cut nearer and nearer to the bone. "As this diagram demonstrates, the value detractors based on combining Beta and returns are principally in your Merchant Banking activities. Gotta recognize that the discount you take for these underperforming, high-asset growth, higher-risk securities activities overwhelms the positives and adversely affects your overall stock price. Pretty fundamental stuff: Winners and Losers."

The answer McCormick proposed was obvious: concentrate on the subsidiaries that were detracting from shareholder value and either fix them so they produced higher returns—or apply the meat cleaver.

The verdict: despite our fond attachment to breadth, diversification, and globality, these were not necessarily good business strategies from the perspective of shareholder value. The combined uncertainty, high risk, and weak performance of the Merchant Bank had imperiled market perception of Security Pacific and had done so significantly.

▼

By late afternoon, discussion focused almost exclusively on the Merchant Bank.

David Lovejoy turned pale as McCormick slashed his way through our overseas operations. For the majority of the Merchant Bank components, First Manhattan's advice was blunt and direct: "Gotta vastly improve or eliminate."

Mont Wilkenson conceded that the Merchant Bank was symptomatic of a general lack of expense control in the entire company. "When you look at what that means to shareholders, controlling expenses at just average peer level versus these meager performance levels, you would increase

ROE by as much as 300 basis points or 3%. And if you make
the leap beyond just average expense performance which, by
the way, ain't no great shakes, to doing top percentile peer
performance. You could pick up another 3% ROE. You have
to control expenses."

McCormick agreed. "That's the bottom line. What we are
talking about is a pretty simple way to allocate missions and
priorities, right? Operate more efficiently and fix or get rid of
the underperformers."

Yeah, simple, I thought. *Simple, but brutal.* Of course it
was logical to control expenses better and eliminate our poor
performers—it was common sense—but it would be a hell of
a lot more complicated than First Manhattan made it sound.
This wouldn't be like chopping off the stale end of a salami.
In the case of the Merchant Bank, the 'Losers' were so inter-
linked with the 'Winners' that we could not remove the poor
performers without eviscerating their profitable counterparts.
After all, the Merchant Bank was a painstakingly constructed
network, not an arbitrary hodgepodge of sovereign operations. What McCormick proposed was akin to removing exactly half the telephone lines from a major city without im-
pairing the service of the remaining telephone customers. If
Hoare Govett and Burns Fry had to go, what was the point of
keeping McIntosh, which depended on its relationship with
the former two subsidiaries for its success? What was the
point of having one-quarter of a Merchant Bank if its strategic advantage and success hinged on its global versatility?

Now McCormick really laid it on the line for us: eliminate
poor performers, improve your costs, and only then will you
have a company with a much stronger market capitalization.
"Then to hit the real home run put together an *in-state merger*
but merge from a position of relative power, or run the risk of
being another bank's target who'll grab you, do the dirty work
for you, and award the benefit to their shareholders."

Yes, I thought, *he's dead right.*

McCormick closed the meeting by throwing the lit torch into our court. "The outcome is in your hands. Let me sum it up by saying, in our view, do it or someone else will do it for you."

Midway through the summit, Flamson became agitated and made a cold-call to the chairman of First Interstate, suggesting a merger. I don't know if he even got through, but the impulsive gesture spoke volumes.

▼

We left that meeting in a complicated wash of emotions. Like Lovejoy, I was disappointed—hardly surprised—that the Merchant Bank had come under such scrutiny. But I was exhilarated by the clarity of the mandate: I had a better idea of what to do and why. We were overwhelmed by what we had to accomplish in a very short window of opportunity—perhaps six to eight months. Rapid turnaround or enormous change was called for if we were to meet First Manhattan's challenge.

Could it be turned around? Could it be turned around in a year or less? If every subsidiary performed flawlessly for six months, could we save the Merchant Bank? Could we save many of the innovations which I was convinced would succeed in the distant future, but which in the meantime were liabilities? Could I risk continuation of a long-term vision we'd undertaken with such high hopes?

We had to strengthen the institution by any means available to compete in the Darwinian banking environment of the 1990s. If Security Pacific was not the conqueror, it would be the vanquished. We had to move in a different direction, or risk being acquired.

▼

In the following weeks, Flamson, Binkley, Kooken, and I spent many hours digesting what we had heard at La Quinta. We shared a concern for the formidable change signaled by

First Manhattan's analysis. Any alarm, even a preventative alarm, provokes a natural round of Monday-morning quarterbacking. Flamson wondered what he might have done differently. "We believed we could be at the leading edge and take advantage of the first wave of a new era of opportunity. But we were so ahead of the wave that time ran out and the wave crashed over our head."

Nick invoked Robert Frost. "I know there's a temptation to wonder at the road not taken, but I like the road we took. I don't think we should be ashamed of trying to be ahead of the curve." Considering the alternative, he said, "Had we stayed with the pack, tried nothing interesting, we would have lost an equal number of opportunities that turned out successfully."

Flamson shrugged. "When you're years ahead of your time, at some point you cease to be innovative and simply become irrelevant."

Binkley resisted the notion that we had failed. "In terms of concepts, excitement, and idea, we have to give ourselves an A-plus."

"In terms of execution," I said, "we have some B's and a lot of D's. We never quite got the collective results we expected, or needed."

"Timing is everything," Kooken said, implying that we'd been too aggressive. "Ambition is not always a precursor to success. In our rush of enthusiasm we entered many of these markets prematurely. Our reach leveraged our capital base."

Nick said, "At least you can't say we were afraid of change. Change was afraid of us."

I felt we should not feel depressed about what we'd heard, but reenergized. "While it would have been handy to come to these realizations earlier, we can in one sense feel relieved. We've been so overcommitted to an expensive strategy that we've been hamstrung. Now we have to let go of those illusions and pursue a less imaginative set of goals."

▼

Privately, David and I commiserated about what had been discussed in La Quinta. The Merchant Bank, ambitious though it was, could cripple the value of Security Pacific stock.

"The problem is that we've deployed massive amounts of capital, locked up billions of dollars in assets, and we aren't seeing the results. The general feeling is that the Merchant Bank is so detrimental to the value of our company that it has to be excised."

"Is stock value the only thing that matters?" Lovejoy asked. "I feel the time will come when analysts understand what we are doing."

"David, I'd love to believe that. Unfortunately, the value of our stock is key. Everything else we might do, from acquisitions to the raising of capital at a fair price, hinges on the price of that stock."

"So we have to correct, liquidate, or eliminate our poor performers," Lovejoy said. It was not so much a question as a reckoning. "You know how tangled up the operations are. We are honestly talking about the entire Merchant Bank. It remains in place, or the whole bloody thing goes. There's probably no middle ground."

"David, the Merchant Bank is a $25 billion operation. The question I have to ask myself as CEO is, *Can I better redeploy the capital it requires someplace else?*"

"And the answer, I suppose, is yes."

"David, you're a wonderful builder, but you've got to raise the performance of certain portions of the Merchant Bank. We've got to turn our weak performers around. If we don't get the numbers up, we are going to have to get out of the business."

"You know I'm 100% committed to this strategy."

"That could be part of the problem. We're entranced by what we imagine it could be. I know you're committed, and I'm committed, but there are triggers that need to be pulled." I urged him to stop building and start managing, to shake out poor people and poor performers and try to get the profits up.

He said he understood. He was on the team.

▼

The board of directors was the ultimate force: God made flesh on earth and attired in three-piece suits. The directors could provide executive management with its highest highs and then take them down to Hades and back in the next breath.

The chief purpose of the board of directors is to represent and express the concerns of the shareholders—the equity owners—of the company. They oversee the corporation's strategy and policies, as well as the broad issues of operations, loans, and the deployment of capital. They rely on management to operate the company on a day-to-day basis. They also direct, appoint, or replace the top management as necessary. Their primary concern is the success of the company as measured by the earnings per share and its growth—overall performance. They are acutely conscious not only of how the corporation serves its shareholders, but how it serves its employees, clients, and community.

The successful governance of a large and complex corporation is a quintessential goal, and the board of directors is the centerpiece of the corporate mechanism. It is the hub of the wheel and in many respect where the buck stops. They are the representatives of the investor-owners and carry a fiduciary responsibility to ensure that the company maintains a stable footing. In the case of banks, the directors are also personally liable. Directors earn up to $40,000 per year for their efforts; this is a lot of money when times are good and their duties are largely routine and structured. But when times are bad, no amount of compensation is worthy of the effort, concern, intellect, experience, and pure, unadulterated guts a good director must provide. The board can make or break a corporation. They can enhance, steady, resuscitate, or completely decimate company value. The most important responsibility they have in exercising their duties is the selection, hiring, and firing of the CEO, the person on whom they must rely for direction and the day-to-day operation of the company.

Security Pacific's board could not have been a stronger, more skilled group. Most of them were or had been CEOs of major, largely California corporations that represented the continuum of industry—aerospace, electronics, communications, food products, construction, and real estate development. They were as skilled, diverse, and tough a group as you are likely to find on a board. To an individual, they had the sheer guts necessary to work through even the most difficult period without a flicker of selfish interest and with one predominating interest at the forefront of their thought process: the shareholder.

At Security Pacific, our twenty-one-member board met monthly and was demographically representative of the geography and range of industries that we served. An average board meeting would last a couple of hours. In extenuating circumstances, a board meeting could last much longer, but this was rare.

In addition to *the* board, we had subcommittees; an executive committee, audit committee, compensation committee, finance committee, and others, most of which also met on a monthly basis.

In every corporation, management is both wary of and dependent upon its board of directors. As president or CEO, you want the board fully engaged in the activities of the company they sit in judgment over. By the same token, sometimes it is painful. Our board was very supportive of Flamson and myself, even during tough times, which is atypical. But in the face of rising exigencies that had not been resolved prior to the transition, some members of the board became agitated and wanted me to tie up loose ends prior to attending to other matters.

On most every board there are one or two individuals who

emerge as de facto leaders of the independent group and generally that person serves as the chairman of the compensation or audit committee. In our case one of those leaders was a young farmer who went on the Security Pacific Board at the age of thirty-nine in the mid-1960s.

J.G. was like a character out of *Amazing Stories*. As a young, struggling cotton farmer, he had lost two fingers in a roping accident. Now in his late sixties, J.G. was semiretired; he had served on numerous corporate boards and was the chairman of the board of the J.G. Boswell Company, one of the largest cotton, seed, and grain growers in the United States. In this respect, Boswell was a businessman with literal roots in the earth. Jim Boswell, or "J.G." to his friends, was not an ordinary farmer but an entrepreneur who'd taken a lake bottom in the San Joaquin Valley, bought it for pennies, acquired water, built dikes, constructed dams, waterways, and storage containment, and transformed this melange into one of the largest cotton-producing areas in the United States. Probably because J.G. had an acute intuition, street savvy, and extraordinary qualities of leadership, he gravitated toward the role of leader and consensus-gatherer of our board. J.G. was also the chairman of our compensation committee and would most often speak in blunt, gutsy sentences with minimal attention to finesse. Entrepreneur of entrepreneurs, best of the best, he was undeniably the strongest voice among the industrial and community giants who comprised Security Pacific's board of directors.

Jim and I would disagree—sometimes *clash*—but I respected his input and sought his insight on issues with the fervor of an apostle in search of the word of a sage. One thing I liked about him was that he never did pretend to speak for the entire board; he spoke only for himself and when he spoke, you were always sure where he stood.

The board of directors was uncertain about the direction of the company and tired of the Merchant Bank. They felt we had given the strategy a noble try but that it had become a detriment to our perception and a drag on our growth, earnings, and stock value.

Second, they wanted me to deal with David Lovejoy. While Lovejoy had done a spectacular job of building the Merchant Bank, they believed—and I agreed—he was doing a mediocre to poor job of operating it.

In the context of discussing key management at a compensation committee meeting, Boswell addressed this issue. "Bob, you've got to do something about Lovejoy."

I explained that Lovejoy was a strategist, a builder, and that he was as dedicated to a global strategy as we were. "I've spoken with him a number of times and encouraged him to manage with a firmer hand."

"His interpersonal skills are so awful," said Flamson. "He's pissing people off inside and outside the bank."

The fact that Lovejoy was personally disliked not only within the institution but outside of it was not news to me. Maybe I'd rationalized his continued presence out of fairness to David or because I was so personally linked to his endeavors. The only way a person who is widely disliked can excel within an organization is to be successful. Now that the Merchant Bank was performing weakly it was perceived as a liability. As such, many people were opening up about and turning against Lovejoy. He was unfairly construed to be at fault for all the failures of the Merchant Bank, and his personality—once tolerable when the Merchant Bank was thought to be successful—became insufferable to those who did not like it as the Merchant Bank slipped.

Flamson had always liked Lovejoy and saw him as an ambitious and creative force, able to attract top talent and always striving for a new and better mousetrap. But as chairman of a troubled company even Flamson, once David's leading proponent, thought David should go. "Security Pacific," Flamson opined, speaking with the authority of a sage, "can no longer afford the Merchant Bank, and can no longer keep David Lovejoy. I feel that both of them are liabilities."

I had very mixed emotions. It is impossible to overstate the degree of pressure I felt to terminate David Lovejoy. Most of my key staff disliked him. I thought it was a shame, because Lovejoy was undeniably talented. He reminded me of a Taoist aphorism; a brilliant man whose personality contained the seeds of his own destruction.

I thought it was too early to leap aboard this dangerous bandwagon. "First of all, I'm not ready to write off the entire Merchant Bank. Yes, it is in disarray, but its future has not been decided. We do, however, have a shortened time frame on its improved performance. Second, Lovejoy has been instrumental in the ongoing management of the Merchant Bank. He's one of its creators. He knows it blindfolded, and to get rid of him before we know the future of the Merchant Bank would be precipitous."

I assured the committee that I would deal with the issue head on. "The problem I have is that the timing is not right. My plate is so full. If he were to leave now, I have no one to back up Lovejoy's position if I get rid of him."

"Don't you have anybody who can take his place?"

"No, that's the problem. Nobody else can run the Merchant Bank."

"But *what are* you going to do with the Merchant Bank?"

"That depends on the performance of its individual units over the next six months. The answer to your question is that there will probably be a major pruning, but not yet."

Despite the board's misgivings about the Merchant Bank and David Lovejoy's leadership skills, I still felt it was necessary to support David. Given the Merchant Bank's one hundred separate pieces, Lovejoy's struggle to control the leviathan was understandable, and Lovejoy might have garnered sympathy rather than antipathy had he not made so many enemies.

I'd never felt such pressure—so pulled in so many directions—in my life. The emotions involved were complex. I loved the Merchant Bank. But evidence was mounting that its continued existence not only jeopardized the bank but would adversely prejudice any attempt at future consolidation.

▼

A smaller but equally strident opposition had closed in around John Singleton as he searched to find his new place within the bank.

Because I'd been unwilling to take Singleton as my chief operating officer, as a consolation or "booby" prize—and one that was foolhardy to bestow upon a man with little knowledge of banking—we elevated Singleton to the rather amorphous position of "chief administrator in charge of other banks in other states." We put him in charge of all non-California banks; Washington, Nevada, Oregon, and Arizona. It was an ashamedly ambiguous, vague, and equivocal position, and one in which Singleton could not possibly excel.

Soon, it was evident that Singleton was not the right person to be in charge of "other banks in other states." Although John made frequent travels to the banks over whose management he presided, he puzzled their managers as much as he had puzzled me. I received apprehensive phone calls from Washington, Nevada, and Arizona. "Bob, I don't mean to be rude: Is it my imagination, or does John Singleton not fully understand banking?"

"Why? What's going on?" I asked.

"Well, John doesn't appear to know the business, and when he tries to talk as if he does, he doesn't make a lick of sense."

At that moment I realized I would most likely have to terminate Singleton.

▼

In private discussions with Nick Binkley, we concluded that the best long-term course of action for the shareholders was to find "the" partner. The 1990s were not going to be like the 1980s; it would be a lean and mean era of changing rules, disparity in global technologies, too many banks fighting for too few customers, and, ultimately, consolidation. Nonbanks were dealing in financial instruments that siphoned business away from banks. Weak and risk-prone banks would limp off the race track licking their wounds. Security Pacific would either be on top or an *also-ran*. However, if we could pull off a friendly merger in California, it would be a tremendous coup. The benefits and economies of a merger, in contrast to anything else we could possibly do—*anything*—would be enormous. And we both knew, without uttering a word, which bank was on our individual minds: Wells Fargo.

Nick and I kept our discussions to ourselves.

▼

On Valentine's Day, 1990, I convened the first in a series of all-day management forums. The gathering included executives from all major Security Pacific operations around the world, and its purpose was to apprise our managers of the important conclusions we had come to in La Quinta and to unite the bank in urgent new purpose.

I brought up to speed an audience of anxious people. "As it was rumored, a number of us convened at the new office at La Quinta where, with the help of First Manhattan, we took a frank look at our company. We had one of the most meaningful sessions that I think has ever taken place in this company, because when we walked out we were absolutely all convinced of where we were headed in the 1990s. There was a lot of debate during the meeting. Points of view were expressed. Feelings were hurt. But it was a very candid meeting. And at the end of the day we all walked out convinced that all of us had a role to play in making Security Pacific a stronger, more meaningful company in the banking community."

After McCormick reviewed the results of our meeting in the desert, Chief Credit Officer Bob Corteway made ominous predictions based on his own analysis. "Looking at the major challenges for the company, from a risk-management perspective the economy is certainly wan, and although there may be disparate views as to the nation's current economic status and prospects for the same, I think we can all agree that we are in a period of uncertainty and slow growth. Historically, we know that during a period of economic downturn and, possibly even more important, from a risk-management perspective, in the months preceding an economic downturn, the issue of asset quality becomes a dominant factor affecting our company's performance. Today, in my judgment, we're witnessing a very classic pattern. The warning signs are here. Corporate profitability is declining, cash flow is coming under stress. We've encountered instances of transactions turning sideways very early on after closing with increased frequency."

Although the ostensible purpose of the forum was to motivate and inspire, many left with an ineluctable sense of dread.

▼

In discussions with Kooken in May, I learned it was likely that our second-quarter results would be nowhere near as good as those of the prior five quarters.

The carcinogenic effects of FIRREA were now being felt across the organization. Internally, our problem loans were now rupturing on many fronts, particularly overseas and the hard-hit regions of the eastern United States. We were witnessing the accelerating classifications and reappraisals of real estate collateral that indicated declines in value of up to 50%. This could not go on. At the end of the first quarter we had shut down our East Coast real estate lending operation.

Soon, it was clear the problem was not limited to only those markets. Bob Corteway had expressed fervid concern. When Grundhofer and Lovejoy echoed his earlier alarm, the four of us met with Kooken, Nick Binkley, and John Singleton to discuss a course of action.

"The economy has been so erratic that I'm reluctant to make any predictions," Kooken said. "The economy is a disaster overseas in the United Kingdom and Australia, and while it's true the economy is showing some strength here, I think we can anticipate a recession to set in by early 1991."

"We've got to do whatever it takes to make sure we don't get in any deeper," I said. "Congress changed the rules after we'd already accumulated a barn full of these loans—nearly fourteen and a half billion dollars' worth plus commitments. I wish they'd given us advance warning. Had I known this revaluation of collateral was coming there's no way I would have allowed us to make these loans."

Corteway spoke with a quiet intensity that I had not seen in some time. "This is going to herald big trouble if we descend into a full-blown recession, especially here in California. This damned FIRREA will stick to our portfolio like leaches on our leg. I think we should direct our future on the theory that a worst-case scenario is realized. But having said that, about the only thing we can do is change our loan policy going forward to ensure that we are essentially FIRREA- and recession-proof."

We unanimously agreed. Security Pacific was an organization teetering on a precipice of unknowable depth and we couldn't take any action that might prod us any closer to the edge. "We have to fulfill any prior credit commitments," I said, "but beyond that we have to shut down real estate lending. That goes not only for the United Kingdom, Australia, and the Merchant Bank, but also Nick's FSS activities and—I hate to say it—California as well."

"Boy, that's not only going to hurt our plan but shock our developer customers and piss off a lot of people," said Kooken.

"I know, it will stun them. But it has to be done," I answered. It would have been foolhardy to get in any deeper, and further lending at this point could come back to haunt us and would look reckless to the regulators. "I don't see any other way to chip away at our potential exposure."

▼

As mid-year approached, I focused single-mindedly on our

poorly performing units, particularly those in the Merchant Bank. With some soul-searching, I acknowledged the innovations that had not panned out, and struggled to put my finger on why they had not turned the kind of profit we'd hoped.

In most instances, the answers were self-evident.

It was a coalescence of management issues, unforeseen rules, and internal hurdles. It was hard not to be emotional when matching the vision of the Merchant Bank against the cold, hard numbers it was generating.

Too perfect not to work. Too beautiful to fail.

I wanted it to work.

The disposition of the Merchant Bank in general, and David Lovejoy in particular, had become overwhelming issues. I was deeply attached to the strategy of the Merchant Bank. My god, I'd been its biggest proponent and one of its chief architects! I had difficulty accepting what now appeared irrefutable evidence of its detriment to our stock value and corporate perception. But even after I had accepted that, it was still an onerous task to have to shut it down. While I respected Lovejoy, I was frustrated by his inability to—I don't know how to put it more simply—*be a nicer person.* Even now, with he and his operation under continuous scrutiny, he would not or could not change.

Cyclically, as the Merchant Bank was openly singled out as our primary albatross—scapegoated—I came under intense pressure from new sources to "deal with" Lovejoy. Many senior officers, even at lower levels, testified to his negative effect on the company. Even my munificent, peace-loving wife, who knew Lovejoy and other senior officers as well, felt his continued stay was bringing me down and embarrassing the company.

▼

Once again I sat down with David for what had become a procession of meetings where we discussed his management of the Merchant Bank.

He still believed passionately in the concept. "Bob, the Merchant Bank is an exceptional strategy."

"David, you're preaching to the choir. 'Too perfect to fail'—but it's failing. We have got to choke some value out of these businesses or eliminate them."

"It's not that simple, Bob. I can't just shake three subs out of the equation and still have the rest of them operate properly. These functions are more than interrelated; they are mutually cohesive."

"But, David, we've been at this intensely for the past four years. As fabulous as the idea is, we are not getting the returns, and we are not getting any stock-price premiums or accolades for innovation—we are getting discounted. Wall Street is pissing on our stock. And now the whole organization is getting pissed."

"We have a mix of outstanding people and some very mediocre people. I'm afraid this is not something we are likely to be able to turn around in a few months."

In the end it came down to this: I told David, "You've got to elicit better performance or liquidate these businesses and improve your relationship with your colleagues."

▼

There was no question that as a result of both a declining economy and the drastic manner in which these loans were to be revalued under FIRREA that our criticized and classified assets—Especially Mentioned, Substandard, Doubtful, and Loss—would proliferate almost logarithmically. Security Pacific could anticipate some big-time problems.

The events of the recent past had cast the regulators in the most pivotal and powerful role; they were now grasping the jugular of the banking system more firmly than at any time since the Great Depression. The sphere of power had shifted. And regulators remembered every one of Flamson's slights, particularly his removal of one of their own from our jurisdiction, and I don't think they looked back on that with fond remembrance.

The regulators were now focusing on large banks—especially those with less capital, high-risk portfolios, complexity, and growing problems, and, no doubt, organizations whose management in the past had inflicted on them some offense or indignity. And that criteria, in the California market, was met by Security Pacific. The sheer unfathomability and moxie of the Merchant Bank provoked their resentment. For these reasons, it was into the nether-regions of our vault that regulators now pointed their flashlights.

Flamson assailed the regulators once more, sputtering about their shortcomings. "Now they think they're some kind of supercolossus."

I tried to calm him down. "Dick, they're just doing their job."

Flamson had his style, and I had mine. There were some things I'd ask Dick's advice on, but some things I'd tell him. I had new rules, and one of them was that there were to be no more wisecracks about the regulators—not a peep.

▼

The on-site OCC regulators continued to breathe down the institution's neck, noose in hand, as they tore through our bank documentation. At the same time, the Federal Reserve held a microscope up to our holding company, nonbank activities, and related subsidiaries.

They'd begun to disagree, sometimes violently, with the classification level we'd given to a number of loans. This did not bode well; it meant that our fundamental methodologies were out of sync with theirs. If our methodologies continued to diverge, it would mean the reclassification of thousands of additional loans. And whereas in the past we could take a regulator to task over a disagreement as to a credit classification, the new atmosphere foreclosed debate. We had to sit there and take it.

Periodically, hopeful stories would surface of government officials imploring bank examiners to use common sense and good judgment when reclassifying loans and subjecting banks to overzealous scrutiny, but if regulators ever availed themselves of this authorized leniency, Security Pacific never enjoyed the benefits. As far as I could tell, our regulators were on a tear.

Flamson would come into my office to pace and say all the things he would rather have told the regulators face to face. "It's almost as if the Powers That Be told the regulators to select one of the major West Coast banks and take it out. If only they understood the Merchant Bank better. Maybe we should send the screw-heads to business school. That would cost a lot less than flying them to the United Kingdom for a month. They always come back empty-handed and more confused than when they left."

"Dick, the Merchant Bank is part of the problem, but we have a bigger problem in our own backyard, and that's the shriveling economy and its impact on real estate."

"Well, hell, why don't they go after First Interstate!"

"Because First Interstate isn't trying to be all things to all people. We've got our hand in too many pies and a gargantuan portfolio of real estate loans."

▼

Soon it was apparent from the manner in which regulators addressed management and the board of directors that they were impatient with our inability to stanch the proliferating level of classifications. Any explanation we proffered that set the blame at the foot of a downhill economy fell on deaf ears.

The regulatory reports expressed concern about our growing level of nonperforming loans and criticized assets, not only in real estate development but in all segments of business. I knew that if we were ever criticized to the point that we were stigmatized with a *Memorandum of Understanding* or, God forbid, a *Cease and Desist*, Security Pacific would find itself in a hole out of which it might never climb. Not only would oversight increase dramatically, but the public notoriety that would result would be a public relations nightmare and effectively foreclose the possibility of a respectable solution. Such resolution would most likely trigger more Draconian measures, such as an admonition to raise additional capital at a cost of significant dilution to our shareholders.

In that event, the board of directors as well as the regulators would most likely call for my scalp.

The Merchant Bank seemed impossible to turn around. The majority of its constituents continued to perform poorly. Was it Lovejoy's fault, or were we expecting the impossible? Six months to turn around a $25 billion operation was not exactly a gracious allotment of time.

There'd been clues—but we were so entranced by the conceptual inevitability of the Merchant Bank's success that we'd tried to ignore them. Hoare Govett had proved the weakest link.

Hoare Govett was 90% broker, 10% dealer. A change in U.K. regulation around 1986—the so-called Big Bang— brought brokers and dealers together, relegating firms that were principally broker companies to the second tier, the second tranche in a hierarchy of U.K. securities firms. Hoare Govett was an important player, but not as prestigious as a Kleinworth Benson, which was a prominent dealer and full-fledged underwriter of securities.

Early in its inception, regulators—like ancient tribesmen confronted with lasers in the jungle—became perplexed by our foreign subsidiaries. They found the Merchant Bank unfathomably complex, and when they consulted their rule books they realized the insufficiency of their own legal statutes and comprehension to deal with the universe of foreign securities. Regulatory costs spiraled as what was once a back room partnership ballooned into a corporate albatross.

Law required us to bring in a team of auditors. Instead of one attorney, Hoare Govett now had to have ten. The Comptroller of the Currency and the Federal Reserve began to subject Hoare Govett to interminable examinations. Exasperated by what they didn't understand, regulators required us to assemble reams of policy books, procedure manuals, and controls; this required that we waste time, spend money, and divert people-power.

The only inherent problems, other than regulatory oversight that devoured nearly 10% of the Merchant Bank revenues, were tremors of cultural incompatibility at Hoare Govett. We discovered that the workers were less skilled than we'd hoped, demanded higher salaries than they were worth, and liked to work shorter hours than we expected.

Hoare Govett represented the flip side of the RMJ dilemma. As in the case of RMJ, we had limited knowledge of the business and were betting on the people; but unlike RMJ, we had not equipped ourselves with the top talent. Our people at Hoare Govett needed leadership, needed to be led by the hand, and sometimes needed to be told *No*.

We dispatched a top-flight executive named Peter Voss to the United Kingdom to handle matters. Voss reported to Lovejoy and was a skilled investment manager, an American expatriate, six foot seven. He was psychologically adept at dealing with the personalities and expectations of our brokers at Hoare Govett.

I flashed back on a phone conversation with Voss in which he expressed his dismay. "These British boys have a different approach to business than U.S. bankers. They are not about to overexert themselves on our account. They want to maintain all the old and costly traditions." Among their traditions were free cars and high bonuses, regardless of performance.

Peter Voss exerted constant effort to rein in Hoare Govett, but it was a most difficult undertaking and a sensitive cross-cultural balancing act. He repaired, as best he could for a

Yank among Englishmen, the cultural issues before him. He confronted the founders of the firm, Richard West and Richard Westmacot, and argued against blind acceptance of ingrained tradition. He impressed upon them the need for sincere effort and disciplined expense control. He advised them on which businesses to exit and where to double the effort. He redeployed personnel based on experience, area of expertise, and degree of knowledge. He brought in additional U.S. expatriate bankers to help manage the firm. Voss and the American members of the team strove to set a good example; they arrived for work at seven in the morning and were usually the last to leave.

To demonstrate our commitment to the Merchant Bank and inspire the lackluster lads at Hoare Govett, we'd moved them from their dilapidated building to a dignified, million-dollar quarters in a spanking new state-of-the-art complex called Broadgate. We'd equipped Hoare Govett with the latest technology and installed several thousand miles of high-density wire to facilitate speed-of-light transactions and spontaneous overseas communication. It was a lot of money deployed in good faith for what we anticipated would be a long-term commitment. Broadgate was a work of art, complete with trading floors, mainframes, and terminals. The purpose of this expansion was to demonstrate our belief in the strategy and the ability of our employees to execute it, to devote ourselves physically as well as monetarily and psychologically to the Merchant Bank effort. We could say we'd put our money on the table, and they could never fail for want of office support, resources, or available technology.

In retrospect, we were trying to make a silk purse out of a sow's ear.

Peter did all he could, but without Lawrence of Arabia at his side, he could neither reprogram deeply entrenched habits nor achieve a unification of morale and purpose. The modern accoutrements had little effect on the culture of the employees. Voss could seldom get a full day's work out of most of them. The more he tried to raise standards, the more petulant the employees grew. Vexed by the pressure to work a full day, some complained and others threatened to "walk" or "move on to something better."

Because of Hoare Govett's position in the U.K. market as a second-stringer, we were never able to penetrate the more attractive high-margin business. The principals of Hoare Govett were brokers—*salespeople*—who lacked the market-making and underwriting sophistication necessary to manage the firm for profitability on a short-term basis and keep pace in the new, highly competitive environment ushered in by the Big Bang.

▼

Time had run out on the Merchant Bank adventure. Security Pacific's capital was spread blade-thin. And patience had waned. Painful though it was to concede, I felt we had given the strategy a fair shake—seven years. We had been at it, and we'd been at it very hard ever since David Lovejoy took over the Merchant Bank in 1987.

While some sectors in our global strategy were performers—Sequor and Foreign Exchange were doing well, and Swaps had for three years straight been the number one division of its kind in the world—their larger counterparts, the *pillars*, had failed to meet our expectations. Hoare Govett had not done very well. Burns Fry was struggling. McIntosh was passable, but useless without the other two.

The Merchant Bank was flailing. Overhead for its ancillary operations was exorbitant. The cost of regulatory oversight was killing us. The outlook for the near term was one of continued struggle. And the Glass–Steagall barrier had yet to be surmounted. It was incredibly frustrating: we had the pieces in place—the outline, the blueprint, the prototype—for a banking revolution, but the puzzle just wasn't falling

into place. Too many pieces had fallen on the floor. The
deadline had arrived. Security Pacific had run out of time,
patience, and money.

▼

In order to lower the final curtain on the Merchant Bank, I
would have to divest myself of emotion and repress the
memories of all the trouble we'd gone to, all the money we'd
spent—all the hours, hope, analysis, and belief. Seven years
of blood, sweat, and tears. The smile I once imagined the
Merchant Bank to have put on Sartori's face by now must
have become a frown. I could hear his ghostly voice mixing
with the whine of the wind outside: *Get rid of it. Dump it.
Dump the Merchant Bank.*

Finally, the morning after I'd reviewed the second quarter
numbers in early July, I rose and took a shower. As the water
cascaded down my face, I thought about the company, its
problems, Lovejoy, and my six months as CEO. *Fuck it,* I
thought. *It's my responsibility to make this decision, it's the
right decision, it's the correct thing to do. This is what I'm
paid to do, expected to do, and up to this moment everyone
but me knew what had to be done: we are shutting down the
Merchant Bank.*

▼

Making the decision brought only minor relief; it was clear
from the poor projected earnings for the last two quarters of
the year that this wasn't going to be like any prior decade for
Security Pacific.

I knew that I had to find a way out of all our problems and
that I couldn't fail. I needed luck, I needed faith, but I also
needed to create the appearance of strength and an environment in which I could meet my obligation to the shareholders—to give them value for the money and trust they'd
placed in me.

The best answer—the ultimate answer—was a merger with Wells Fargo, maybe sooner rather than later. That would represent a ninth inning, two outs, two-strikes home run hit out of the ballpark. It would be the biggest, most rewarding deal possible.

Dear God in Heaven, I thought, *let it be Wells Fargo.*

7

A Passing
Stage(Coach)

Prudential Securities' bank stock analyst George Salem stepped into my office for a short visit. Salem had carved out a reputation as one of the more outspoken bank analysts on Wall Street. A stocky, outspoken man in his fifties, Salem was a first-class curmudgeon with a moon-pie face and resonant voice. Salem rejoiced in his own ability to surprise an audience with totally off-the-wall comments and observations. At serious gatherings he could provoke gasps by going for the jugular during Q&A sessions, asking questions that were the banking equivalent of, "Are you still beating your wife?"

He was respected by many bankers—albeit grudgingly—for never having been co-opted, as some analysts are, by the banks whose stocks they recommend. Although he was fascinating and entertaining, I was inclined to dislike him only because he was so thoroughly negative. If it was white, he saw it as black; if it was black, he saw it as a neutron star. He was the Black Mariah of analysts, the walking Melody of Doom, and—like the morose reverend in the movie *The Right Stuff* who comes calling only to announce the death of a test pilot—I knew Salem was here to relay bad news.

He entered my office looking even more dour and moribund than usual, sat down, and immediately intoned, "Bob, I have a warning that you'd do well to take seriously: the economy is going to nosedive, it's going to crater. And when it does it's going to take real estate with it. Real estate loans will be the sinkhole of this decade."

"Whose economy? I hope you're not talking about California."

"Yes, California! And Security Pacific is poised right on the precipice. Mark my words. There is going to be a catastrophe, sooner rather than later."

"Really?" I tried not to smirk. "George, what indication— what evidence—leads you to this conclusion? Since so much is at stake, can you be a bit more specific? Have you been running numbers? What do you know that we don't?"

With the hush of a Vatican representative about to reveal the Third Secret of Fatima he said, "I spoke to some real estate brokers out in the Valley."

"Which valley is that? The Central Valley, the San Fernando Valley? The Valley of the Shadow of Doom?"

"The San Fernando Valley."

I was distinctly underwhelmed. He talked to some real estate brokers—big fucking deal. "George, is that why you came all the way up to my office? What the hell do the real estate brokers out in the Valley know about the future of California that the economists don't know?"

He flashed a melancholy smile at the folly of my ignorance. "Oh they *know*. Bob, don't kid yourself—they know."

"George, come on now. You're telling me that you base this calamitous prediction on what a few real estate brokers out in the Valley tell you?"

With an ample measure of foreboding, he said, "Make what you will of my information. You ignore it at your own peril."

I blew this gem of insight off and chuckled as he left the building.

What I didn't know was that George Salem had an unsettling record for sniffing out problems before they erupted into industry-wide calamities. In the 1970s he'd been the first analyst to go on record questioning the elephantine risk implicit in tanker loans and real estate investment trusts; both eventually caved in on banks.

And in the case of our meeting, *he turned out to be right.* And, as he promised, it would be sooner rather than later.

▼

We had made money through early 1990. Net income for the first quarter of that year was the second highest on record, up 5% from the first quarter of 1989 to $188 million. Return on assets remained "steady as she goes." Then, suddenly, financial reports began to buckle under the combined strains of the Merchant Bank and declining credit quality.

There was a simultaneous eruption of problems on many banking fronts—credit quality, liquidity, and economic downturns in the United Kingdom and Australia. By the close of the second quarter 1990, the U.S. economy in general had transmuted from sluggish to diseased. Arizona had been thrashed. Texas, New England, and the Southeast were hard hit. Our nonaccruing and past-due real estate loans had doubled in one year. Real estate development loan charge-offs under FIRREA had nearly quadrupled from their 1989 figures, forcing us to take significant loan loss reserves that pierced into earnings. Also on the rise were charge-offs in other areas: domestic commercial and industrial, foreign commercial and industrial, and monies lent to foreign governments. Recovery of troubled loans had also dropped.

In John Kooken's segment of our second-quarter video report, he dutifully prepared employees for the worst: "Favorable news was offset by a higher provision for credit losses as a result of increased loan losses. We expect our loan losses to remain at higher levels for the next two quarters, so it is important that we continue our efforts to control expenses. All of us have to continue to focus hard on minimizing all elements of operating expenses. Our new War on Waste Campaign provides an ideal vehicle for all employees to participate in this effort. And I hope that each of you will take an active part in this campaign."

We expected the third quarter to be worse. The winds of war were stirring in the Middle East; Operation Desert Shield would soon become Desert Storm. Oil prices were up, the stock market was down, and even Japan—the Land of the Rising Sun—was in trouble. Job growth was as slow as it had been in eight years.

▼

Early in the third quarter of 1990, it was apparent Security Pacific was developing dangerous weaknesses that would be difficult to reverse because our trouble areas were so vulnerable to paroxysms of the economy.

Our board believed the California economy would reverse its downturn in short order. Buoyed by overoptimistic economic forecasts, they often said, "The worst is most likely over. California cannot possibly be hit hard."

It reminded me of the many scenes in *The Towering Inferno* where William Holden ridicules Paul Newman for worrying that a tiny electrical fire many floors below could adversely affect a gala party on the top floor. "There is no way that little fire in a closet a hundred floors below could possibly disrupt the splendor of the evening. So calm down, put on your jacket, and join the party."

"Bob," the litany went, "a handful of bad loans in Australia or the United Kingdom can't possibly affect us here in jolly California. . . . "

"One or two underperforming subsidiaries in London can't possibly. . . . "

"One tiny clause in a five-hundred-page law called FIRREA can't possibly take down an entire real-estate portfolio. Now, put a smile on your face, slip into your best jacket, and come join the party."

While analysts and economic historians often pinpoint LBOs as the principal cause of bank problems and failures in the late 1980s, for Security Pacific the primary cause of the menacing downturn was in our largest area of concentration: real estate. Whether we looked at England, Australia, the East Coast, or, ultimately, California, real estate was the focal problem.

Between late 1989, when FIRREA's potential to disembowel our valuations was first detected, and now, when its impact was recognized directly on our balance sheets, we experienced in rapid succession the five stages of death: Denial, Anger, Bargaining, Depression, and Acceptance.

My initial response was, "I don't believe a word of FIRREA. Show me where it is in the law."

Flamson bypassed *Denial* and plunged immediately into *Anger*: "That doesn't make any goddamn sense. That's bullshit! They can't do this to us!"

Within weeks we were *Bargaining*. Flamson stuck his head in my office one day and said, "This will not stand, and they know that, and I'm going to talk to them."

I asked Dick what he intended to do about it.

"Well, by God, I'll call Greenspan and Clarke personally and talk to them—talk sense into them!"

"Good luck," I said.

He returned, hours later, in a state of Acceptance. "Well, it's true, it's real, it's happening, and we're in trouble."

Revelation hit Flamson like a freight train. The volume of his voice dropped. His eyes moistened. His face transmuted to the color of plaster. "If the California economy goes down,

Bob, and the regulators continue to impose this edict, we are in very serious trouble. I mean, I don't know if the bank will *survive*."

I went before the board of directors, to prepare them for the possibility that our situation might worsen before it improved. They were beginning to get the picture. "You are all aware," I said, "that the valuation process was critically altered by FIRREA. But you should also be aware that Security Pacific is not as well prepared as other institutions to weather both regulatory changes *and* economic downturn. We have lower relative capital levels, lower relative reserves, and are fragmented and diversified in a handful of the most volatile and hardest-hit markets in the world. Worst of all, we are heavily, heavily invested in California real estate."

I reiterated for them the figures we all knew. "Of $13.5 billion in currently outstanding real estate land and development loans, $7 billion of it is in California. We have another $4 billion in commitments and standby letters of credit." I added, lest anyone miss the gist, "We have nearly a $2 billion annual pre-tax pre-reserve cash flow, but if we have to write off $2 or $3 billion in loans each year, our earnings are *dead*. And we'll be on the regulators' intensive care list."

Flamson sat forward, expressionless. Then he said, "We have to focus every available resource on preventing our collapse."

▼

Meanwhile, the Federal Reserve was intensifying its oversight of Security Pacific. They focused on what they perceived as the inability of our holding company to fend off adverse business conditions and full-blown recession.

The realization that the Federal Reserve intended to downgrade us was a shock—a blow to morale and a black mark on an historically stellar report card. The only comfort to be found anywhere originated out of the Fed's belief that because of our overall strength and financial capacity, the likelihood of an irreversible crisis was remote.

As a result of this first round of regulatory tightening, Security Pacific was required to issue quarterly status reports through an ad hoc committee of the board on our progress in meeting recommendations set forth by regulators, and to provide projections for the following quarters. Regulators admonished us not to pursue further acquisitions without their approval.

The comptroller of the currency's first-half 1990 report, produced around this time, echoed the warnings. While our overall condition remained the same, credit quality deterioration had accelerated. The OCC questioned the reliability of our internal risk-ratings and recommended we reevaluate our credit policies. Regulators pored over our commercial and construction real estate files, found our overall credit quality to be adequate, but downgraded an enormous number of our loans.

Their concerns were appropriate, but our credit people disagreed with many of the downgrades regulators imposed on our classified loans. We were intimately familiar with our construction real estate development portfolio and horrified by their unwillingness to compromise on the strictures imposed by FIRREA. Whereas in the 1980s we could aggressively take a regulator to task over a discrepancy in credit classification, the new atmosphere foreclosed debate. We had to swallow hard and accept their downgrades.

We immediately undertook restructuring measures. We would devote the second half of 1990 to clarifying our objectives and comply with the demands of our regulators: strengthen the composition of our assets, improve capital adequacy, and reassess our dividend policy. We would review the methodologies used to calculate our loan loss provisions and renovate procedural manuals accordingly. We would adopt a plan to liquidate outstanding commercial paper. We began work on a funding contingency plan that, with its catastrophic scenarios and lists of backup credit lines, would guide us in the unlikely event that a financial calamity triggered a crisis in depositor or investor confidence.

These plans sounded good, but we were beginning to realize that the die was cast. Unless there was some give on FIRREA—unlikely—or an instantaneous turnaround in the California economy, it would be virtually impossible to stave off future deterioration for the simple reason that we could not unmake loans.

▼

By the close of the third quarter, *John Kooken Reports*, a much-loved segment of the Security Pacific quarterly video, began to elicit fear and loathing: "Net income was down 27% from the same quarter of 1989. As I mentioned to you in my report at the end of the last quarter, we expected credit losses to remain at high levels. In light of the difficult and uncertain economic and banking environment, we felt it was prudent to further add to our reserves for credit losses. These factors, combined with the fact we had no growth in noninterest income, produced this decrease in earnings. . . . It is extremely important that we continue to focus on expenses in these difficult times."

To skirt the bad news, we began to stuff our videos with fluff: footage of me announcing the recipient of the annual George F. Moody Community Service Award, a profile of a Securateam charter member who'd given six thousand hours of community service, and Jerry Grundhofer initiating a largely cosmetic program called Simply Better: Take Pride Every Time. We devoted one-third of a fifteen-minute video to an honor bestowed upon Security Pacific by the National Center for American Indian Enterprise Development, and more time still to our selection by the Asian Business Association as Corporate Partner of the Year. We talked about the number of ATM machines we'd installed, and about a highway we helped finance in Scottsdale, Arizona—anything to keep the shareholder's mind off the miserable reality. Then we would speed-roll the bad news over happy music and production credits: *Performance Highlights*: *net income down*

27%, provision for credit losses up 110%, nonperformers up, noninterest expense up, net income per common share down 32%, return on average common equity down.

▼

I didn't know how to interpret the baseline economic forecast I received from our economists at the start of the fourth quarter. What I read clashed with common sense: "While overall economic growth is forecast to decline in early 1991, the economy does not appear to be severely unbalanced. Assuming there is no *hot war* in the Gulf, the recession should bottom out in the spring of 1991."

As far as California was concerned, "the economy will show a slowing trend similar to what is anticipated for the nation as a whole. There will be higher unemployment rates but the rise will be limited by the mildness of the downturn and by slower labor force growth than we saw in the 1970s and early 1980s." Recovery was "anticipated" in the second half of 1991. But I didn't see it, and I didn't feel it.

▼

The dream of a consolidation of equals—a merger that would enable Security Pacific to continue to exist as a viable entity—now became a more immediate priority.

With fair excitement, I held private discussions with my team about the possibility of a major in-state consolidation. We agreed this option was the most desirable and beneficial to our shareholders. We acknowledged our disadvantaged state: we were in a weakened condition and our stock value was suspect, but not so bad that a merger of equals was out of the question.

In light of our compromised state, my desire to find the right merger partner now intensified into something approaching fever. I was tantalized by the mere thought; the strength and value to be achieved through a California mega-merger would avoid subjecting our shareholders to the possibility of two or three years of unrealized value as we struggled independently to fix our problems. The disembowelment of the Merchant Bank—while imminent—would be lengthy, complicated, and expensive.

I saw few options: the selection of a potential partner and its culmination in a major in-state consolidation was the most expedient way of achieving the primary goal of maximizing shareholder value during this decade.

▼

As Security Pacific drifted into troubled waters, Dick Flamson could not have been more supportive. I believe Flamson felt partially responsible for some of the problems and, consequently, wanted to be partially responsible for a solution. More than once he asked, "What could I have done differently?" He was frustrated that he couldn't fix it all himself, and that I had been handed a ticking time bomb.

Flamson and I openly discussed the possibilities. There were only three realistic in-state candidates: Bank of America, First Interstate, and Wells Fargo.

Clearly, the bank we most wanted to merge with was Wells Fargo. I respected their CEO, Carl Reichardt, enormously, as did Dick Flamson and several members of Security Pacific's board of directors. We regarded him as *the* contemporary leader in banking. Wells Fargo had an immaculate reputation among West Coast banks; as far as analysts were concerned Wells could do no wrong. While Security Pacific was complex and global, Wells was a high-performance, conceptually traditional California bank. It was the Emerald City.

Furthering our odds for success was the fact that we had talked merger with Wells perhaps a half-dozen times over the past quarter century. As recently as 1989 Reichardt had flown down from San Francisco to speak with Flamson and myself about that possibility. So this was not a new idea. Like bashful schoolchildren at a first dance, we had blushed, walked toward each other, giggled, and turned away. But I felt that maybe the time had come. At least I surely hoped so.

So I asked our investment bankers to run some hypothetical numbers on the efficacy of a variety of potential mergers. The preliminary results of these matrices with Wells were awe-inspiring, approaching 20 to 30% accretion—as opposed to dilution—to shareholders on both sides of the deal because of the massive expense saving in a consolidation. We knew that following the marriage of two California banks we could rapidly consolidate branches in overlapping geographies. And we knew branch tightening would work because we had not only done precisely the same thing, internally, in 1987, but had based our blueprint on the Wells model. We were absolute believers in a new way of banking that Reichardt had created: Build on a sales culture, expense control, and centralized processing. Culturally, Wells and Security Pacific were very similar. We had chemistry; we had *simpatico*. It looked right on paper, it felt right, and if I had my way, it *would be*.

Flamson agreed that the possibilities were enticing. "Do it," he said. He gave me the license and autonomy to go forward, and agreed to back me with the board of directors.

I made a brief presentation to the board in which I reiterated the conclusions we'd come to at La Quinta, and filled their imaginations with the limitless possibility of an intrastate marriage. They granted me what I termed a "hunting license" to talk to Carl Reichardt and, once again, explore this possibility of a merger of equals.

▼

Carl Reichardt was a legendary figure in California banking, a man with an uncommon amount of common sense, the kind of guy who could reduce banking to one sentence: lend to people who pay you back and control expense growth. Carl had emerged out of the real estate side of lending at Union Bank. There was nothing phony about him; he lacked a banker's polish, but he was bright, articulate, and easy to

approach. He had a warmth of personality that was engaging.
I also concluded that the key to getting the deal done, if
Reichardt was so inclined, was that the new organization
would have to be called Wells Fargo, and I would not be the
chief executive officer. Reichardt would have to be the number one guy. I was willing to give that up for the deal. Carl
probably would be willing to make me the president, but I
had no preconditions that I survive the merger so long as the
goal was achieved.

I phoned Reichardt and proposed a revival of our talks.
"Maybe we should discuss *the thing* we talked about last
year," I said, reiterating my belief that so much could be
achieved if our two institutions amalgamated into a super-
power.

"Well, it is interesting, Bob. The potential is clearly enormous, and I agree that consolidation could well be the real
game plan for the 1990s. But let me think about it."

In the first part of October he called me back. "I'm interested in talking about *the thing*. Let's get together."

My talks with Reichardt would have to occur beneath a
shroud of secrecy.

Our first meeting was held in mid-October in San Francisco at the Ritz Carlton. We surprised each other by how
rapidly we wanted to proceed. There was much common
ground, a cautious but undeniable enthusiasm, and an unarticulated momentum.

"We will have to be very quiet about this," said Carl, "as
we go forward."

"Of course. There's no reason this can't evolve relatively
quickly."

"Let's do it."

"Let's," I agreed.

Following this preliminary encounter, we began to meet in
stealth in a reserved room at the Park Hyatt Hotel in the financial district of the city. The lengths we had to go to keep
these discussions private was mind-bending. I took cabs,

transferred from one vehicle to another, followed convoluted walking routes, kept my collar up and my head down. We reserved rooms using third-party names and checked in with the anonymity of Mafiosos planning to make a move on a major casino.

At the second meeting, I told Carl about the work First Manhattan Consultanting Group had done, and the conclusions I'd come to about the need for Security Pacific to eliminate our poor performers and, hopefully, consolidate.

"My one concern is your Merchant Bank Division," he said. "You know my feelings about that operation." I did. He despised the Merchant Bank.

"It's done," I announced. "I'm going to get rid of it."

This pleased him. "And Lovejoy?" Even Reichardt knew about Lovejoy.

"Lovejoy goes right along with it. Deep six."

Reichardt was delighted. "Once you get rid of the Merchant Bank, our institutions will have so much in common. A consolidation is almost irresistible." He noted my shift in focus to shareholder value, and this appealed to him.

▼

We met approximately a half dozen times in San Francisco. On these excursions I went into town very low-key, on the premise of either meeting with customers or visiting with officials at the Federal Reserve. Banking journalists and analysts swarmed these streets and virtually all of them knew me. If even one of them suspected that I was meeting on the QT with Reichardt—especially with this kind of frequency, under assumed names at hotels—it would be headline news that we were contemplating a merger.

One brisk afternoon on my way from a meeting with Carl to the Federal Reserve I was approached from behind by Sam Zuckerman, at that time a well-known reporter for the *American Banker*. I felt a hand on my shoulder and whipped around.

"How's it going, Bob?"

"Very well," I stuttered.

"What are you doing up here?" A deceptively simple question which, uttered in this particular cadence, indicated to me Zuckerman was already looking for a story.

I swallowed hard. "Just up for a routine visit with the Fed."

"Another meeting with the Fed? Weren't you just up here last week? And, jeeze, I could have sworn I saw you in San Francisco the week before that— ."

"Gotta run," I said as I propelled myself into the building. Zuckerman looked startled by my rush of anxiety but, fortunately did not inquire as to why I was so uncharacteristically peremptory, or why I was visiting the Fed without any of my colleagues.

As Reichardt and I made further progress, we agreed to employ Ted Hall of McKinsey & Company to nudge our negotiations forward, memorialize in written form our conclusions, ensure follow-up, and track open issues. Ted joined us in our secret meetings and served as a facilitator.

Negotiations took off. The more we met, the more we agreed on. And the more we agreed on, the closer we were to a written agreement to merge. We fixed the exchange rate based on our most recent stock prices. The benefit ran equally to both companies and their shareholders. We formulated what was very nearly a coherent and complete plan. We determined that the consolidation offered unquestioned strength and unprecedented levels of economization and expense cuts. We decided on the name of the company and on our respective roles. Carl would remain chairman and CEO and I would be the president and chief operating officer. We concluded that Paul Hazen, who later became the chief executive officer of Wells, would have a lesser position but would probably not stay following the merger.

We were exuberant; we had outlines, procedural manuals, organizational charts, business strategies, and five-year projections. I began to consult with our outside investment bankers and attorneys on the mechanics of the transaction. We told people about the plan only on a need-to-know basis.

By late November, everything was falling into place. The planets were in alignment. Carl and I had spoken to our respective executive committees and boards and had obtained their support for this influential transaction. *What a major event in the history of California banking*, I thought, *and it's really gonna happen.* We were so enthusiastic that we set a tentative date to get formal board approval.

"I think we should wind this up with a written agreement and announce the deal in the second week of January, right after the holidays," Carl said.

"That's a perfect time frame," I agreed. "We'll get the year-end pageantry out of the way."

"In tying up the loose ends, however, there are certain aspects of Security Pacific that I need to understand better."

"No problem, Carl. Tell me what you need and I'll get it for you."

The following day, Reichardt requested more complete— sometimes highly specific—information about particular businesses and subsidiaries, which I then attempted to obtain without provoking a lot of suspicion. One area in which Reichardt showed marked interest was our Swaps operation in the United Kingdom. This was a complex area that involved arranging the exchange of different foreign currency and interest rate obligations, in equal amounts and within similar time periods. Swaps, in more complex arrangements, become derivative transactions. One of the top swaps "books" in the world at that time, this operation had garnered Security Pacific a streak of accolades and a lot of publicity and media attention. But Reichardt wanted to know very specific information about Swaps so that his people could assess its risk.

Trouble was the Swaps operation was decentralized and did not share the technological loop with the rest of the banking operations—much of the documentation was in the

United Kingdom. It was particularly hard to obtain Swaps information without animating the paranoia of many people; to seek this kind of documentation was practically an admission that a fairly drastic undertaking was in the works. My attempt to do so would look exactly like what it was—a sneaky type of due diligence—and would invariably set off warning alarms throughout the company.

For these reasons I had no luck producing the information Reichardt had requested in exactly the configuration he'd requested.

And then toward the end of November, John Kooken, Bob Corteway, and I did a last-minute inventory of our loan portfolio and arrived at the unsettling conclusion that, pending further analysis, we would most likely have to set aside more loan reserves than we had planned for the fourth quarter. If and when this augmentation was deemed imperative, I would have an immediate obligation to announce both the decision to reserve and the dollar amount to the public. The timing was *awful*. If required to make this public exposure, I would arouse enormous industry speculation and set off warning bells and cries of doom. It would be patently obvious to analysts that this was not business-as-usual for Security Pacific, and that we were going to have a very poor year.

The first week of December was a pivotal one. Kooken and I had yet to decide absolutely on the necessity and size of our loan loss reserve. We had to make the decision soon, and announce it promptly.

Reichardt and I met early in the week to finalize our plans. While I had produced what I could in the way of information on the Swaps operation, it was not quite what they wanted. The truth is that Carl and I both had some difficulty deciphering the information because neither of us understood the finer points of swaps ourselves. We decided that our respective chief financial officers, Rod Jacobs and John Kooken, should get together and attempt to reconcile whatever issues needed to be resolved.

I also informed him that I might have to announce an additional reserve for our loan portfolio and report a poor quarter. Fortunately, this didn't appear to faze Reichardt, who expressed his continued enthusiasm for the merger.

Then, toward the end of this optimistic meeting, I received an urgent call from Kooken. "Bob, we've got a considerable problem."

"What's the problem?"

"We issued securities this morning and, as you know, we are forbidden to do that."

"Oh, hell. Well, what happened?"

Carl closely watched my reaction from his side of the table.

Kooken—normally cool, calm, and reserved—now sounded close to panic. "Damned if I know! Knowing full well you were in discussions with Wells and that we might have to announce an extra loan loss reserve provision, I told our guys to *stop* issuing securities in the near term! Obviously, somebody didn't get the word or didn't understand the directive. Here we have this historic merger pending and they went ahead and issued it anyway."

My mouth went dry as sandstone. Of course John was right. We both knew it was a violation of securities law to embark on any public offering while important announcements of a material magnitude were pending. "John, let me wind things up here with Carl, and I'll come back to Los Angeles."

I set the phone down in its cradle.

"Is everything all right?" Carl asked.

This was the damnedest screwup I'd heard of in some time. And the timing was impeccable—a masterpiece of tragicomedy. Here I was, as deep as I could possibly be into negotiations with Carl Reichardt—a legend, a local hero, and someone I didn't want to look like a fool in front of—and I was mere *hours* away from pulling the trigger on the announcement of an extraordinary loan loss reserve. I thought, *The last place in this world we should be is out on the market issuing securities.*

I was pissed off and embarrassed and I could not hide it. "Carl, there's been a development." I solemnly briefed him on the problem. "I apologize, but I've got to get back to Los Angeles. I will call you when I know more." I felt like I'd shown up for my prom date with my shirttail hanging out of my fly.

I hustled back to Los Angeles, where Kooken and I gathered with our attorneys, including Russ Freeman.

I was nearly livid. "I don't understand *how* this could happen."

Kooken shook his head. "I told them not to."

"But it happened." At this point I didn't care who was at fault. I wasn't going to shoot anybody over it because I had so many other problems. *First let's fix it*, I thought, *and then I'll fire the moron.*

I pointed out how inept we would look if we had to pull the offering. "Not only will it create a suspicion that something major is in the works, but we will really be parading our ineptitude to the world. It demonstrates a lack of organizational control. I mean, it just isn't done."

Kooken felt there was no choice. "We have to withdraw the offering of these securities right away."

Immediately, on Thursday morning, December 6—and as discreetly as such a clumsy thing can be done—we pulled the issue. As anticipated, warning bells sounded up and down Wall Street. Reuters, AP, BusinessWire, the *Wall Street Journal*, *American Banker* and a myriad of analysts wanted to know what was in the offing. *Why has this issue been pulled? What is it you're not telling us?*

The irony of this is that throughout the industry, people had come to the right conclusion for the wrong reasons: *Yes, something was up.* One potentially good thing was up, one bad thing was up, but neither one was decided and the sand continued to slip through a juncture in the hourglass.

I phoned Reichardt. Doing my best to sound confident and cool, I filled him in on the pulled offering.

"That's not good," he said.

"I know," I admitted. "It's terrible. But we can survive this." I continued. "Carl, we've simply got to bring our negotiations to a head. I know that you don't like to be rushed, but I've got a problem. I'm going to have to announce why I pulled the securities issue."

"How soon do we have to decide?"

I resisted the urge to tell him, *In the next thirty seconds.* "Like, in the next three or four days. By Monday I would hope. I have to know if I can announce a Wells–Security deal and the reserve as the reason for the pulled offering. If I can do that, it's going to play much better for our stock. Our stock price and yours are the basis for the fixed exchange rate. If our stock plummets with the reserve announcement it will later make the deal look like a distressed sellout. I don't want that and it could jeopardize our merger."

"Right. A lot is riding on this."

A hell of a lot was riding on this. "Now that I have to announce that I'm setting aside the loan reserves, I've also decided to set aside other money to accelerate the shutdown the Merchant Bank." I'd withheld any announcement about the disposition of the Merchant Bank pending a decision about the merger because I intended to announce it in tandem with my announcement of the deal, suggesting by implication that it was the natural and expected consequence of our monumental undertaking with Wells Fargo. Without that triumph, I would just be issuing a list of incomprehensible goofs and disasters.

"Carl, we ought to be in a position to decide one way or another on our deal. If you feel we have to wait, we have to wait. But I would really prefer that we go forward with the announcement of this transaction. We have everything decided and agreed. We have drafts of a definitive agreement. We have done so much and come so close. Why not go to our respective boards this weekend and finalize and sign this contract so that it's done by Monday?"

He said he would think it through and call me back.

In the meantime, I had a lot of thinking to do, and some heavy decisions to make. Kooken and I were closing in on an accurate loan loss reserve number; it was going to be significant, and I had to decide on the precise figure soon. Late on Thursday afternoon I decided that the following morning I would inform David Lovejoy of my decision to shut down the Merchant Bank, and that he would have to leave the company. It was one of the most painful decisions I ever made.

I woke up on Friday, December 7, a day that will always live in infamy in my mind. I arrived at seven, made some notes, and called David Lovejoy into my office. Lovejoy had been largely excluded from news of my negotiations with Reichardt. I let him know what was up, and that I was confident that the Wells merger would succeed as planned. Now the hard part:

"David, as you might have guessed, whether we merge with Wells or not, I'm going to shut down the Merchant Bank." I confessed I'd arrived at the decision some time ago, but had held off on executing such a disruptive event pending a possible merger. I reiterated my reasons. The Merchant Bank, as ambitious and brilliant as the strategy was, was simply too costly and too unprofitable. "It's hurting shareholder value. You know my heart was in this thing just like yours, and it was not a decision I made with any kind of joy." I told him that I had fully enjoyed working with him, admired his brilliance, but that he would no longer be a part of Security Pacific.

Understandably, David was upset. He didn't see the reason for completely shutting down the Merchant Bank. We talked for some time, and David left my office about 10 A.M.

I was restless. I found it hard to sit still, but I wasn't the type to pace. We were down to the wire. I longed for my phone to ring and to hear Carl Reichardt's voice on the other end of the line telling me effusively that he had decided to go forward with the merger. To distract myself I caught up on some paperwork. I called Kooken and we further discussed the numbers related to our loan loss reserve.

Then at 11:30 A.M. my secretary, Amelia, put through a call from Reichardt. *Great,* I thought, *the call I've been waiting for.* I was positive Carl was going to say, "Let's go ahead. Let's get our boards together this weekend, sign the definitive agreement, and announce it on Monday." I picked up the phone. "Carl, how's it going?"

His voice kicked in with uncharacteristic abruptness. "Say, Bob. You know, this merger is a tremendous idea, just tremendous."

"Damned right it is."

"But we simply feel there are too many uncertainties."

Oh shit, I thought, *it ain't gonna happen. Unbelievable.* "Maybe I can clarify some points. What uncertainties, Carl?"

"Well, too many uncertainties about your company. Bob, Wells is a fairly simple and straightforward organization. Security Pacific, I've discovered, is a rather complex organization. It's hard to get a *grasp* on it. You know what I mean?"

My throat tightened. "What are you saying? You don't want to do the deal?"

"That's about the size of it. We just can't do the deal."

I stammered, "I just fired Lovejoy and set in motion the breakdown of the $25 billion Merchant Bank." The subtext here was that I thought my major announcement would be explicable in light of the announcement of the merger, and injurious to Security Pacific without the merger.

"You were going to do that anyway. You said that was imminent."

My guts churned. "Carl, that is true, but this is undeniably a sour outcome to a lot of understanding between you and I, and immense contemplated value for both of our shareholders. Our stocks will go off the charts. This is an enormous disappointment, Carl. Now I have to go out there this morning and make nothing but crummy announcements."

"I understand, Bob. Like you, I was enthusiastic about this possibility. It just isn't going to happen."

Holy shit, I thought, as I imagined having to announce the huge loan loss reserve, pulled offering, and turmoil in the Merchant Bank—with no upside whatsoever. The sequence of events and timing were horrendous.

"Can you be specific about the uncertainties?" I asked humbly. "Are you sure these uncertainties are so great that they should derail this merger?"

"Well, you were unable to give us the exact information we requested about the swaps book. Zundt has some concerns, and Hazen's got some uncertainties."

"What concerns? What uncertainties? Can I resolve them?"

"No, I think the concerns are complex and unlikely to be cleared up in this phone call. Don't get me wrong: I still think this was a fantastic idea. We just can't pull it all together."

I knew that Carl didn't like to be rushed. He was extremely cautious by nature. One of Carl's favorite phrases was, "If you've got to have the answer now, the answer is *No.*" Probably I'd applied too much pressure by asking that we arrive at a decision within a matter of days. Yes, I was pushing. Maybe if I backed off a little he would reconsider. I cleared my throat. "It's kind of hard to believe it's dead after we've come so close. The economic benefits of this transaction, as we agreed, would be so overpowering. I mean, Carl, the deal is an absolute home run. And I'm sure that with a little more time we can answer all your concerns. Is there any chance you might reconsider your decision, or resurrect it at a later time? Can we keep the exchange ratio fixed so our stock price won't affect our negotiations and pick this up again next month? Maybe we can get together after the first of the year."

Reichardt sounded somewhat apologetic. "No, Bob, I'm afraid our thinking is that we are just going to back away from the whole thing."

This phone conversation—the culmination of all our efforts—lasted about five minutes.

I was stunned, paralyzed. The past five days had bowled me over. I stared at the wall in silence for five minutes. *So close.* What went wrong?

I liked Carl, and looked up to him—but his explanation was clearly lame. Later I would I learn the real reason for Reichardt's exit, but at this moment I was mystified. We had pounded this merger out on a table like a lump of potter's clay for months. We'd laid all our cards on the table. He'd seen all our numbers. He knew the location of every compartment, closet, and desk drawer in Security Pacific. That the merger had to be terminated because we couldn't produce a piece of paper related to our swaps book—in proportion to the enormous value of this transaction to both corporations—was a weak excuse. It was feeble.

And I was left with my ass hanging in the wind.

▼

That weekend, Flamson and I convened an emergency session of the Board of Directors. I don't know what was going through the minds of the Board members; perhaps they were certain they'd been called in to hear tremendous news of how the Wells merger would bring about enhancement to shareholder value. Feeling like one of Ingmar Bergman's scythe-wielding incarnations of Death itself, I opened with a frank *mea culpa* for the collapse of the Wells deal and gave them an explanation for the withdrawn issue. Then I promptly subjected them to a blizzard of disaster:

1. "The Wells deal fell through.

2. "On Friday I terminated David Lovejoy and shut down the Merchant Bank.

3. "We are faced with significant economic downturns in all of our key real estate markets, which means higher classified loan levels and higher loan losses.

4. "Monday morning before the market opens we're going to announce that we've set aside $200 million in reserve to shut down and dismantle the Merchant Bank.

5. "At that time we'll also announce our intent to set aside an extraordinary $600 million addition to our loan loss reserve and another $100 million to write down our other real estate taken back from defaulted borrowers.

6. "The regulatory agencies have intensified their oversight of Security Pacific and have expressed real concern about our generally lower capital, short-term funding, and deficient reserve levels.

7. "We have had a very poor year.

8. "We've had a terrible fourth quarter."

There was nothing left to say, but I did outline strategies for the immediate future. As part of the breakdown of the Merchant Bank, we would sell particular subsidiaries; others would be managed down, closed, restructured, or reassigned to the auspices of either Nick Binkley or Jerry Grundhofer. We would preserve the dividend if possible. For the time being, we would cease acquisitions. We would concentrate on improving our standing with the regulatory community. "We have a very tough year ahead, but I believe we are up to the challenge."

They accepted my explanation and approved my proposed action plan.

▼

I desperately hoped that this five-day assault on Security Pacific—a pulled bond issue, firing a top executive, scrapping my lifelong dream of a Merchant Bank, the heartbreaking phone call from Reichardt, an unprecedented and depressing emergency session of the board of directors, and the humiliating Monday morning announcement of our worst year in recent memory—would represent an anomaly, a singular abyss from which we would emerge, scathed but alive.

But I was wrong. I was naïve to the bone. Reichardt's phone call was merely an aria in a two-month opera of disaster.

8

Apocalypse Now

On the executive floor, tensions ran high.

George Moody was still on the Board and still despised the Merchant Bank. He was furious at the estimated $200 million price tag for dismantling the Merchant Bank. Following a board meeting he pulled me aside and, with an undercurrent of I-Told-You-So, chastised me for an experiment that had been a folly. "You're ruining the bank. You're destroying this institution."

"Well, George, you hate the Merchant Bank. I'm tearing it down."

"I don't know what's worse, creating the Merchant Bank or the cost of getting rid of it."

"Hey, George, I'm the man that the board has challenged to run this bank. They agree this is a step in the right direction. This is my job. If you don't like it, then take it up with the board."

"You're going to have minor insurrection all over the globe. There are some twenty subsidiaries that we have to sell or exit."

"George, are you proposing we keep the subsidiaries?"

"Absolutely not. But why does it have to cost so much to tear something apart?"

"Because of what you just said: we can expect minor insurrection as we sell or exit twenty subsidiaries."

When I publicly announced the shutdown of the Merchant Bank, everyone involved—brokers, swaps, you name it, from Asia to Australia to Canada—was pissed off. No longer was it possible to camouflage our deterioration on Wall Street. Everyone wondered what was happening to our bank.

By mid-December, as the result of that month's dismal announcements, our creditworthiness was challenged when one of the most closely watched credit agencies, Moodys, reduced Security Pacific's own commercial paper rating, calling our own financial health into question. At that time we were using $4.5 billion of commercial paper within Security Pacific's holding company to support a variety of loans made to businesses and individuals through our higher-risk FSS subsidiaries. With our commercial paper ratings reduced below levels that connote unquestioned safety, we were now struggling to get funded, and there was the very real possibility that Security Pacific's holding company—the parent and primary financial source for our hundred-odd subsidiaries—could find itself technically insolvent.

I'd never heard of such a thing. Clearly, fifteen years of unbroken success had come to an end.

Every investor was watching us now.

Some analysts believed we had it coming; they felt Security Pacific had been riding high on the hog and that our stock was overpriced. Rejoicing in our debilitated state, some sectors of the press kicked us in the balls with headlines like *SECURITY PACIFIC'S SAFETY NET IS FRAYING FAST.*

▼

In early January I found an agitated, cigarette-smoking Russ Freeman waiting in my office.

"Bob, we might have an issue."

"Great—another problem?"

"Not necessarily a problem. Burns Fry called. As you know, we own 30% of that operation. Now that we've called for the shutdown of the Merchant Bank, they are calling on us to complete the acquisition of the rest of the company—100%—and they feel we are legally obligated to do so."

"No, Russ, not an issue—this is a problem."

Freeman and I sat down with the contract Lovejoy had co-engineered. The wording was murky on some points, not the least of which was the most important: whether or not Security Pacific bore a legal duty to acquired 100% ownership of Burns Fry by the last quarter of 1990.

"But this is '91," I said. "Where has this been?"

"It's one of those open items associated with the Merchant Bank shutdown."

There was an inherent trapdoor built into that deal as a result of poorly phrased legalese, and the trapdoor sprung at the worst possible time—when Security Pacific was already facing crises on virtually every front.

I waived my no-smoking policy. Russ lit another cigarette and with a confident singsong voice that contradicted the moment of his words, said, "The dilemma is this: Burns Fry feels we are committed to purchase them and we don't feel we are. Unfortunately, the contract is unclear and can be interpreted either way."

"How much will it cost?"

"To acquire the remaining 70% will cost us about $200 million."

"No, no," I said. "We can't afford that. Even the reserves I allocated for the sale of Hoare Govett won't cover that."

"I don't think Burns Fry will rejoice when I tell them. We may have to go to war on this one."

This was no trickle of problems; it was a deluge. Security Pacific had the ebola virus, leprosy, hemorrhagic fever; first there was a rash on the back of its hand, then a wound that refused to heal on the arm, then pneumonia, and now the brain was turning to mush.

We were broke. What could we do?

I sat down with a forlorn John Kooken. "Because of our downgraded commercial paper rating, we can no longer sell to most of our traditional commercial paper customers because they are prohibited from owning more than a small percent of paper that is rated below top grade."

"They wouldn't buy it anyway because it carries more risk. John, we have to find a whole array of new buyers for four and a half *billion* dollars' worth of commercial paper."

"Within six weeks," he added, blood draining from his face. "That entire portfolio matures the second week of February!"

▼

Then, impossibly, the situation worsened: our traders—the very people we now relied on to sell the commercial paper—staged a walkout. They wanted higher bonuses and had cunningly waited until their boss, the head of the Investment Department, went on vacation to hunt quail in Mexico.

To prompt our brokers back to the trading floor, we acceded to their demands. "Pay them what they want," I said, "and we'll kill them later."

Nick Binkley and I commiserated on a related issue. We doubted even our ace traders would be able to sell $550 million in Floating Rate Preferred—attractive nouveau instruments—which was reviewed and repriced every week, and whose sale added directly to capital. "The loss of our A1/P1 Commercial Paper rating and all of the other bad news makes the sale of these instruments virtually impossible."

"Then we'll have to repurchase them ourselves," I said. "And preferred counts as capital."

Nick shook his head in amazement. "That will leave us with

an additional $550 million to fund, and that's $550 million less cash, directly out of capital."

"We don't have nearly enough time to sell any of our other balance sheet assets to raise needed cash."

"That leaves us only one alternative for the short run—borrow cash from another source."

I reminded Nick that we had about two and a half billion dollars' worth of short-term commercial paper backup lines from fifteen other banks that we could tap. "But if we utilize these lines of credit, everyone will know we are in the middle of a liquidity crisis, and if the whole world knows we're in trouble with basic funding, then everything else will crumble; it's a fait accompli."

"The final backup," Nick offered reluctantly, "would obviously be the Fed."

Yes, the Fed—the lender of last resort. The hair on the back of my neck stood up at the prospect of having to approach the Federal Reserve for emergency funding. "I'm loathe to do that, Nick. It would permanently destroy Security Pacific's reputation. Even if we borrowed for only a few days, it would be a public relations catastrophe. We'd be a Wall Street laughingstock. The regulators would be all over us."

"We'll be an even bigger laughingstock if we run out of money."

Christ, I thought, *Nick's right*. "I suppose I had better put the Federal Reserve on alert." If we couldn't find buyers, I would have to do the unthinkable—approach the Federal Reserve for a nearly unheard-of use of the Fed Discount Window and secure a colossal loan from the U.S. government to preserve our liquidity. "That would be humiliating. Let's do everything we can to avoid the Fed."

▼

That night Flamson and I worked late. I told him I was worried that we might have to ask the Fed for a loan, and that I was prepared to put them on notice. Although neither one of us wanted to do it, we argued back and forth. During this contentious discussion, Flamson's phone rang.

We'd often answer the phones ourselves after the secretaries had gone home, talking to our customers without the intermediary screening of a receptionist. I took my calls seriously, but Flamson occasionally saw them as an opportunity for hijinks.

Flamson listened for a moment, winked, and put the irate caller on the speaker phone: "I want to speak to the man in charge. My branch manager—that bastard—turned down my application for a loan for no apparent reason!"

I practically had to stuff a handkerchief in my mouth so as not to laugh when Flamson adopted the manner of a jubilant but inept custodian. "Oh, you want Mister Richard Flamson the Third, the chairman of this big bank."

"If that's the guy in charge, yes!"

"A nice man, a nice man! Unfortunately, I regret to inform you that Mr. Flamson and all of the important people have departed for the evening, but I shall attempt to take a message."

"Who the hell is this?"

"Why, I am the executive janitor."

Flamson asked the man two or three times to spell his name. It was a simple name, like Jones or Johnson.

"Sir, is that second letter A as in 'apple' or E as in 'Elvis'?"

"No! It's an 'O' as in 'Orson Welles.'"

"Oh, he was a fine movie director, a fine director! Didn't he make that fine picture *Citizen Kane?* Spell it one more time please, slowly, and I shall attempt to write your name on this message pad."

Afterward, Flamson abruptly got back to business. "We've got a hell of a problem."

▼

Kooken monitored the progress of the brokers and kept me informed. He and I contacted Dick Thornburgh, an investment banker at First Boston. Thornburgh had worked with us before and had a thorough familiarity with the intricacies of Security Pacific. He knew we were in trouble and, in mid-January, offered a suggestion to help us out of our dilemma. "I think First Boston can provide you guys with a loan of probably $1 billion. Would that help?"

"Yes," I said, "that would help." It would save our ass.

"This would be a short-term loan—payable in perhaps a year or two—but if you want it I believe it can be accomplished."

"We would like to accomplish it," I assured him.

"There's one small catch. If you agree to accept the loan, it will have to be secured by all of the stock of the FSS subsidiaries, meaning that in the months ahead you'll have to securitize asset pools of these companies to pay back the loan. First Boston would, of course, expect to lead these offerings."

"I think this is a great partial solution to our problem. But I'll have to discuss it with Nick Binkley."

I didn't think Nick would be crazy about placing the future of FSS on the line, but I thought he would prefer this idea to a continuation of our funding crisis. We would essentially be placing Security Pacific's family jewels on the line to ensure our continued viability as a company.

I also bounced the idea off Flamson. Flamson agreed with me that it should be done. "It's difficult and it's humiliating," Flamson acknowledged, "but we have to do it."

Nick understood that it was a needed escape hatch. "It's like the guy who pawns his wife's wedding ring to put food on the table."

I dispatched Nick Binkley to New York to see if the deal could be assembled quickly enough to help. I put Russ Freeman, our chief legal counsel, on alert; he would have to swing into action if the deal was approved.

The next day, Binkley phoned us from the First Boston office with an update. Flamson and I huddled around the phone. "The consensus here is that the deal is doable."

I gave Flamson a thumbs-up signal.

Binkley continued: "But we're pressed for time. I'm ironing out details as quickly as I can."

Flamson asked for the phone. He took the handset slowly. I thought I saw a flash of despair in our chairman's eyes as he began to speak to Binkley. "Nick, I just want you to know that I appreciate what you're doing. I know this isn't easy for you. But I also want you to know that this deal *must* get done. We need this loan desperately. Call us back the minute you have something in writing so that we can begin the documentation."

Flamson hung up the phone and just sat in my office for several lingering minutes without saying a word, undoubtedly reflecting on the sequence of events that had landed us in this awful mess.

Nick phoned back an hour later to tell us the terms and conditions he had agreed to and the time frame for completion and funding of the loan. Flamson was ecstatic; we all were. Dick said, "Now we have a substantially better chance to make it, to stay out of the Fed and remain self-funded."

▼

The last day of the second week of February we made it. We were funded. We did not have to go to the Fed on our hands and knees or access backup credit lines. We had about $100 million in cold, hard cash. Our levels were low, but we were liquid.

That night, Nick Binkley and I huddled in my fifty-fourth-floor corner office, hours after everyone else had left. The sun sank beneath the orange Los Angeles horizon, the lights had been dimmed by the security staff, and outside the office window was a blaze of fluorescence from the skyscraper across the street.

The unrelenting trauma of the past two months had put me in a nostalgic mood. "You know, Nick, in my first formal presentation before the annual stockholders meeting a year ago, I had the honor of announcing record earnings of $740 million."

Nick remembered. "An increase of 16% over 1988."

"And when I began my speech, asking rhetorically, 'You might be asking, where do we go from here?,' I never imagined the answer might be, 'Right down the crapper.'" I shook my head. "In a broad but very real sense, these two months have become a joke."

"At least you have a sense of humor about this."

"Yeah, but there inevitably comes a point where things just aren't all that funny anymore."

"We were blindsided. Some of it was our fault, but not all of it. Who ever thought real estate—*terra firma*—would crater?"

"Nick, our situation is not going to improve. On a crisis-by-crisis basis we've managed to survive, but this can't go on forever. Another stretch like this will kill us."

"The trick is to stay funded," he said.

"Ultimately, we have to extricate ourselves from the reliance on commercial paper, because this problem is going to recur."

Nick—a genuine renaissance man—had a charming habit of memorializing quotations; sayings, parables, aphorisms, and poignant or profound vignettes on life and business that he found insightful and he scribbled them down in a small black book that he carried in his breast coat pocket at all times. He referred to them frequently. Whenever a problem or unusual situation arose, Nick would consult his pearls of enlightenment. "There is an old saying. 'The art of good business is. . . .'" or "Confucius said. . . . " or "Mick Jagger said. . . . " I stared at the book leaning out of his pocket. I asked, "Is there any wisdom in your little book for a situation of this magnitude?"

Nick chuckled grimly, loosened his tie. "We've met our immediate funding obligations, but we have to consider the long term. Do we—a major bank—want to keep scrambling for money like this? I suppose we could raise capital by selling off or, as First Boston suggests, monetizing some of our more valuable assets—raising cash, shrinking the company assets, and, where possible, booking profits at the same time. We can also wind down some of our most cash-intensive activities."

"That would look awful," I pointed out. "The whole world will see us having a gigantic fire sale; Wall Street is going to smell panic and that could kill any chance we have to find a new merger partner who would regard us as an equal."

There it was—the "M" word. *Merger*. Like Morse code—and even when unarticulated—the unuttered concept now accented every meeting, every utterance. *Merger* had not been an undesirable concept when Security Pacific was powerful and funded, but now that we were deteriorating it sounded like an admission of defeat.

"I know," said Nick. "The last thing we want anyone to suspect is that we're desperate, especially if we are to pursue *that option*."

"Isn't that our ultimate solution?" It was a rhetorical question, because I knew the answer.

Nick scratched his throat. "This is a huge institution. Given our size and deteriorating condition, any merger would by definition be a daunting transaction. Would the Fed support or move to block a merger of that magnitude?"

"I don't see why the regulators would block us from pursuing the one objective that so directly addresses our and their concerns. The alternative—a government intervention—is inconceivable. It could throw the banking industry into turmoil."

"We would have to move quickly, before another crisis." Nick reached for his little black book, flipped through the pages and stopped. "'Fighting it out would be like climbing Mount Everest without an oxygen bottle. It can be done, but few make it, and those who do lose so many brain cells in the process that they can neither enjoy the vista nor get back down the mountain.'"

I felt our path was clear: "Let's solve our funding problem permanently so it no longer hangs over our head. We'll doll up the company as best we can and find a partner with lots of capital."

The notion that our only realistic course of action to overcome and, frankly, mask our problems, lay in a merger was, to me, surreal. I'd worked for Security Pacific for my entire life. It was a company that had survived traumas and thrived for more than one hundred years.

Nick was thinking aloud. "If our primary goal is to maximize the value for our shareholders over the next few years, a merger of two California banks would be the slam bang winner of all time."

I thought for what felt like a long time. "I'd want it to be a merger of equals and not a sell-out."

"Bob, if a merger of equals is going to happen it has to happen very quickly. We have some muscle left, but there's enormous propensity for further deterioration—and the greater the deterioration, the less leverage we'll have in any negotiations. We need to engage a partner from a position of some strength." Nick tried to look on the upside. "But if we can pull it off, it will be the coup de grâce of your tenure, short and sweet as it's been."

"Not so sweet," I said, without a whisp of a smile.

Nick Binkley had a depth of understanding that went beyond numbers and statistics. Realistic and objective in his observations, he was a man whose philosophical range and compassion engendered confidence. He loved this bank as much as I did and understood how badly it felt to admit that Security Pacific—with its hundred-year tradition as a family bank, a vital engine to the California economy, philanthropic contributor to the community it served, and, now, an international player—might be, in essence, forced out of existence as an independent institution under my brief reign at the helm.

"Security Pacific is like a racehorse, Bob. It was strong for one hundred years, and it ran faster than hell for the last fifteen."

"Maybe too fast," I responded.

"We can try to maintain the upper hand, but I think any merger—whether it's exactly equal or truly a sale—is preferable to having a broken-down horse."

Nick stood up straight and looked at me. "Bob, we must not fight this thing to the death. It's painful business, but we've got to sell our horse before it dies."

Sell your horse before it dies.

The phrase was provocative in its subtext, poignant in its simplicity.

For a number of weeks, Nick's horse analogy continued to reverberate. If Security Pacific was indeed a race horse, was it sick enough to die? Second, was it well enough to sell? If not, could it be made to appear healthy?

Shareholder value, I thought. The phrase rang in my mind and, like a persistent dream, the ringing never stopped. *Got to merge. Merge quickly, merge now, merge at any cost. I've got to get us out of this.*

The reality was that a merger would be no simple matter for this bank. Nearly 45,000 lives would be disrupted and the history of an extraordinary institution would most likely be lost. We were significantly weaker now than we had been even months before, when we'd engaged Wells Fargo from a position of relative strength.

Was there any alternative? For a brief moment I imagined what the father of Security Pacific, Sartori, would do were he in my shoes. How would he have dealt with this outbreak? Would he have demonstrated his trademark grace under fire in the face of the real estate provision of FIRREA, or would the decorous little man have raged against the system? Would he have deferred to the regulators, or slapped them around a little?

Throughout my thirty-year career at Security Pacific, I'd never been able to gain a reputation as a great manager or

leader. And now that I finally had my chance as the chief executive officer, I would have to become a liquidator.

▼

We had come far too close to a disaster, and there was fallout.

During this crisis period Bob Corteway staggered lethargi-
cally into my office, ragged and near tears. "I basically can't
handle it anymore. The problems are too severe."

"What are you telling me?"

"I'm going home. Please don't call."

That was it. Corteway turned slowly—the way a wrecking
ball changes directions—and walked out.

He appeared to be having some sort of meltdown. I knew
in the past months he'd suffered through onerous disagree-
ments about credit requests with David Lovejoy. But what
else was going on?

Some of the prophetic words he'd spoken at our management forum echoed now in my mind: " . . . during a period
of economic downturn and possibly even more important
from a risk-management perspective, in the months preceding an economic downturn, the issue of asset quality becomes a dominant factor affecting our company's performance, and today, in my judgment, we're witnessing a very
classic pattern. The warning signs are here. . . . "

Corteway probably felt like a lone voice crying out in the
wilderness.

I was enormously sympathetic for Corteway because he was
an extraordinary human being who had done a lot for Security
Pacific; by the same token, the fact that he had simply called
it quits scared the hell out of me. Corteway was our chief
credit officer—my God, were things *this* desperate? What did
he know about our credit situation that I didn't know? Was it
even worse than we suspected? How could it be?

I hurried to Jerry Grundhofer's office. "You're not going to
fucking believe this. As if we haven't got enough problems,

Corteway just went home. He's totally upset. He nearly collapsed in my office."

"You mean he just *walked?* Will he come back?"

"Damned if I know."

I couldn't tell if Jerry was surprised or not. "What was the straw that broke the camel's back?"

"Well, shit—look at 1990. Look at this quarter. The last two months have been positively hellish. The Wells deal collapsed, bad loans arc skyrocketing, we have a funding crisis, we've lost 15% of our capital with the redemption of the preferred, we've lost our A1/P1 rating, and now the credit agencies are threatening to downgrade our remaining debt. Corteway probably just saw a couple new loans go bad and absolutely couldn't stand it anymore."

Grundhofer exhaled. "Every man has a breaking point."

▼

Two weeks later Corteway had still not returned to work. I called on George Benter and Dick Heilman to pick up the slack in Corteway's absence. Heilman was responsible for credit quality control, and George, who had vast experience in credit, was to be our final lending authority.

If our lending apparatus had a systemic weakness, perhaps it was the result of our emphasis on growth. Because growth was a function of the number—rather than the quality—of loans we made, no one wanted to say *No*. No one wanted to be the messenger who issued a caution that resulted in a drop in earnings. We'd prided ourselves in growth, and frowned upon any gesture that restrained it. We'd built an inherent paradox: if we'd stopped lending, our earnings would have been less impressive, and Dick Flamson or I might have called for a scalp. But if we kept going until the bottom fell out, we also would have called for a scalp. The credit officers were damned either way. Something had to give.

▼

Corteway returned to work several weeks later. He looked great, but I couldn't place him back in his prior position. He needed to be out of the credit approval loop. Unfortunately, word had spread about what had happened. At an outside meeting held at San Diego's Hotel Del Coronado, J.G. Boswell—our senior board member—asked me to join him for a stroll around the bay. Never one to mince words, he began what I thought would be a casual discussion by saying, "The credit is going from bad to worse and you can't have your chief lending officer walking out of the building. I think that Corteway succumbed to pressure from Lovejoy and others to extend credit in cases where it was not advisable to do so."

"Corteway himself admitted that he had yielded to pressure on some credits that he didn't really like." I was torn; I didn't entirely blame Corteway. I was pissed that Lovejoy had applied a jackhammer to Corteway. "He was overwhelmed by Lovejoy's perceived importance in the company."

"That may be true, but I think you should get rid of Corteway." This was not the first time J.G. had issued such proclamations. A year earlier he'd wanted me to axe an employee named Tom Thomas for not pulling our Arizona interests out of the quagmire quicker. I had refused Boswell then, and would do so now.

"No way, J.G. I need him. I won't fire him. Bob Corteway won't make credit decisions for this company anymore, but I need him because not only is he an excellent credit administrator, but he knows the inner mechanisms of the portfolio. He lives and breathes this stuff and he knows the condition and status of all our major loans. I depend on him for his knowledge of individual loans, especially right now. Cutting him loose would be stupid."

J.G. was upset. "Somebody's got to take responsibility for this."

"I'm not going to get rid of Corteway," I repeated. "He's a good banker and he would never do anything intentionally to harm Security Pacific. Firing Corteway is not in the best interest of this company."

I assigned Corteway as the overall administrator of the credit function without approval responsibilities.

▼

Now more of the big southern California real estate developers—some of them long-standing and well-established companies—began to fall into the abyss of declining values, sales, and cash flow. These were the companies who had been developing real estate for aeons and had been tremendously successful at developing land into residential communities and selling the homes. They were the cardiovascular system of development in California, performing the most basic and necessary function to its historic growth.

Southern California had sustained recessions, but had never suffered an economic setback that came even close to what we now faced in early 1991.

Coinciding with all this, one of our largest California real estate developers found itself in a *cash crisis*—code words for the inability to sell houses or move land. Security Pacific had a long history with this company and, jointly with Wells Fargo, lent them $100 million secured by personal assets. Four months later, before any payment was due, the regulators marched in, examined the loan, classified it a "Loss," and ordered us to write off our $50 million.

What made this loan unique was not only its size but the prominence and historic quality of the borrower, one of the largest developers of single-family and multifamily dwellings in the nation. The deterioration of the company was directly attributable to the downturn in the California housing market, which had adversely affected home sales and, consequently, cash flow.

When I questioned regulatory decision on this matter, their response was shocking. They essentially said, *Security Pa-*

cific is no longer permitted to bail out any real estate developers, ever.

Shortly thereafter I flew to Washington, D.C., to meet with our old examiner, Jimmy Barton, at the Office of the Comptroller of the Currency. I liked Barton as much as any banking executive could like a bank examiner. He was honest, straightforward, and intelligent.

He was friendly but standoffish as I enumerated the measures we'd taken to reverse our descent. "We've tried very hard to improve our oversight and our entire process of evaluating credits. We overhauled our reserve methodologies."

"Does that mean you wouldn't make any more loans like the $50 million bailout deal we made you charge off?"

I tried to laugh but I couldn't. "You think I'm stupid? No, I think I got the message your deputies were attempting to impart—that there's no money available in the banking system to bail out any of the real estate developers."

"Bob, you know what we're trying to accomplish."

"I know, but I don't feel this is the way to go about it. The regulators are going to take down a lot of decent people."

The government wanted to siphon excesses out of the economy—now—and if that meant taking out developers and even major banks in the process, so be it.

In the spirit of a Sartori, Dick Flamson—who remained as chairman with a determination to resolve ongoing difficulties by sheer force of will—wanted Security Pacific to bail these guys out. "How can the regulators tell us not to help these guys? They are our customers! When we don't help our customers we cut our own throats and we renege on our part of the bargain. Our mission has always been to promote growth, and we do that by funding the real estate developers. This is land—this is what we have stood for since Sartori opened shop a hundred years ago!" Dick took the impact of this crisis on developers so personally that I thought he would dip into his own pockets if he could afford to do so. He felt their resuscitation was essential not only to the vitality of Security Pacific, but the welfare of California. He was devoted to the Sartorial vision of bank as savior.

"Dick, what can we realistically do? We are struggling too."

He was unusually intense. "I have thought carefully about what I'm about to say, Bob. I feel very strongly that we should pool some funds—say, $400 million—to bail out our real estate developer customers until the economy turns."

Uh-oh, I thought, *so we're back to Denial*. Words failed me. I was simultaneously touched and frightened: this sentiment, as sincere as untrammeled snow, carried unparalleled risk if the economy did not mend. Second, the regulators were adamant that no assistance was to be provided to developers. When my voice returned, I whispered, "Say that again."

Flamson continued. "Real estate in California is such a fundamental part of our economy—it is the cornerstone. As long as there's been a Security Pacific we've put money into California. It's always been that way. We just have to ride this damn thing out and help our developers along, otherwise they'll go down and most likely take us with them. That's why I say we've got to pump another $400 million or so into California to support the development of real estate." My silence provoked him to add, "I'm dead-ass serious!"

In his eyes I saw a reflection of Sartori. He so badly felt we had an obligation to our community. I ached to agree with him—my heart said 'yes' but our financial state, and the message from the regulators, said 'no.'

I rose from my seat. "Dick, we can't do that. Even if we wanted to. Even if it was financially sound."

"We cannot walk away. We risk our own company if we do. What do we stand for?"

"Jesus, Dick, this is not a Frank Capra movie. Remember the $50 million we put in with Wells? We tried to be the Good Guy, we tried to be the heroes. The regulators don't want us making these loans. There is no mistaking their message. The government is *forcing* us to walk away from our communities."

"We've got to keep our people healthy. If they get sick, we get sick."

"We *are* sick. On what logic do you base our capacity to help the developers? Dick, even if we *wanted* to, how are we *able* to?"

"The most likely economic scenario is that the recession in California will be a short-term economic setback."

No, I thought. *We wanted to believe that, and we've believed it for too long*. It wasn't true. "There's no evidence for that."

"Its always been that way. California has historically been resilient."

"This time it's different."

"Bob, we have to put money out to help salvage these guys. They are our customers, our friends, our community."

His sincerity took my breath away. I thought he was in denial. "That . . . that's not in the cards, Dick. I'm sorry. We can't do that."

"Why not?"

I was put in the strange position of instructing my instructor. "Because we've done it once and the regulators didn't like it. We tried to play our part to help solve the liquidity problem and what did we get? The regulators pushed it back in our face: they *punished* us. They don't want us trying to be heroes, and you want us to do it again. What makes you think it will work this time?"

His fingers trembled in outrage. "How can they do this to us? How can they do this to California?"

"Dick, the regulators are adamant and the message is crystal clear: don't bail out the builders. The government wants some scalps. If real estate doesn't kill us, the regulators will."

My heart broke for Dick. The historical antecedents of this company *mattered* deeply to the people who ran the bank. Our predecessors imbued contemporary management not only with a sense of lineage but a philosophy, a vital affiliation with the development of California and its real estate. There was a steadfast belief that Security Pacific was intrinsically linked with the land and that this land would never let us down. Flamson didn't want to let down the developers.

He was 100% right—in spirit. And in another economic environment, or with a stronger balance sheet, or less inflexible regulation, we could have injected money into real estate. But under the circumstances, it was impossible.

It was a poignant delusion based on historicity, but a delusion nonetheless.

▼

Two and a half months had elapsed since the aborted merger negotiations with Carl Reichardt and on one of the few free evenings I had, I found myself reflecting on what might have been. I found it difficult to accept that within such a brief period of time our circumstances had shifted so dramatically, but I tried to evaluate our situation with a clear head: we'd become trapped in a cycle of overaggressive growth in an environment whose complexities and technologies our founder, Sartori, could not possibly have imagined.

In a very real sense, this came about because we felt an obligation to Sartori's vision. It was impossible to walk through the anteroom to the board room, see his portrait, as well as those of my predecessors—Sartori, Wallace, Shelton, Austin, Larkin, and Flamson, as well as Chairmen Hartnack and Robinson—and not be cognizant of our founders and the path they staked out for Security Pacific. How could we not think of our history? The culture of the institution, our commitment to growth, especially in California, was still there and always would be. There seemed to be no question about it.

And when, in the dark days ahead, we had to ask ourselves, *Why were we so extended in real estate?*, that allegiance was part of the reason: a sense of obligation to continued growth, particularly in California. We wanted to be the leaders of the Sartori vision. It was a torch that was passed from one leader to the next.

Even if we'd been prophetic enough to decline further participation in California real estate, the mandate to fund California was so intrinsic to our culture that any alternative was never contemplated.

▼

I now realized that a Security Pacific–Wells Fargo merger would most likely have been a disaster, and I could only ascribe the breakdown in negotiations to Divine Intervention. Carl had come to the right decision but for the wrong reason. The merger would have been a catastrophe because of a factor neither Carl nor I had strongly considered: both institutions had enormous California real estate development portfolios—the two biggest portfolios in California. If there was a good reason to have terminated that merger, it was the prodigious size of our combined California real estate development portfolios, which—unbeknownst to us at the time—would have become unmanageable in this bottomward economy. There was a good chance that had we conjoined those portfolios in a merger, both institutions would have been crippled, maimed, or killed.

Years later, Carl and I spoke and agreed that in hindsight *not* to merge was the wisest decision we could have made. During that later conversation, Reichardt revealed to me that prior to our December 7 phone conversation, he had consulted with Warren Buffett, who held a 10% plus stock ownership in Wells Fargo. It would be difficult to overstate the importance of this relationship. Buffett is the most legendary investor still living.

Reichardt was one of the few bankers Buffett respected enough to invest in substantially. Buffet was, as a result of the size of his ownership, someone with whom Carl frequently discussed strategic moves. While talking about our deal with Buffett, Carl focused on the difficulty in obtaining the requested information pertaining to our swaps book.

Buffett noted this and said, "Carl, wherever there's one cockroach in the organization, there's always more than one roach. If you do this deal, you may find yourself with an entire army of roaches."

I tend to believe that Buffett's advice was a decisive factor in Reichardt's decision to abort the deal. When one of your major shareholders—and the savviest of businessmen to boot—warns you off a deal, you listen.

Warren was right, but perhaps not in exactly the way he intended; that army of roaches he referred to would soon emerge in the form of California real estate development loans.

Amazingly, word of my discussions with Reichardt remained private until they were leaked to the *Wall Street Journal* in mid-January 1991. These leaks, mildly irritating at the time, had a beneficial side-effect: they embedded the embryo of fear in a man named Richard Rosenberg. A thing that was undetectable to the eye and never once mentioned during the course of negotiations would become the Rosetta stone of the biggest merger deal in bank history.

Part II

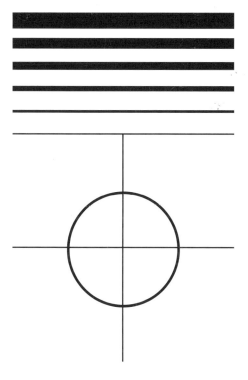

THE MERGER

"O! For a horse with wings!"

—Shakespeare, Cymberline (III:1)

9

Looking for
Mr. Rich(ard)

Following our liquidity crisis in early 1991, I contacted First Boston—our investment bankers—and asked them to run a series of more thorough reviews of what would occur were Security Pacific to merge with either of our three major California counterparts—Bank of America, First Interstate, and, despite the breakdown in negotiations, with Wells Fargo Bank. The study results confirmed the overwhelming opportunity that existed to magnify shareholder value—beyond any other conceivable alternative—through an in-state merger. Reichardt and I had discussed a fifty-fifty exchange of Wells Fargo and Security Pacific stock—a true merger of equals. At this exchange ratio there would have been a 32% accretion to our earnings per share, and a 22% accretion at Wells. A 10% accretion is generally considered enormous; these numbers were *gargantuan* and virtually guaranteed that had my talks with Reichardt borne fruit, our stock price would have jumped immediately.

While these numbers were compelling, the figures generated by hypothetical matrimony with Bank of America were positively lyrical.

In the event of a merger with Bank of America, I guessed at a realistic exchange relationship of Bank of America, 2/3; Security Pacific, 1/3, with combined expense savings of $1 billion. First Boston confirmed the benefits of this merger in a second analysis issued under the dramatic title of *Project Clint*. Once again using pseudonyms in homage to the Sergio Leone western, Security Pacific was "Good," Bank of America was "Big," Wells Fargo was "Bad," and First Interstate was "The Ugly." For my part, I wanted to merge the bank while it was still worth more than a "Fistful of Dollars."

Project Clint provided ample evidence that by targeting Bank of America as a merger partner we were making the selection that would best reward our shareholders. Security Pacific and Bank of America shareholders would, respectively, receive roughly 50% and 40% accretion.

This confirmed that, barring the real estate loan concentration, a merger with Wells Fargo would have been attractive. But Bank of America was undoubtedly the awesome target. Unfortunately, we still had a number of problems to resolve before I could approach them.

▼

The last week of February 1991 my secretary, Amelia Di-Pasquale, buzzed me on the intercom to say that Dick Rosenberg, chairman and CEO of Bank of America, was on the line.

I thought, *He probably wants some commitment to the Boy Scouts or the San Francisco Opera.* I had never spoken to Rosenberg on the phone before and we'd had only a handful of casual discussions at Reserve City Bankers meetings.

"Hi, Bob. This is Dick Rosenberg. How's it going?"

"Well, okay, but if this economy would improve things would be going a whole lot better."

The foreplay is almost over, I thought. *I wonder how much money he wants, or perhaps he wants a job for one of his children.* I would try to give him what he wanted, because I wanted to be able to approach him later in the year—if Security Pacific was still standing—about a potential merger.

"Say, Bob: I read in the *Journal* that you guys engaged Wells in discussions about a possible merger. Is that a fact?"

"Yeah," I confirmed. "Carl and I nearly assembled a company that could have given you guys some real competition. We were just two small players trying to make a buck," I joked.

I can't remember if Rosenberg laughed or not. "Bob, we all know that consolidations have become a great play for shareholders and—when it's an in-state merger—my economists tell me that the numbers fly right off the charts."

"Our numbers show the exact same thing," I said.

"Jeez, Bob, if the two of us were to get together it would make one heck of a company."

My heart skipped.

We *needed* a merger.

The dream partner *was* Bank of America.

Unbelievably, Rosenberg was calling me to propose the idea!

And . . . I wasn't ready. I needed at least six—most likely *nine*—months to stabilize our deterioration, close issues related to the shutdown of the Merchant Bank, and obtain an accurate forecast of asset quality so that I would be representing an institution that someone would want to buy.

In a puerile sense it didn't seem fair; Rosenberg was dangling "merger" in front of a bank almost too weak to refuse. So why not try?

"Bob, what do you say?"

"About what?"

"About a Bank of America–Security Pacific merger?"

"Hmmm," I mused—as if I'd never given it a single moment's thought. "It would certainly be some hell of a deal."

"That's an understatement. Bob, I think we would be creating the second largest bank in the United States."

"I just wonder if we could possibly overcome the Department of Justice issues involved."

"My legal guys think we could."

Obviously Rosenberg, like me, had given this enormous thought.

"So, what do you say, Bob? How about you and I get together and throw some ideas around?"

"Sure, what the hell."

Rosenberg and I scheduled a private meeting for the following week.

▼

Our banks had danced before—Security Pacific and Bank of America.

A little-known and patently ironic footnote to Security Pacific's acquisition binge involved a fusillade of overtures we made to Bank of America in the Autumn of 1986. At that time, Bank of America's spine was so eroded by bad loans and poor management that rumors had begun to circulate that First Interstate was preparing to launch a hostile takeover. Flamson and I, like others in the financial community, were dumbstruck by Bank of America's decline and the growing possibility of its failure.

While it was probably bad karma to rejoice at the prospect of Bank of America's demise, banking is not unlike other industries, and the setback of a major competitor was regarded as our good fortune. Not only would its extinction broaden our potential customer base, but Bank of America possessed propitiously located branches in desirable California markets and a handful of "crown jewels" that Security Pacific badly wanted to call its own—especially Seafirst, Bank of America's Washington State affiliate bank. I yearned for Charles

Schwab's operation, which had become the nation's pre-
miere discount brokerage firm, with 1985 revenues of about
$200 million.

Banks are like ships navigating the Bermuda Triangle;
when one goes down, the captains of the other ships begin to
sweat, but only after they salvage for themselves any treasure
fallen from the sinking vessel.

Bank of America made no secret of the fact that it would
prefer to survive and continue to operate independently. Like
Security Pacific, Bank of America was one of California's
premier financial institutions and had no intrinsic desire to be
torn apart by sharks.

Between Labor Day and Christmas, Security Pacific performed a peculiar, whimsical, and two-faced mating dance
with Bank of America. Our own motivations were mercenary. We wanted to exploit, in any way possible, their staggering deterioration. We approached the beleaguered corporation with a succession of propositions, ranging from the
humble to the grandiose, and culminating in the suggestion
of an outright merger in which Security Pacific would clearly
be the survivor.

We buddied up to Bank of America, we buddied up to First
Interstate. We wanted a piece of the action, all or part, and either side would do. Dick Flamson wrote directly to Paul Volcker, chairman of the Federal Reserve. The September 2,
1986 letter began with a heartrending lamentation for Bank
of America, a melancholy expression of shock at its weakened position, and the stark realization that the banking giant
might now have to consider the sale of precious assets.

The tone of the first two paragraphs was reverent, somber,
gracious, reserved, and deeply concerned as it reflected on
the decline of Bank of America—it probably brought a tear
to Volcker's eye. Then Dick got down to business, proffering
Security Pacific as Bank of America's knight in shining
armor. To help Bank of America rebuild its capital adequacy,
Security Pacific would spare no expense. We would be glad

to assist by purchasing Charles Schwab, and/or purchasing Seafirst Bank, and/or purchasing as many retail branches in northern, central, and southern California as Bank of America would care to sell. We would also carefully evaluate any other divestitures Bank of America might wish to throw our way. And if these efforts were not sufficient to relieve Bank of America of its sad and considerable burdens, Flamson was willing to discuss the more comprehensive exigency of a full-scale merger.

This offer was wild, it was crazy, it was ambitious—but it was worth a shot.

Unlike the first half of Flamson's letter—remorseful expression of an altruistic desire to lend a helping hand to a struggling brother—the second half metamorphosed from tender elegy to legal contract, composed with the calculated eye of a vulture stalking prey—a barrage of acquisition scenarios, document requests, and financial projections based on the prospect of a Security Pacific–Bank of America shotgun wedding.

In early October, we learned that First Interstate, under Joe Pinola's leadership, would make an overt and hostile run at Bank of America. While Bank of America continued to display a stiff upper lip, their financial stability was so compromised that they were forced to evaluate the militant merger proposal.

"It's not right," Dick decried. "If Bank of America doesn't want to be acquired, they have got to stand their ground." The implication here, of course, was that unless Security Pacific was involved, we didn't want a deal to occur at all. We didn't want to be shut out of this once-in-a-lifetime opportunity.

Security Pacific graciously extended the olive branch to Bank of America.

But behind the scenes, we simultaneously began to court First Interstate—how could we help First Interstate to facilitate this merger? Would it help First Interstate to make their move on Bank of America if we were to pick up some of the slack? For example, if we took Seafirst off their hands? Or how about if we purchased a bunch of California branches or bought, say, Charles Schwab's discount brokerage operation?

It was as bald-faced an example of playing both sides of the street as one could find.

On October 7, Flamson wrote to Bank of America's board of directors, offering Security Pacific's helpful and willing hand to help save a bank in dire straits. The spin we put on this is that we cared deeply about Bank of America's survival, valued its prominence in the market, and would do anything in our power to help a pal in its time of need. Our thoughts and prayers were with them. We would do what we could to help and if by some coincidence our munificent actions, as an unanticipated side-effect, happened to benefit Security Pacific in the process, well, so much the better. We certainly didn't want to give the impression we were trying to take strategic advantage of their attenuated state—which we unabashedly were.

Dick expressed our desire to purchase at least $4 billion in branch deposits in northern California. "These actions could relieve some immediate BAC capital concerns and so alleviate the need to pursue FIB's proposal," he wrote to Bank of America.

I watched the ominous tango between First Interstate and Bank of America with apprehension. I was doubtful that First Interstate had the strength and capacity to overpower even an anemic Bank of America. Indeed, within days, Standard & Poor's, alerted to First Intestate's intentions, responded to the news by placing First Interstate on S&P's Creditwatch Surveillance list, with negative implications. S&P believed that such a unification would adversely affect the credit quality of $6.5 billion in debt securities and $2.3 billion in commercial paper. S&P cited the combined entity's projected below-average equity capitalization, substantial level of nonperforming assets which included an onerous LDC port-folio, and anticipated mediocre profitability as heightened risks to bondholders.

When First Interstate publicly disclosed the price it was willing to pay for Bank of America, it was an anemic num-ber—a feeble pittance—that provoked laughter on Security Pacific's executive floor.

"We can do a hell of a lot better than that," Flamson said.

But to cover our bases, on October 8, I wrote to Joseph Pinola, chairman and chief executive officer of First Inter-state Bancorp: in the event that First Interstate was success-ful in merging with Bank of America, "it may be that you will find it necessary to divest of certain assets or businesses in order to raise capital or alleviate Justice Department con-cerns." To help out First Interstate, Security Pacific would be happy to discuss the purchase of branches in northern Cali-fornia, as well as Seafirst. And incidentally, in the event that First Interstate's strategy should shift from one of merging with Bank of America to an outright *sale of itself* or finding a merger partner, Security Pacific might be interested in ex-ploring that option as well. Yes, if we could not have Bank of America, we would happily make do with its pursuer and arch nemesis, First Interstate.

I assured him our offers would be competitive. "And we would be willing to work with you to conclude these trans-actions in a timely manner." Our proposal, I reiterated, was in the best interest of First Interstate, the competitive mar-ketplace, and the banking industry. In other words, we had our nose under every side of the tent with our ass sticking up in the air like the Space Needle.

Of course, history would subsequently bathe our efforts to acquire all or part of Bank of America in the glow of bitter irony, but at the time we were as serious as Pope John Paul.

While I remained in contact with Pinola, Dick continued to pursue Bank of America. He placed a call to Sam Arma-cost and offered to make an unsolicited bid for Bank of

America. Armacost, whose humorlessness was legendary, was apparently not amused. What had first appeared to be a helping hand had turned into a two-tier attack on the independence of Bank of America. Armacost restated his desire to remain independent.

As a result of rumors and press leaks, Flamson pulled back and immediately issued a conciliatory press release: Security Pacific would be the good guys, stand on the sidelines with a watchful eye, and offer "help" only if and when it was desired. "We think," Dick announced, "it is important that the Bank of America remain an independent organization. That is in the best interest of the competitive marketplace. . . . "

That same day I issued an internal statement: "It has been and continues to be Security Pacific's position that we are interested in seeing the Bank of America remain independent, and we will work with them in any way that we can to that end."

A more candid statement might have read: *"The last thing on God's green earth we want is for First Interstate to acquire the Bank of America without any participation on our part in this potentially historic and lucrative deal."*

But we couldn't bear to throw in the towel just yet and, behind the scenes, I ran dozens of spreadsheets, merger matrices, and stock conversion equations in an attempt to extrapolate the efficacy of a Bank of America acquisition just in case their situation fluctuated for the worse.

In order to pull it off, Security Pacific would have had to raise a minimum of $1.5 billion in additional capital. We had to protect Security Pacific shareholders in the process and guarantee they would be shielded from dilution and future Bank of America loan losses. In the event that loan losses were to exceed Bank of America's equity level, the assistance of the FDIC in the deal would be required. So we quickly concocted a capital scheme that did just that.

Another alternative I explored was to assist First Interstate in their acquisition of Bank of America to Security Pacific's advantage. Our rationale was that the purchase of Bank of America would present First Interstate with a hornet's nest of anti-trust and capital adequacy issues. In the event First Interstate needed to divest, Security Pacific would step in and acquire their current California Bank. This purchase would raise Security Pacific's market share from 12.6% to 20.6%. I also felt that because First Interstate already had a premier performing bank in Washington, it might wish to divest itself of Seafirst after the merger.

Our overtures were rebuffed. We immediately bifurcated our strategy. Working at cross-purposes even to ourselves, one division at Security Pacific strategized on how we could help First Interstate achieve its domination of Bank of America while another figured out ways to make the acquisition impossible—to chop it, thwart it, annihilate it at the root. Even I was beginning to lose track of who was on which side. The attempted conquest took on the ambiance of an Abbott and Costello routine.

Dick phoned Rudy Peterson, former chairman of Bank of America, and proposed an ingeniously perverse plan Flamson and I had hatched at one of our weekly meetings on the subject. This scheme would make it a virtual impossibility for First Interstate to acquire Bank of America. Flamson's idea was to concoct—there is no better word for it—a joint Security Pacific–Bank of America "Operating and Technology Company" with an unbreakable, long-term contract whose legal ramifications would so convolute the acquisition as to make it cost-prohibitive and hopelessly befuddling to even a coliseum full of corporate attorneys.

A week before Christmas we were still trying to goad Bank of America into a partnership arrangement in which we would pay a premium for desirable assets, make an equity investment in Bank of America so large as to frighten First Interstate off the takeover track, or convince Bank of America to allow Security Pacific to purchase it outright. There was an element of grandiose fantasy in our mischief, but I can't say it wasn't fun.

Soon, rebuffed by Bank of America and perhaps dumbfounded by Security Pacific's peculiar intervention in the deal, First Interstate withdrew its "offer." Bank of America's board of directors declared its intention to remain independent, ousted Armacost, and reinstated Tom Clausen, who over time was enormously successful in reversing Bank of America's near disastrous deterioration.

In the end, that Bank of America remained independent turned out to be a godsend for Security Pacific. The dance had been exhilarating while it lasted.

Now we would dance again, only this time the other partner would lead.

▼

Rosenberg's call couldn't have come at a better time. Security Pacific was not yet a catastrophe, but was well on its way. The economy continued to slump and showed no indication of near-term reversal. We had suffered more than a financial fender bender. Mercifully, our car was still driveable; in fact it *looked* better than it ran. I was confident the lemon could last long enough for Dick Rosenberg to drive it around the block and make an offer.

Over the next week or two, Rosenberg and I met three times.

Rosenberg has been described as cherubic, childlike, mischievous in a discerning, gentle—not nefarious—way. Our discussions were pleasant, but Dick and I were two very different people. Rosenberg, while unquestionably a bright and very able businessman, preferred to keep his cards to his chest. Nor was he the type of person to probe deeply; he either liked an idea or disliked it.

In discussions, Rosenberg sounded and appeared as if he had rehearsed or been well coached. He knew exactly what he wanted in a merger. When I assured him I fully expected him to be the number one officer, and that Bank of America was the best and only name for our potentially merged organizations I thought he would have an orgasm.

"Bob, I really think this is going to work."

I hadn't expected negotiations would go so well; in fact, I had engaged Rosenberg in negotiations knowing that Security Pacific had problems to resolve before we were in any condition to effectuate a merger of this size.

The Burns Fry dilemma had yet to be settled and fizzed on my forearm like an open sore. Still to be decided were potentially enormous issues associated with the Merchant Bank shutdown, including the intended sale of Hoare Govett and the twenty other businesses that we were simultaneously either trying to sell or exit. And our real estate portfolio was no great shakes; trying to halt the proliferation of troubled assets was tougher than balancing on top of a rollicking beach ball.

I wanted to keep talks going—but in good conscience I couldn't.

I had to first tie up these loose ends. I didn't want to waste Rosenberg's time or my own, scare the hell out our employees, and raise the hopes of our shareholders all for nothing. I figured I had one, clear shot with Rosenberg, and I had only one golden arrow left in my quiver. If I blew this opportunity—out of eagerness or desperation—there would be no going back. Security Pacific would be on its own; we would have to sell a large part of the institution outright, or struggle along until the wheels fell off and burned.

After some soul-searching, I phoned Rosenberg. It killed me to have to make this call. "Dick," I said, "I'm thrilled with how our talks are going, but the truth is that right now I have some unresolved issues. Let me see if I can put them to bed first. Then, if you're still interested, we can get back together."

Rosenberg was understandably disappointed—a good sign that signaled he really was interested in the deal.

▼

I raced to clear the issues from the deck. Burns Fry remained a predominant concern. Not only was it performing poorly, but its management was convinced beyond a shadow of a doubt that we—Security Pacific—were legally obligated to purchase the remaining 70% of their operation. Even as we struggled to sell them, they harangued us to buy them out. We didn't think we had made any such commitment, nor did we want any such commitment. We faced the imminent prospect of a prolonged and public legal battle.

Attorney Russ Freeman flew up to Burns Fry's Toronto head-quarters, sat down with management, and maneuvered us out of any immediate obligation. The next day Freeman flew back to Los Angeles. "They are not bending over backwards to compromise. I would call them inflexible."

I honestly didn't know if we were in the right or not. "Can we really beat them in court?" I asked Freeman.

"We've got a shot," Freeman said, with the dispassionate candor of an experienced attorney. "Let me sit down with our outside counsel and see what they think."

Security Pacific's outside counsel wanted to take Burns Fry to court. They believed the contract was ambiguous, equivocal and riddled with uncertainties; it was their consensus that the case, if tried in a sympathetic venue, was ours to lose. But they conceded that such proceedings would be a time-consuming and costly pissing contest.

To complete the acquisition would require about $200 million, of which perhaps $100 million would have been good-will—the amount by which the price paid exceeds the book value. A transaction of this magnitude would obligate us to make a formal application to the Federal Reserve. There wasn't a snowball's chance in hell that the Fed would approve such a transaction because Security Pacific was low on capital, under the close scrutiny of the regulatory agencies, and entering a period of severe tumult.

Out of prudence I'd penciled about $75 million of the $200 million year-end Merchant Bank reserve to complete the Hoare Govett sale. If we were legally compelled to purchase the remainder of Burns Fry, I would have to reallocate those reserves to this new exigency. Even then, we would not be able to cover the cost. Even our attorneys were ambivalent. Half of them believed it was our duty to attempt to purchase Burns Fry; the other lawyers wanted to "go to war" with the subsidiary. The latter was not a prospect that evoked my enthusiasm. We'd enjoyed an amicable and productive relationship with Burns Fry. Any lawsuit filed by their principals would most likely be tried on Canadian soil—another stumbling block on an already steep incline.

I needed objectivity. I turned to my old friend Tom Collins, a shrewd lawyer and a no-bullshit Irishman who would call a spade a spade whether I or our attorneys liked it or not.

Tom traveled to Canada with two goals in mind: first, examine their books to see if the financial evidence reflected an accounting based on the eventuality of a 100% sale to Security Pacific; and, second, assess the psychology and expectations of Burns Fry principals and employees to gauge the sincerity of their beliefs and determine how "soft" they might be if it came down to negotiating our way out of this quagmire.

Tom Collins returned from Canada. "Bob, there is ample reason to assert that Burns Fry honestly has believed all along that this was an agreement written in stone. For example, they have bought back and sold partner shares as if there would absolutely be a completed sale."

"Son of a bitch. Are they open to compromise?"

"I suspect you could find some middle ground, but it's going to cost you."

"How would they react to a countersuit?"

"They would almost certainly fight you in court, and they

have a lot of legal ammunition. They *believe*. And circumstantial evidence falls on their side."

Tom convinced me to attempt to resolve this in a friendly way.

We sat down with the management of Burns Fry and eventually arrived at a costly solution that would not require the approval of the Federal Reserve. We negotiated our way out of full ownership of Burns Fry, but did so only by paying an exorbitant premium for a minuscule 5% increase in ownership. To finance this transaction we gutted our reserves and wrote off the excess.

We paid a lot for a little, but we bought peace of mind and a second opportunity to engage Rosenberg in merger talks.

▼

Other obstacles remained. Before I could approach Rosenberg, I had to make an accurate assessment of our asset quality problems and project any future deterioration so that if Rosenberg was still interested in our bank, he knew exactly what he was getting.

CFO John Kooken and I anxiously awaited the result of the comptroller of the currency's belated third- and fourth-quarter 1990 examination of Security Pacific. The report arrived in late March. While the new report was largely a regurgitation of prior findings, the OCC sounded fresh alarms on the topic of asset quality: deterioration had escalated to unacceptable levels.

Obviously, the regulators themselves—effervescent with advice and tough talk—disbelieved that we could ever turn our crisis around. But we had to try. In a desperate attempt to understand the pace of our decline, I asked the leadership of each division to project a realistic classified loan and operating plan for the remainder of the year. I could stomach no more surprises; I knew Rosenberg wanted no surprises.

▼

The solemn addendum to the operating plan entitled *Asset Quality Projections* was nothing short of a last rites. It had been prepared by our Credit Department along with our account officers and was guaranteed to provoke cardiac arrhythmia even in hard-core marathonists. This grisly memorandum began with the frank reminder that from the close of 1989 to year-end 1990, our non-LDC criticized loans had proliferated from $6.8 billion to $11.4 billion. "Under the baseline [economic] recession analysis, non-LDC criticized loans are projected to increase by a further $1.2 billion to $12.6 at year-end 1991, after peaking at $13.0 billion in second quarter 1991. . . . Similarly, non-performing assets [are anticipated to] increase from $2.7 billion at December 31, 1990, peak at $3.6 billion in third quarter 1991 and decline on a quarterly basis thereafter to $2.7 billion at year-end 1992."

However, the report chastened, in the event of a severe economic turndown—which now appeared imminent—we could expect criticized loans to hit $15 billion. "Similarly, non-performing assets [would] peak at $4.6 billion."

In the instance of "modest" recession, charge-offs would approach $700 million in 1991, anchoring at around $660 million in 1992. But if the economy truly caved, we could expect to charge off $1.1 billion in both 1991 and 1992.

The report implied that even the installation of our new asset quality improvement plan could not be expected to mitigate these damning numbers.

While it was probably too late to reverse the trend, we nevertheless had to enhance internal awareness of the need to reduce classified assets. Criticized assets above a certain threshold had to be restructured and upgraded or liquidated. We had to get them off the balance sheet, or our constant deterioration would jeopardize any attempt to merge.

What, I wondered, would Dick Rosenberg think of these numbers?

In order to reapproach Bank of America, I had to have an explicit accounting of our criticized assets. In April I asked for a loan-by-loan breakdown, sorted by type classification—Watch, OLEM, Substandard, and Doubtful—and apportioned by department, division, unit, and subsidiary.

By June I had a slender but staggering document that—Divine Intervention notwithstanding—was a blueprint for anticipated future deterioration.

I slid my calculator to the center of my desk. Drawing a quintet of columns and rows on a yellow legal pad, I scratched out the numbers that synthesized loans by type, size, and division. Using groupings to represent loans, the grid slowly tessellated into three dimensions, then blackened into a constellation of humongous loans whose redemption was unlikely. This simple process provoked a catalysis of emotion. As the matrix unleashed itself with metamorphic frenzy, and the enormity and sheer bulk of the troubled assets fixed itself on the page, I experienced a simultaneous sense of gratitude and dislocation; gratitude that the problem was here in front of me, but surreality at the realization that real estate—our bread and butter, the thing we thought we could always count on—had so turned against Security Pacific, a bank that owed its success in nearly a primordial way to the fecundity of California. Real estate *was* Security Pacific; now it had become the enemy.

Reading the list of loans was like taking an unwelcome stroll down Memory Lane. I saw many familiar names; Trump, Hemmeter, Hawaiian Airlines. Unbeknownst to me, we'd even lent money to Conley Wolfswinkle, partner in Keating's Phoenix-based megalopolis Rancho Vistoso. The list read like a Who's Who of Americana.

No single loan could topple Security Pacific—but the sheer number of mega-loans took my breath away. Sixty-three criticized loans over $25 million, some of them in the $300 million range. Add to that the 314 criticized loans between $10 and $25 million, and a litany in the $2 to $10 million range—it was incredible! How could Security Pacific continue to be the "Engine of the Economy" when all these customers were not paying us back?

But at least it was here, on paper—incontrovertible, comprehensible, and ready to show to Rosenberg. Also in place was a procedure to update and reissue this report monthly.

Early that Summer, our ad hoc compliance committee of the board revised our procedures manual, a document that helped our managers to sculpt future plans with an eye toward regulatory compliance in areas of asset quality, solidification of capital, and improved liquidity.

"Like many others in the industry," the preamble read, "Security Pacific was obviously unable to adequately foresee the rapid economic and market changes in some critical geographical and product markets. Those changes, which accelerated during the final three years of the 1980s, created adverse circumstances in certain of SPC's subsidiary operations. Due to . . . uncertainty, Security Pacific has made the decision to completely refocus its resources on the basic and fundamental businesses at which it has been very successful over the years. . . . Steps have been taken, with more planned for the near-term, to sell, downsize, or close businesses which do not fit with SPC's fundamental and basic business."

Even the dividend was on the chopping block: "Dividend payments will be reviewed each quarter. . . . Management and the Board of Directors are prepared to reduce the dividend"—which we had already done earlier that year—"or eliminate it entirely should economic conditions warrant."

We decided to sell every perquisite and disposable asset we could. We sold our airforce. We put on the auction block a number of subsidiaries, some of them precious. We contemplated selling a myriad of satellite buildings and offices that housed many bank activities. We even contemplated vacating our headquarters, shifting our downtown activities to a cheaper, more ascetic—not *aesthetic*—building, and selling another magnificent skyscraper that ten years ago had puffed us with pride. There would be no more ice sculptures and Bacchanalian American Banker Association parties. We were tightening the belt in humility.

We cut every unnecessary expenditure. We shut down the executive dining room and got rid of our economists. We sweated over every penny. We had to hurry.

The last major undertaking was to dump Hoare Govett. The sale of Hoare Govett was no simple matter, for the reason that its key employees wanted a voice in the deal. It was like the worst players on a baseball team demanding ownership of the franchise; nevertheless, I couldn't allow Hoare Govett to hold me up. In April we set into motion negotiations to expedite an emergency exit via a modified buyout of a portion of Hoare Govett. We agreed to spin off the Asian operation to the employees in Asia and found a capital investor to put up the money. We finally signed an agreement with the management of Hoare Govett relative to the sale of the U.K. operation so that they had a say in their future. We were now, theoretically, in a position to wash our hands of what had been a noble but unsuccessful experiment.

▼

I sat down with John Kooken. "I feel confident we've done about everything we can to stabilize the health of the institution. My plan is this: wait a couple of months to make absolutely certain that we caught all the problems, and then go back to Rosenberg. Any thoughts?"

"Now that we've refunded, we've got to stay refunded," he said.

"Any suggestions on how I might present our liquidity issues to Rosenberg?"

Kooken thought aloud. "We pulled through our funding crisis in large part by procuring that billion-dollar two-year secured loan through First Boston. By securitizing blocks of assets—which we will continue to do—we have been paying down the loan. With this effort combined with the general shrinking of activities we will soon be able to pay it off and at the same time entirely *eliminate* our dependence on commercial paper. It has been a crutch for too long."

Good, I thought. *The last hurdle is behind us*. I was somewhat relieved but scared to death we had missed something, or that an unforeseen problem would surface. We were still at the mercy of a fibrillating economy.

For these reasons, I balked.

I was reticent to contact Rosenberg or even inform the board of directors of my immediate intent. Frankly, I was gun-shy. The economy was like a reversing escalator in a carnival funhouse. I was afraid the moment we committed to Rosenberg, something else would shift—a trapdoor would open, a step would drop out from beneath us, or a shrieking ghoul would pop out of a closet. I was in a momentary holding pattern, frozen and skeptical.

▼

Flamson remained chairman until June 1991, when I was named chairman of the board; fortunately, Dick remained on the board.

Since 1989, Flamson's illness had progressively worsened. So vigorous for so long, he now suffered constant bouts of fatigue and listlessness. Despite the ailment, his advice continued to be perspicuous and acute. I was amazed by the loyalty, passion, and zeal he brought to his work and the caring eye he focused on the future of the bank.

Even on days he did not come to headquarters, he phoned. He was deeply unnerved by the way we were coming apart at the seams. "You're doing what needs to be done, you're dealing with it. Keep in mind that you have a responsibility to the board. You've got to keep them informed."

It was his way of urging me to take action. "You know I want to move forward, Dick, but I'm nervous I haven't caught everything."

"I sympathize. But sometimes you just gotta make your move and let the chips fall where they may."

▼

The day before our July 16 board meeting, Flamson underwent a full blood transfusion at the Hoag Cancer Center so he could be an alert and active contributor. On the executive floor the following morning there was peculiar uneasiness. The corridors were unusually silent and the quad was vacant but for one secretary. I heard few computer keyboards, printers, ringing phones. Apprehension clung to the air like ozone. There was a sense of oppressed waiting.

Orange smog creased the sky. It was going to be a heavy, hot day. I could sense that Flamson had arrived. I sat at my desk, drawing checkmarks beside items on a list of issues that had been resolved. I was anxious about this morning's board meeting.

Dick peered into my office. "Bob."

Dick moved across the threshold with intent. He looked good this morning, almost iridescent. His eyes were unusually sharp. "Have you, to your satisfaction, cleaned up our difficulties enough to reconsider Rosenberg's offer?"

"I believe so. The sale of Hoare Govett, while not accomplished, has been set into motion."

"I'm thinking. . . . "

"What? Say it."

He sat on the corner of my desk, arms folded. On the credenza behind him and to his left, the minute hand on my clock advanced. A phone rang in the office next door; no one picked it up. The office assistant in the hall knelt to the carpet where she'd spilled coffee. Dick rose, graciously closed the door.

Flamson's acumen and intuitive sense of timing asserted themselves. "Take it to the board."

I paused. "I'm inclined to wait one more month and present it at our August meeting. I want to make absolutely certain that we have a full reckoning of our problems. I want to take a look at the upcoming regulatory report to ensure that no new catastrophes or large credit problems emerge." His pause invited further explanation.

"Dick, the patient has been stabilized—true—but he's so critical he could bounce either way."

Flamson shook his head. "We should do it today."

"This morning?"

"We'll just walk right in there today and go for it. Just lay it on the table. We're going back to Rosenberg."

"I don't know, Dick. I'm not even prepared to make a formal presentation to the board. Things are moving awfully fast."

"That's exactly why we should seize the moment."

"No, I think I want to wait until next month."

"Bob, my gut tells me we've got to get this done. We have a narrowing window of opportunity. Let's not wait for next month; let's do it today. The clock is ticking."

To hear this man say those words at this moment in his fleeting life indicated something beyond the inherent meaning of the words.

I trusted him. Our eyes locked. "You think so?"

"I *know* so."

I said, "All right."

▼

Thirty minutes later Dick and I converged near the smashed automobile sculpture on the executive floor. We took the elevator down one floor and walked through the anteroom to the board room. J.G. Boswell greeted me, gestured in the direction of the paintings of my predecessors, and chuckled: "Say, Bob, have they started your portrait yet?"

I quipped back, "So far all I've got is the charcoal sketch and the artist isn't sure if he should bother to fill it in."

▼

The directors took their seats around the oval marble and hardwood table. I passed out Security Pacific binders outlining the agenda; of course it meant nothing now, because I intended to throw the meeting in an unexpected direction. Many directors poured themselves a cup of coffee; others drank water. By the meeting's conclusion, some would yearn for something stronger.

I stood to open the meeting. "Good morning, everybody." I dove rapidly in, outlining the gravity of our predicament. I replayed in rapid succession the events of the past six months. "We entered into negotiations with Wells and that didn't work out. I had subsequent conversations with Dick Rosenberg but pulled out because we had too many open issues that I had to resolve—operations we were trying to shut down, deals we were trying to close, situations we were trying to adjust."

I ran down my handwritten list: funding was stabilized; Burns Fry, stabilized; Hoare Govett, well on its way to stabilization.

Boswell asked about our criticized assets. "And what is the state of our real estate development portfolio?"

"FIRREA took no prisoners. But I believe we have a realistic projection of our problem assets and I feel comfortable that I can make an honest representation in the event we pursue the merger option."

"Merger? Now? Is it the right time?"

I glanced at Dick. "There are, I believe, three potential solutions to our problem."

The directors were silent; everyone had stopped drinking and shuffling paper.

"Now that these immediate issues have been resolved—and I do believe our problems are for the moment stabilized—we have three choices. We can continue on our current course and try to fight it out, *or* we can sell the institution and seek the best price, *or* we can try to find a merger partner.

"Gentlemen, we are on a very slippery slope. For us to continue on and fight this thing through, we've got to be assured that we've found all the problems. We also have to be assured that the economy is going to rebound, especially in California. And I honestly can't assure you of either one. I know what and where all the problems are, but the economy is changing so quickly that I can't begin to estimate the magnitude of losses we might experience in the future. I can say this: in a worst-case-scenario, we could suffer a disaster. Keep in mind that if we try to fight it out and we fail, the outcome will be cataclysmic.

"Option 2: we can sell the company and try to get the best price from whomever. But whatever price we get will have an adjustment factor which—if things get worse, and I think they will—could also be catastrophic for us and for the shareholders."

"We're still one of the most respected institutions in the country," Boswell said. "Why couldn't we get a premium?"

"The reality is that there are not many institutions who can afford right now to pay a premium to acquire us. Any interested party that gets a good look at our credit portfolio will balk at the idea of paying a premium."

"That leaves the merger as an option," Flamson prompted.

"Right. Option 3: we can try to find a merger partner who will come together with us in a fixed, unalterable, hell-or-highwater deal. That is what I suggest we do. We failed with Wells Fargo, but given the magnitude of interest expressed by Bank of America, we could continue to pursue a merger with Rosenberg. I think I can pull it off."

"Why Rosenberg?" Boswell asked.

"Because I sense that he wants us badly. I would characterize Rosenberg as sincere, anxious, and ready. If his attitude hasn't changed, I'm convinced this deal can be done."

This gave the directors pause; such a deal would be huge. It would be the biggest bank merger to date. It would create a bank of unparalleled size and reach. For that very reason—the unknowability of attempting such a deal—some of the directors were reticent.

One of the directors leaned forward. "Bob, what is your sense: Do you think the economy is going to turn around any time soon?"

"I honest to God don't know." Who did I look like—the Amazing Criswell? If I could anticipate every twinge and convulsion of the economy, Security Pacific wouldn't be in this mess. "All the California economists are bickering with one another. I think we should not count on a turnaround any time soon."

"When you say 'fight it out,' I accept that at face value. But is it possible?"

"I think it would be an uphill fight. Although we project moderate economic improvement, every bone in my body tells me to proceed on the assumption that a miraculous turnaround is unlikely. We could lose everything."

"What are we talking about, logistically, when we say fight it out?"

"Sell our best assets, with the exception of California, in order to raise capital and bolster reserves. This strategy is a variation on what we proposed in our contingency plan. We reduce Security Pacific from about an $80 billion institution to a $40 billion institution. Basically, we would be left with a California bank."

"Is that something we would like to contemplate?"

"It's not something *I* would like to contemplate. We would have to sell our top performers—businesses that are worth a hell of a lot to us—and for what? What do we get in return? When you put the pencil to it, in this current economic environment, there are no premiums being paid for these assets. Our shareholders would get clobbered."

Boswell said, "You clearly lean toward a merger."

"J.G., I can't help it. To me it makes the most sense. If we attempt options 1 or 2 and fail, we stand to lose everything, including any realistic opportunity of a merger. But if we try to find a merger partner and fail, then we can proceed with one of the other two plans."

Flamson put his knuckles up to his chin and nodded. "Who can argue with that?"

"Although I opened this meeting by saying we had three choices, I believe we have no choice. We *have* to find a partner with a lot of capital, cut the deal, and merge at any cost. We have to try to negotiate the best deal we can for our shareholders and structure the transaction as a fixed deal. Otherwise, we may be penalized in the event of unanticipated future deterioration."

Boswell said, "I understand why a merger is the most appealing choice of the three, but what makes me nervous are the tendrils of desperation."

"J.G., I think it is desperate."

One of the newer members of the board spoke up. "Bob, I ask this somewhat naïve question philosophically: Is merging good or bad for everyone concerned?"

I understood what he meant. "As CEO, my hardest job is to balance the interests of our constituent groups: shareholders, employees, customers. With effort and attention, it is often possible to make sure all these groups are served. But as we get into trouble, this equation shifts dramatically." I thought but did not say: *When a corporation enters a Dark Age, it is the shareholder who holds the gun to your head.* "Is losing jobs good or bad? Well, compared to what? If I could create an environment in which every constituent is satisfied that would be a remarkable achievement. But that's not the way things are shaping up. Our gas tank is empty. The short answer: no, it is never desirable to lay our people off, to confuse customers, to provoke turmoil in lives. But I know one thing: if given our current circumstances we try to please everybody, everything will crumble and all the constituents will be left with nothing but a wall plaque, the final edition of *Security News,* and a souvenir T-shirt. If we want this corporation to survive in *some* capacity—to have any muscle left at all—we have to consolidate. I see no other way."

"What is the upside?" Boswell asked. "What is *the story,* if you know what I mean? What are the objective benefits of a consolidation?"

"Enormous, Jim. Not only for the shareholders through the nearly $1 billion in expense savings we project in an in-state merger, but for the entire institution. There's a certain inevitable logic to it. I've been aware for some time that the industry today suffers from overcapacity, and overcapacity means inefficiency. Bringing two large institutions together fosters efficiency, and improved efficiency means we are able to compete better, and if we can compete better, we can price better. With that efficiency we can develop products and services and price them competitively for consumers and businesses. The opportunity is that the capital strength of two combined companies, as it would have been with Wells, is potentially so awesome that it gives us the ability to develop and provide products and services on the most efficient basis."

I thought: *Maybe I've said too much, given too many details. Boswell probably sees this and wants to strangle me.* I sat down and gave my mouth a rest while the directors contemplated the three options. Some made notes. Others drew pictograms and arranged impromptu columns enumerating pros and cons. I opened my binder and found the notes I'd made that morning. Discussion was quiet and candid on the strategy, but cryptic on the topic of Bank of America.

"Is it possible to go back to Wells?"

I told them why it didn't make sense because of the size of our combined California real estate portfolios. "Also, I personally couldn't stomach another fiasco with Reichardt. He said no, and I think he meant it." I sensed resistance to Rosenberg. "What is the board's opposition to Bank of America?"

"There is no chemistry between our banks," one director put it bluntly.

The street buzz was that Rosenberg, who had left Wells in the mid-1980s, was not a huge fan of Reichardt's. The directors worshiped Reichardt and held this against Rosenberg. I argued that this could be used to our advantage. "Rosenberg is scared shitless of Reichardt's interest in Security Pacific. I think because of that very fear Rosenberg might easily agree to a lockup deal."

The directors didn't see Rosenberg as a world-class banking leader in the same league with a Reichardt or a Clausen. They saw Rosenberg as not having a relationship with the industrialists. He wasn't a classic banker. Rosenberg was seen as a retail specialist; aloof, difficult to approach personally, and alienated from the southern California banking establishment.

Again, like a jackhammer, the question: "Why not go back to Wells?"

Others assented. "We came so damned close with Wells. Reichardt seemed so eager. Don't you think your best shot is to go back to Carl?"

I was operating on pure adrenaline and logic. "No, that won't work. I can't do that. Carl said *No* and there was a reason Carl said *No*, and I have no reason to believe that his *No* will turn into a *Yes*. Trust me."

"What was Carl's reason?"

"Carl's reason was bullshit—excuse my French. Nevertheless, it was firm."

"Are you sure it was firm?"

"Look, even if Carl did say yes—which he won't—the pricing deal with Wells would not be as advantageous to Security Pacific or its shareholders as a deal with Bank of America. Reichardt would want to discount everything he didn't understand. He'd want to buy us cheap. Our combined real estate portfolios demonstrate too much concentration in this economy and would put both institutions at grave risk. Most important—and this is crucial—if I am rejected by

Wells for a second time, then Rosenberg will know for certain that Reichardt is uninterested, and I believe this would vastly diminish his appetite for Security Pacific. This is very important: Rosenberg cannot know that Carl has absolutely said *No*."

Strategically, I wanted—no, *needed*—to be able to use Reichardt's implied interest in our institution as psychological leverage to motivate Rosenberg to do the deal. I felt ego might play an important role in a merger with Bank of America.

I implored the board to have faith. "You'll just have to trust me on this, and trust me to get it done." That was a fairly bold statement to make. I'd only been president and CEO for eighteen months; I'd only been chairman for thirty days.

Flamson spoke on my behest. "Bob's our best shot. He knows what he's doing. Let him play his hand."

In the end, they did trust me. They knew they could—my balls were on the line, and if I didn't get the bank out of this jam I would be dog meat—and they knew they *had* to.

After the tense meeting, Flamson patted me on the shoulder. "Run with it. They've given you a license to hunt; go hunting."

In retrospect, Dick's hunch was dead-on. If I'd waited another month to present our ideas to the board and move forward with a merger, it would most probably have been too late.

▼

I wasted no time. I phoned Rosenberg that afternoon. He was eager to talk. "Good to hear from you, Bob. So, do you feel you've got all your issues resolved?"

"I think so. I can show you every loan, all our files, every classification—everything. I can show you the status and resolution to the Merchant Bank activities." Then in a bold, spontaneous, and cocky move I added, "You know, Dick, we'll want to take a close, hard look as well at your loans and other activities. I'm a bit concerned about your LDC exposure and want to know how you're dealing with it."

"Of course," he said. "I understand."

The earnestness of his response truly amazed me. It was like a 150-pound offensive guard challenging a 285-pound defensive lineman with "trash talk" which Rosenberg had taken seriously.

We figured out a way we could meet without arousing suspicion.

The desire to merge was the same, but the equation had shifted. We were, as Boswell sensed, a bit more desperate. But to execute a merger, we had to conceal the perspiration.

What none of us realized—not even Dick Rosenberg, who would soon agree to merge with Security Pacific—was that the economy was going to get materially worse.

10

Wheeling and Dealing for Survival

Two weeks later—on Tuesday, July 30—I flew to San Francisco and met Rosenberg in a private room at the Ritz Carlton. It was just he and I—no facilitators, no attorneys, not even an assistant to record the minutes.

Richard Rosenberg had joined Bank of America in the mid-1980s, after a short stint at Crocker Bank following numerous run-ins with Reichardt. This was a period of unbridled decline for Bank of America, whose board sought to turn things around by rehiring its one-time boss Tom Clausen. Initially, Rosenberg ran the retail side of Bank of America's Seafirst operation in Washington State, but was shifted to its San Francisco headquarters in 1987. In late 1989, Rosenberg took over the top job at Bank of America as its chief executive officer. He was as new on the job as I was.

The first thing that Rosenberg insisted we do was sign a confidentiality agreement stimulating the free flow of classified financial data between our two organizations and, most important for Rosenberg—for reasons that would become crystal clear in a matter of days—stipulating that during the course of our discussions I would not engage in probatory merger discussions with any other banks. The exclusivity clause forbade either one of us from talking directly or indirectly with others. Rosenberg wanted no leaks about what we were doing.

Rosenberg's single-minded fervor was a godsend. I speculated that the thing driving this man was his uncertainty about the interest Carl Reichardt might still have in Security Pacific. Dick's worst nightmare realized would be for Reichardt to learn of a possible deal.

During the eleven days of negotiation to follow—and extending through the next nine months of the process—Rosenberg never uttered Reichardt's name. Not once, not ever, not even in casual passing—he didn't even want me to think about Wells Fargo. He didn't want me to joke about Wells Fargo. And I didn't want to invoke Reichardt's name for fear that Rosenberg might ask me point-blank if Reichardt posed a threat to the deal. I would have to confess: as far as I knew Reichardt had no interest whatsoever in reviving discussions.

By divulging Reichardt's disinterest, I would have lost an important component of my negotiating power.

As recently as July 19, Reuters News Service had unwittingly aggravated Rosenberg's fear of Wells Fargo by regurgitating the rumor of a Security Pacific–Wells Fargo merger and reporting that I still felt such a merger was "attractive and compelling."

This first meeting went well in rekindling the initial discussions we'd had back in February. We reiterated our belief in the strategic significance and benefits, the understanding relative to the Bank of America name and that he would be the ongoing CEO. We briefly discussed the exchange ratio but demurred on setting it firmly until we'd exchanged data, done additional analysis, and consulted with staff and our respective investment bankers. We agreed to meet again on Friday to discuss our findings, specify the ratio, and explore the social issues of such a large merger.

Over the several days following our initial meeting, Rosenberg and I exchanged information like two men playing Beat the Clock in what amounted to an accelerated due diligence. A very small circle of executives at both companies knew about the discussions.

Rosenberg's people commenced an examination of our loan portfolio; mine of his. We quizzed each other. Our financial and credit people, along with our investment bankers, burnt the wick at both ends in an effort to comprehend the financial health of the respective institutions. Their ancillary diligence freed Rosenberg and I to consider the exchange ratio and sociological issues: the ongoing management team, who's in and who's out, location of headquarters, board membership, savings benefits, and the reality of layoffs—displacement, compensation, and the impact job cuts would have on our customers and communities.

Because we had both done abundant "homework" on the deal already, these were not cold and calculating marathon debates. The mood was brisk and cordial. We discussed issues openly and frankly, without any unusual differences. Rosenberg was a good negotiator who communicated clearly and listened well.

But he also wanted absolute control. He could not abide the presence of one loose shoestring, or a single department or subsidiary whose complexity eluded his understanding. The depth of his knowledge was unquestionable in many areas, but shallow—as if by design—in others. He appeared to have limited curiosity about our most unusual—and often lucrative—subsidiaries. This I found ominous.

Frank Newman was Bank of America's chief financial officer. He had moved from Wells Fargo to Bank of America around 1986, just prior to Clausen's return. Newman was highly respected, dry but humorous, and a solid communicator with a spectacular range of knowledge. He was also one of the more brilliant financial people I'd ever met; I felt I was doing business with a former chess master who was always six moves ahead. He was mustachioed and wore a beret much as a French boulevardier. He was without the classic banker's appearance but was a strong complement to Rosenberg.

To confront the problems that faced Bank of America in the latter half of the 1980s, Rosenberg, with Frank Newman in place, brought in two other members recruited from Wells Fargo.

Mike Rossi was Bank of America's chief credit officer. He'd moved from Wells to Bank of America in 1987, at a time when Bank of America's loan portfolio was in tatters. To his credit, Rossi set into motion a process that largely cured the credit problems and ensured that policies and procedures were locked into place within Bank of America's culture to prevent any recurrence. His efforts bore fruit quickly: the improved credit quality and renovated culture ignited admiration for Rosenberg among regulators, banking insiders, and investors. Unfortunately for us, as we would soon discover, in doing so Rossi established for himself a "tough guy" persona that sometimes emerged in areas unrelated to his view of our credit. Rossi was outspoken and could be intimidating, but I perceived this as a measure of his loyalty to Rosenberg and to the high standards he had set for Bank of America.

Lew Coleman was the head of Corporate International Banking. He had also come to the Bank of America from Wells in 1987 and was generally regarded as Rossi's mentor and Rosenberg's *heir apparent*. Undoubtedly intelligent—a banker's banker—Coleman struck me as an individual with more to offer than he was permitted to demonstrate. He was always on the periphery of the business at hand, always watching, always absorbing. Perhaps intimidated by Rosenberg, he seldom volunteered his real thoughts. I often wondered what was going on inside his mind.

▼

We met again on Friday, August 2. Our discussions were positive, at times euphoric.

Rosenberg was delighted that we had set into motion the sale of both Hoare Govett and our interest in Burns Fry, its Canadian counterpart. We were clear of uncertainties and ready to proceed with the social issues.

Rosenberg wanted to keep the new Bank of America's monolithic headquarters in San Francisco at its present location but agreed to retain Security Pacific's downtown office space in Los Angeles as the new Bank of America's southern California headquarters.

Whereas in February 1991, at our first encounter, Rosenberg had expressed some reluctance at the notion of equal boards, he now relented: "Bob, a true merger has equal boards, and I think we should have equal boards, and I think you want equal boards."

We agreed. The new board of directors would consist of fifteen Bank of America directors and fifteen from Security Pacific. The name of the surviving entity would be Bank of America and would be known throughout the consolidation process as the *New* Bank of America.

Rosenberg and I enumerated a joint-staff approval policy for key management, stating that beyond the selection of the eight or nine senior executives, any other nominees would require the signatures of both Rosenberg and myself. This was important in formulating an equitable personnel program: in every position we would choose the candidate most qualified for the job, based on skill level, experience, and track record—the best and the brightest; the best auditor, the best attorney, the best chief credit officer, and so forth.

Then we discussed key management staff. David Lovejoy was already gone. John Singleton would go and in his absence Bank of America's Marty Stein would assume the position of head of data processing.

Nick Binkley would run financial services, which would be a desirable adjunct to Bank of America, which had no comparable activities.

John Kooken wanted to retire, leaving the CFO slot open to their Frank Newman.

Jerry Grundhofer would run the retail business and interstate banks, and Russ Freeman was expected to retain his position as chief legal counsel. Finally on our side, Kathy Burke would become the new head of human resources.

On their side, Lew Coleman would run the wholesale, international, and trading business. Mike Rossi would be chief credit officer.

In preparation for personnel discussions with Rosenberg, I'd rated top executives on ten factors, including intelligence, leadership ability, commitment, strategic thinking, and stature within the banking community. Steven Carpenter, who ran our business banking activities with great success, had received one of the highest scores, and I thought his value to a combined corporation would be immeasurable. Carpenter was a known commodity—highly respected—and I could not for the life of me understand why Rosenberg was so fiercely against the idea of Carpenter coming to the New Bank of America. We debated Carpenter's future role for almost three hours. Finally Rosenberg revealed the source of his antipathy. In his prior position at Bank of America, Rosenberg had attempted to attract both Lew Coleman and Steve Carpenter to exit Wells Fargo for Bank of America. Rosenberg said he had a deal with both of them, but within a few hours of the transplant, Carpenter backed out of the deal.

It was obvious to me that Rosenberg had never forgiven Carpenter for what he perceived to be a deception and overt betrayal, and in reprisal he wished to blow Carpenter's rear end out the door.

Carpenter did not make the senior-level cut and, when he learned he would have to leave, he did not take his oversight well.

Finally, Rosenberg offered—and I agreed—that following Rosenberg's retirement in about four years at age sixty-five—and contingent upon board approval—I would replace him as chief executive officer. This would be part of any agreement that we finalized. While not a game-breaker for me, I accepted this fact. But down deep I was not sure I wanted to succeed Rosenberg and run the New Bank of America.

Now we got down to brass tacks—the exchange ratio. I had reviewed the analysis and was decided on what I thought was a fair exchange ratio. Rosenberg and I compared respective analysis and considered what this consolidation would mean, in a broad sense for both institutions, and arrived at an exchange ratio based on the market value capitalization of the companies, and one that gave respective shareholders the benefits of the combined efficiencies we expected to realize.

The exchange ratio we agreed upon worked out to 0.855; for every share of Security Pacific stock, we would receive 0.855 shares of Bank of America stock. Following a merger, Bank of America shareholders would hold 2/3 of the total shares while Security Pacific's owners would hold 1/3. The resulting accretion to our earnings would be a whopping 49%; the accretion to Bank of America's earnings would be 35%. This was possible in part because for the combined organizations we projected combined cost savings of at least $1 billion and potentially $1.2 billion over a three-year period, preferably sooner.

The meeting ended on this high note, with our agreement to attempt to finalize our understanding by the conclusion of the following week.

▼

With our agreement on the exchange rate, Dick Rosenberg and I turned the calculations over to our investment bankers to let them fine-tune the numbers. Bank of America hired Morgan Stanley; we brought in First Boston who, under the direction of Dick Thornburgh, studied the exchange ratio and discussed it with representatives from Morgan Stanley. Thornburgh was a young, bespectacled partner who through many years of working behind the scenes with us on a variety of deals—realized and unconsummated—had become a trusted confidante.

On Monday morning, August 5, he strode into my office in a mischievous mood. "We've completed our analysis and they've completed theirs. We believe, after discussing the numbers with Morgan Stanley, that we can obtain a better exchange ratio."

"Better than we already have?" I asked wonderingly. "Why would they?"

"In a word: *terror*. Morgan Stanley's people feel that Rosenberg believes Wells Fargo poses a lingering threat to the potential deal. Rosenberg knows about your discussions with Carl and he knows that Carl is familiar with the numbers and could step in with a preemptory bid, a higher offer that might be better for the Security Pacific shareholders."

"But the exchange ratio is good," I said. "It's fair to both sides. This is supposed to be a merger, not an auction." I was grateful for the deal we'd arranged; the last thing on my mind was putting the squeeze on Rosenberg, and I told Thornburgh as much. "I'd rather not disturb the equation we already have and risk jeopardizing the deal. I mean, I almost don't want to *breathe* on the exchange ratio."

"Understood, Bob. I just want you to be aware, and as your investment bankers we would be delinquent not to say so: we think the money is there."

Thornburgh smiled, shrugged, and walked toward the door.

"Hold on, Dick. Come back."

Thornburgh turned around.

"Lookit, I'm quite satisfied with what we've arranged. And it's my job to make this deal happen. But, having said that, I'm not stupid. If you honestly think you can maneuver more money for the shareholders, go ahead. But, Dick, for god's sake I'll kill you if you blow the deal."

"Okay."

"The moment they blink, you back off."

"Right."

I held my breath as Thornburgh and his team returned to the bargaining table with Morgan Stanley.

▼

During the week of August 5, a great deal of paper changed hands.

I'd promised Rosenberg we would show Bank of America everything—the good, the bad, and the ugly.

"We will do this with total honesty," I said, "so that you can never say there was a single loan, a single document we didn't show you."

"I know and I appreciate it."

"But, in return for that, you are on notice that our situation may worsen. We both know that as the economy nose-dives, our problems compound."

"I know that, Bob. I understand that, and I assure you that economic deterioration is not a consideration."

As if further evidence of our proliferating woes was needed, our bank's letter of credit ratings were lowered by Fitch. Again, the downgrade reflected reduced profitability prospects due to deteriorating asset quality.

▼

The afternoon of August 5 I convened an emergency meeting of the executive committee to update them on the progress of my discussions with Rosenberg. The executive committee urged that we call the full board together and inform all the directors of how quickly talks were moving.

While our administrative assistants scurried to round up the other board members, I received a phone call that blew my mind.

"Guess who?"

"Carl?" I couldn't believe my ears—it was Carl Reichardt. I had probably not heard from him in eight months, around the time of our aborted merger. I wondered at the coincidence of his timing and came to the conclusion it was probably no coincidence. "How's it going, Carl?"

"Oh, not too bad. Say, Bob. I wonder if you and I could get together for lunch."

I stammered, "What's up? Any urgency?"

Five days before I'd signed a confidentiality agreement. I buttoned my lip. I felt my palms go sweaty.

"Nothing urgent. Just thought we ought to touch base on where we stand. I still love the benefits of in-state mergers."

"So do I. Carl, I'd like to but I honestly can't right now. How about September, after vacations?" Silence lingered in the air like an animal trap. He was waiting for me to say too much, to trip up, pop off, and blurt out everything. I knew that he knew. I didn't know *how* he knew it, and he never *said* he knew it, but he *knew*.

We set a date for late September and ended the conversation. *Life was so damned peculiar.* Reichardt wanted to alert me in a wordless way that he might want to get his oar in the water. How the hell did he know? What had suddenly possessed Wells Fargo? I could only marvel at the irony. Since last December, when Reichardt had called off our merger at the last possible moment, Security Pacific had *deteriorated*. Was our institution suddenly now more appealing because Rosenberg wanted to merge with it? In any event, if I was correct that Reichardt's ears had perked, this was good news. Perhaps, notwithstanding our collective real estate loan exposure, Wells Fargo would be waiting in the wings if a deal with Rosenberg collapsed. This would be preferable to other alternatives.

I hurried downstairs to the full board meeting. The directors were exhilarated by the progress I'd made with Rosenberg.

"Good work," said Boswell, our most senior and outspoken director. "One of the first things we've got to do is arrange golden parachutes for the executive officers participating in the negotiation of this deal. That includes you, Nick Binkley, and Jerry Grundhofer."

"It just makes sense," said Flamson. "We have to protect you and because of your proximity to the negotiations vitiate any potential appearance of a conflict of interest."

Golden parachutes have a bad reputation, but there is logic behind the madness. The board wanted us to negotiate on the behalf of the corporation, unfettered by visions of sugarplums—in other words, Binkley, Grundhofer, and I had one purpose and one purpose only: keep the deal on track. We were not there to strike a bargain for ourselves, or to the detriment of the corporation and its prevailing constituents. Second, what is agreed upon tacitly is not always realized. While Rosenberg said Binkley, Grundhofer, and I would play key roles in the New Bank of America—and I had no reason at this time to disbelieve such assurances—executives were commonly squeezed out in the bloody aftermath of big deals, especially following the consolidation of two giants. None of us wanted to be ejected and unsalaried at the same time. In the event of a management shakeup, the parachutes were the premium Rosenberg would have to pay to dislodge current management and, in essence, banish representation of Security Pacific from the executive platform.

▼

Dick Thornburgh arrived at my office early the next morning, a cat smile on his face. "Bob, we've successfully tweaked the exchange ratio. We've slid it up from 0.855 to 0.880, or nearly 3%. Morgan Stanley's analysis shows that this number is high enough in their view to preempt anything Wells

Fargo might toss across the transom. That means the stocks will split at 65.7 to 34.3."

This precious 25-point increase in the exchange rate was worth, to Security Pacific shareholders, $88 million in stock. Our accretion rose from 49% to 52%.

Awesome numbers. I was elated. "Good going."

"Thanks. Say, do you have a moment?"

"Sure, Dick. Have a seat."

Thornburgh's brow furrowed. He folded his hands. "What is it?"

"Well, Bob, what it is: I'd like to discuss our fee."

"I see. I've already thought some about this and I think perhaps one-tenth of 1% is probably appropriate. We're talking about a $4.5 billion deal. That's $4.5 million for a few days of really good work. That's a pretty fair day's pay."

Thornburgh's eyes brimmed with moisture. I thought I saw a tear appear as I defended what I thoroughly believed to be a plentiful figure for a few days of numbers crunching and the enhanced deal value they'd achieved.

"Bob, this is not so much a money issue."

I promptly apologized to Thornburgh for my naïveté and asked him what he had in mind.

Thornburgh somberly reminded me, "First Boston has done an awful lot of speculative work for Security Pacific on deals that never got done and we didn't get paid."

"Yes, you've done great work, for which I am grateful and Security Pacific is grateful. But, Dick, how is $4.5 million unreasonable? What's the problem?"

"Like I said, it's not the money."

"What is it then? Tell me."

"Morgan Stanley's getting paid about $9 million. How will it look if we get paid so much less than Morgan Stanley on what by all indications could be the banking deal of the century? Bob," he pleaded, "we'll be the laughingstock of the industry if our take is half that of Morgan Stanley."

The fact of the matter was that First Boston had done Security Pacific an enormous favor by renegotiating the exchange rate. More than that, Thornburgh was right that his people had done a vast amount of work for us on the come—running matrices and hypothetical projections on deals that had never seen fruition. They were absolute professionals and good people, and this merger—if it went through—was the jackpot for which they'd been praying. How could I in good conscience deny them an equal fee when they'd finagled another $88 million for our shareholders? "What the hell. You've done a tremendous job, Dick. We'll pay you what you want."

"Thank you, Bob!" His smile connected both ears. Now I was the one with the tear on my cheek.

Rosenberg agreed with the decision of my board that Binkley, Grundhofer, and I should be equipped with golden parachutes. "Naturally," I said, "your people should be protected as well."

"Of course, that would be appropriate." Rosenberg then informed me he was already protected and working under a written contract of employment stipulating that he would be taken care of in the event he lost his job. I was surprised; this was rather unusual for the chairman and CEO of a major bank. To my knowledge, no executive at Security Pacific had ever worked under a similar arrangement. We agreed that Bank of America's Frank Newman, Mike Rossi, Lew Coleman, and Tom Petersen—vice chairman of their Retail Division—should all be granted parachutes because they were intimately involved in the mechanics of the deal and should be protected.

In the assembly of the agreement, each bank eked out advantage where it could.

Frank Newman and his attorneys collaborated on a way to

execute the deal on a purchase-accounting basis, rather than pooling. The reason for the structuring of the merger this way was Bank of America's desire to write down Security Pacific's weaker assets at consummation and avoid a future drag on earnings as a direct result of the need for additional reserves or write-downs. As this was a straight stock-for-stock exchange by definition it would have to be a pooling agreement; but if there was some cash aspect of the transaction that was offered by one side to the other, and not reciprocated, this would constitute sufficient disparity to permit a purchase-accounting transaction.

In order to achieve this disparity, Bank of America's people now offered to purchase the executive-held Security Pacific restricted stock for *cash*. Everything else would be exchanged for stock. This would meet the conditions and technical criteria for a purchase accounting treatment.

Restricted stock is stock that is issued to company executives on a conditional basis, most commonly on the basis of position and as an incentive to maintain employment. Normally, restricted stock vests under a change of control; thus, Security Pacific's restricted stock would be exchangeable for Bank of America stock without any further conditions. Nine executives at Security Pacific held restricted stock. The Bank of America had not granted its executives any restricted stock.

Jerry Grundhofer, Nick, and I met to discuss the proposed cash-out of our stock. We all agreed that we would prefer to exchange our restricted stock for Bank of America shares; that is how much we believed in the future success of the new combined company.

Jerry said, "Another downside of this is that if we accept cash for the restricted stock, then we'll have to pay taxes on it now."

Only Jerry would think of that. When one accepts stock in an exchange, the taxes are deferred until the exchanged stock is sold.

"Jerry's correct," said Ed Herlihy of Wachtell Lipton, who was helping us understand the implications of decisions.

A bold treble seized Jerry's voice. "We should go back to Rosenberg and tell him if he wants his purchase accounting, and if he wants to pay cash for our restricted stock, he should pay our taxes as well."

My first thought: *That's nonsense. Rosenberg will never agree to that.*

My second thought: *Oooh, that's a damned good idea.*

"Furthermore," Jerry said, "if they're going to pay the taxes too, they should also pay the *taxes* on the *income* that is *represented* by the *taxes!*"

"You mean gross it up?" Herlihy asked.

"Sure. They should gross it up so there is no detrimental tax effect on us whatsoever."

"I dunno," I said. I was astonished by his chutzpah. "Can we afford to be that cocky? Is it the smart thing to do?"

"Look at it this way: this is the price Rosenberg pays us for helping him get his purchase accounting and getting the deal. I think he wants us bad enough."

Herlily thought the concept was shrewd and just might fly. Eventually I was persuaded that the idea had merit. We had been asked to make concessions, and it was Bank of America's design—in all our best interest—that they pay cash for restricted stock. Why should we be penalized?

"The spirit of togetherness I want now yields to the spirit of greed." I said this in a jocular vein, but I believed it was true.

I approached Rosenberg with this proposal and, to my astonishment, he bought it.

"That's probably a lot of money," Rosenberg said, "but we'll do it. You'll get all your restricted stock acquired on a tax-free basis, and we'll get our purchase accounting. That settles it. I think we have our agreement."

▼

On Thursday, August 8, Rosenberg called to confirm that
their due diligence was complete and within their limits; all
of the general terms of the loan agreement looked good. We
agreed to go to our respective boards on Friday, August 9, to
receive their formal approval.

Our outside attorneys, O'Melveny & Meyers, promptly
swung into high gear. Collaborating with Bank of America's
outside counsel, Pillsbury Madison & Sutro, they hammered
out the final agreement. To see it in indelible ink, to hold it
in my hand and to know it would be signed by both Rosenberg and myself, was a supreme comfort.

The deal was to be done in eleven days, from the moment
of first contact to board approval.

▼

The next day, in secret, separate meetings, Rosenberg and I
made formal presentations to our respective boards. Security
Pacific's meeting was long and it was intense. The agenda
was crammed from floor to ceiling. I reviewed with them the
terms of the agreement, our rationale for the merger, Bank of
America's incentive, and the history of my talks with Rosenberg. First Boston gave a rundown of the financial benefits
and offered a Fairness Opinion. There were pie charts, slides,
and bar graphs. The paper on the conference table weighed
perhaps several hundred pounds.

It was the high drama of numbers, formulas, discussion of
social issues, and final resolution.

I discussed the distasteful alternatives to the merger, especially trying to dispel any yearning that lingered for a Wells
combination. I compared the prospect of a Wells merger to
the more advantageous Bank of America merger. I argued that
the accretion to our shareholders was virtually unbeatable.
"Any other combination pales in comparison. Wells, though a
stupendous bank, is a California-only institution. Bank of
America is a world-class institution with a wider scope and a
fully developed long-term strategy. It's a stronger company

going in, it's better capitalized, has a stronger asset base, has lower nonperforming loans and a stronger emerging stock multiple. Wells stock is now so high that I honestly don't see it going much higher."

Flamson agreed. "Bob, you might explain to us the semantic difference between a *sale* to Bank of America and a *merger.*"

"Right. A merger has significant advantages. First, we retain the ability to influence the new company going forward. We'll have equal board representation, thus equivalent say in immediate and long-term strategies. If this was a sale, chances are we would retain no board representation. Second, we will have an active say in personnel selection and a real hands-on ability to protect our employees. The smoothness of this transition should assure that there is minimal trauma to our customers and the communities we both serve."

"How are we going to take care of the employees?" Flamson asked.

I outlined our plan and was emphatic that the burden of displacement was to be borne equally by both companies. "The best employee will get the job. This is Rosenberg's wish as well, and I believe his intent is to approach it honestly." Employees faced with termination would be treated with dignity, offered a pantheon of services, and provided with as generous a severance package as we could afford.

Boswell asked about the golden parachutes. "We're covering you, Nick, and Jerry. But are your equivalents at Bank of America all covered as well?"

"Yes, Rosenberg and his board are amenable to providing parachutes for his key people."

The final hours were devoted to the contemplation of catastrophic *What Ifs*? What unforeseen contingencies might thwart the deal? I reminded them that only a material adverse change (MAC) could blow the deal. Material adverse change is a relative concept—some resourceful attorney's work of art. What in fact might constitute a material adverse change? It would require the full cast of a large law firm to determine what was *material*, what was *adverse*, and what constituted *change*.

I told them I didn't foresee that happening. "We've shown them where all the skeletons are buried and they are aware of our state. The MAC generally would exclude any further atrophy that is a consequence of this awful economy."

At the conclusion of the marathon session, Security Pacific's board blessed the merger unanimously. I told the directors it was our intent to issue a public announcement on Monday, August 12.

This same conversation—or a close facsimile—was just now beginning, four hundred miles north in Rosenberg's board room in San Francisco, and I hoped it would proceed as smoothly.

I emerged from the meeting and discovered that Security Pacific stock had, that day, dropped another half a point.

▼

Early that evening I was seated in a Pasadena Mexican restaurant called *Arriba* with my family when my cellular phone rang. I hoped it was Rosenberg, confirming his board's approval. I was famished and it required superb leadership and managerial discipline to abandon my steaming burrito for a dark but loud corner in the restaurant.

"Bob." It was Dick Rosenberg. "I've just come out of our board meeting. Can we talk?"

I couldn't hear him over a traveling trio of mariachis. "Yes, let me go to my car phone. I'll call you right back."

I pocketed my cell phone, hurried out to the parking lot, climbed into my car, and called him back in at atmosphere more conducive to talking business.

"Bob, our board doesn't believe that our officers need parachutes. Thoughts, comments?"

Thoughts? I'll say. "I thought this was supposed to be equal. We are supposed to be in this thing together."

"We are in this thing together," Rosenberg said. "I don't feel it's that major a complication. But I do want to hear your thoughts."

Here it was, two hours after I'd put the deal to a vote, and our corporations were already falling out of step with one another, wandering in slightly different directions.

"None of your people will be 'chuted? Newman? Rossi? Coleman?"

"No, none of them," Rosenberg said. "At least that's what the board wants. And I sense our people don't feel that parachutes are necessary."

"Dick, did your board have any comment on our parachutes?"

"No, that's fine. Your people can and should be protected. Is that okay?"

I wasn't certain. Here I was, half in and half out of a car on a hot August evening, two margaritas in my stomach, traffic roaring past, and I didn't know whether it was okay or not. It certainly wasn't what I wanted—but could I stand for it? My brain starved for food, I said "Okay." At first blush this arrangement didn't sound right—and in hindsight it wasn't—but neither did it sound like the End of The World. I wanted this deal so badly that the important subtext of his board's wish to withdraw Bank of America parachutes eluded me for those few pivotal moments when I had an opportunity to speak up.

We concluded our phone call.

It didn't take long for me to absorb the inference behind Rosenberg's last-minute board room razzle dazzle. As I stepped out onto the concrete of the parking lot, it hit me: this obviously implied that Rosenberg's people felt comfortable that their jobs were not in immediate peril because their boss, Rosenberg, was to be the guy in charge. It was a way for Bank of America's board to assure executive management: "Don't worry, we're calling the shots, you're going to be okay." Without parachutes, his top people wouldn't become spooked and leave Bank of America.

By the time I regrouped with my family in the restaurant, I already sensed that I had just been witness to a conspicuous red flag. But running through my mind like a mantra was the thought, *I can't let this deal get off track.* Did I like the fact Rosenberg's people felt no need for protection? No, of course not. Did it ever-so-slightly tip the scales of equality in Bank of America's direction? Yes. Was it worth raising hell over? No; I didn't want to go back to the board with what was essentially a social issue: I was determined not to allow a personnel issue get in the way of the desired goal. Rosenberg and I were a minute or two from finalization of an agreement that was for Security Pacific a life preserver. I could not allow a dispute over parachutes to erupt into an issue. It was philosophically highly questionable, but in the end it probably didn't matter. I'd always believed that deals fell apart less often because of numbers than as a consequence of verbal indiscretions, recalcitrance, and pride— usually over frivolous matters.

But I did wonder to myself, *Was this the beginning of disparity? How many more times would I be called upon to make similar concessions?*

▼

This inauspicious phone call marked a pivotal turning point; it was the first indication I had that, although Rosenberg took pains to present the deal as a merger of equals, his actions betrayed our deeper understanding that he was maneuvering from a position of greater power.

And the more I thought about it, the more it bothered me. It *stunk.* Not only did it disequalize the merger, it shifted the equation of power. This small gesture was a psychological manipulation in disguise, a subtle declaration by Rosenberg: *I have just an edge over you.*

▼

But on Monday morning, August 12, Rosenberg and I issued

a press release to the media announcing our intent to create the New Bank of America. It stated, in part:

"Bank of America and Security Pacific today announced a definitive agreement to merge, creating a banking institution with approximately $190 billion in assets, and combined equity capital of approximately $12 billion."

Security Pacific stock jumped 35% to nearly $30 a share.

Prior to the upcoming joint press conference, Rosenberg and I huddled in a ground floor holding area of the Security Pacific headquarters while electricians strung cables from outlets. Cameramen mounted halogen lamps on tripods and assembled reflectors. I wasn't nervous, but I was pensive and reflective. I'd been so focused on doing the deal that I hadn't yet completely absorbed the reaction or fully reckoned with the magnitude of what we had agreed to accomplish.

"This whole thing is so heavy," I muttered.

Rosenberg was taciturn. "This is a big deal."

If there was something vaguely oppressive about the details to come, it surely had to do in part with the fact that 12 to 18% of our combined workforce would be let go. Even if the merger was ultimately good for California, the images of consolidation and power it evoked were astounding. We would have to absorb—and truthfully address—a lot of criticism.

"Dick," I said, "maybe it would be a good idea to start this thing out on a lighter note. Perhaps I could introduce you with a little joke."

Rosenberg, who was kind of a straight arrow, stroked his chin, shrugged. "Any ideas?"

Something about sitting here with Rosenberg in this awkward holding pattern had triggered in my mind a vision. "What if I open by saying, 'I'd like to welcome Dick Rosenberg here. Carl Reichardt picked him up at the airport and drove him over.'" I chuckled. "Get it?"

Rosenberg didn't crack a smile. His lips didn't even widen.

"I get it all right."

No go. This guy, I thought, basically has zero sense of humor. He'd won, and he still couldn't lower the impenetrable shield, not even for a second. He couldn't even say the words: *Carl Reichardt.* Rosenberg had an intensity that went beyond the pale.

Dick and I took our seats at a small table with twin microphones. Rosenberg presented the opening comments. "The New Bank of America," he began, "will have more capital, greater pro forma market capitalization, more domestic assets, and the largest branch network of any existing or proposed U.S. bank. . . . Clearly, this merger creates a preeminent banking institution. Bank of America and Security Pacific are an extraordinary strategic fit; one that will enable us to build on the strengths of both organizations to create a highly profitable new banking enterprise that we intend will become the leader in the United States, and will be in an even better position on a global basis."

When it was my turn to speak I addressed the issue of why we were interested in pursuing a merger. Without mentioning Security Pacific's weakened position, I discussed overcapacity in banking and the economic benefits of an in-market merger. "When two large and successful companies operating in the same market combine resources they can clearly provide superior customer service, substantially reduce operating expenses, increase profitability and shareholder value, and have the broader base of resources and strengths to grow. It is that simple. That is why we have seen several smaller in-market mergers in New York, the Southeast, and Texas, and I think there will be more in the months to come."

Were there ever—although it took six years, not months.

"This particular in-market merger between Bank of America and Security Pacific is unique because of the strategic fit of the two organizations. In addition to the very strong and very similar operations in the Western states, we have strong and similar operations in the Pacific Rim countries, and our national and international strategies are remarkably similar. Perhaps even more important are the similarities in corporate cultures and management styles."

I would come to eat those words.

We opened the floor up to questions.

A journalist shot upward, notebook balanced on the crook of his arm. "How many people will lose their jobs, and will they be Security Pacific or Bank America employees?"

My stomach churned. Knowing that we could not cut $1 billion in expenses without massive job elimination, Rosenberg and I had estimated displacement of between 12,000 and 18,000 individuals. This was a big number, a lot of people; a repercussion we could not casually or unemotionally set aside. We had rehearsed a nebulous, circumspect answer to this question—an answer we both knew wasn't completely true, to a question we knew damned well would be the first to arise.

Rosenberg grimaced. "We have not made any projections as to the number of people who will lose their jobs, and as far as the second part of your question, we will be selecting the best person in each category for each job regardless of which company they originally were from."

The press conference proceeded smoothly and was well received by Wall Street, the banking community, and local business reporters: SECURITY PACIFIC, BANK AMERICA MAKE BANKING HISTORY; THE BIGGEST BANK IN THE WEST, RIVALS CREATE MEGA-BANK: THE WEST IS WON.

Immediately, the social pundits of the press began to take their licks. California was in a serious economic downturn and we were going to put a lot of people out of work. Few wrote that this solution was far preferable to a sale or a total failure, which would leave most everyone at Security Pacific out of work.

Layoff estimates riddled the headlines: MERGE AND PURGE; 10,000 JOBS MAY BE LOST IF DEAL IS OKD; 13,000 MAY LOSE THEIR JOBS; AS MANY AS 400 BRANCHES, 15,000 JOBS MAY BE SLASHED; LAYOFFS COULD HIT 20,000.

They were very close to the truth. What they didn't pick up on was the other 80,000 or so who would remain as employees once the deal was complete but who would have to cohabitate with uncertainty for at least six months until the position assignments were finalized. A lot of employees were dazed and confused.

The merger was the subject of cartoons, limericks, and editorials. An August 15 cartoon by Skelley depicted Security Pacific as a bride and Bank of America as her groom, saying, "What a coincidence! You're marrying me for my money and I'm marrying you for yours. . . . "

Analysts rushed to fix the blame for the fall of Security Pacific.

In an August 18 *Los Angeles Times* article dripping with invective, Tom Furlong likened Security Pacific to a "sinkhole," failed to mention one advantage of the merger, and crazily asserted that firings had become prevalent after Flamson took over. Furlong turned his flame-thrower on the Merchant Bank, excoriated management in the 1980s, and alleged that Flamson—the now-ailing genius who'd quadrupled our size in ten years—had destroyed the bank. That was unforgivable, dumping the blame for all our problems in the lap of a dying man.

At this point I still believed in the abiding principle that Security Pacific would continue, albeit under a new name, and felt that the eulogies—which ranged from the sympathetic and heartfelt to accusatory and bitter—were premature. In one or two instances I took newspaper editors and journalists to task for what I felt were unduly negative portrayals of what I still felt to be an astounding step forward for both institutions. The deal, I argued, was less a death than a reincarnation.

11

The Million
Loan March

R osenberg and I left no stone unturned.

During the eleven-day time frame in which the agreement was struck, in the interest of secrecy and discretion, we'd avoided a thorough due diligence that would have cemented any unresolved issue because a full-blown due diligence would have signaled to employees and observers that something major was in the works. We had addressed only in very broad terms the condition of our loan portfolio. We gave them all the facts—numbers, names, methodologies, reserve computations, a true but general flavor—but Bank of America had not yet conducted a file-by-file review of our activities.

Rosenberg was well aware that Security Pacific had financial troubles. He felt that we had been more than candid and, while neither of us could be assured there would be no further economic deterioration, he was convinced our portfolio was manageable. We'd even shown his people projected loan classifications and extrapolated questionable loans far out into the future, taking into account the deleterious consequences of continued economic slide.

It was a complete, unambiguous picture.

The scope of Bank of America's full due diligence, now under way, was wide and comprehensive. They evaluated most every loan and identified credits that could be potential candidates for the separate asset pool or "collecting" bank they proposed.

▼

Michael Rossi, Bank of America's chief credit officer, fired off a memo to Rosenberg outlining the terms for the second—and official—due diligence. The diligence had to be coordinated and conducted rapidly in order to accommodate regulatory filing deadlines. Rossi wanted to interview key people at all of our major business units. He mobilized battalions of senior managers, attorneys, auditors, and credit experts to conduct the examination. While we had a signed, unconditional agreement to merge, the details Rossi outlined and the tone of the plan gave me concern that if their intensified review turned out to vary substantially from their initial conclusions, they would claim that material matters had not been properly disclosed at that time. I wasn't worried about the veracity of our disclosure, but I found the temperament of the memo foreboding. They would now probe our portfolio in enormous depth. I didn't want to be cut out of the process and needed to maintain direct communication with Rosenberg.

▼

During my continued inquisition of Rosenberg, I finally got a clue about their pre-agreement review of our loan portfolio: they'd come to the conclusion that in order to equalize our asset quality and loan loss reserve level with theirs—and cover projected loan losses—Security Pacific would need to augment its reserves by another $1.2 billion.

This number was important, insofar as Rosenberg had plugged this number into the deal matrix and used the result to demonstrate to his board of directors how the consolidation would impact Bank of America's financials. This was the number Rossi's due diligence team would in theory validate. A number much higher could jeopardize the deal or result in an attempt to renegotiate the exchange ratio.

I held my breath, watched closely, and communicated frequently.

Rosenberg and I met on September 5 to discuss the progress of Rossi's army.

"The due diligence is going very well," he said. "We've found no significant problems. It's coming out just about as expected."

"Good." Internally, I was ecstatic, but I didn't want to show any emotion that might expose my lingering concern that we might have missed something important during our preliminary due diligence.

▼

The deal's historicity had by now dawned on all of us. But even I was surprised by the depth and duration of media coverage.

In an article headlined "No Promises For Smith Except Riches," *American Banker* journalist Sam Zuckerman predicted that were I not selected to replace Rosenberg, I would pull my parachute. I knew Sam, I liked Sam, but his sour analysis was precipitous and ill-timed. It unnecessarily shifted the focus of the transaction to what I stood to gain personally and, in that respect, was not conducive to the spirit of the deal. His speculation that I would "cash in" if not made CEO was cynical. I knew there were other options, a wide gray area between taking over and leaving. If I had a role to play at Bank of America, I would stay. I wanted to stay. I felt an honest obligation to stay.

▼

Rosenberg and I met in Washington, D.C., in mid-September at the Reserve City Bankers Meeting. He said the due diligence was still on track.

"How does the credit side stack up?"

"Based on the preliminary data I've seen, the credit due diligence is also passing muster. We feel you're underreserved; I see how momentously that provision in FIRREA impacted your loan portfolio. On the upside, your LDC exposure is minimal. Your LBOs pose no major obstacle. Prior to last year you had no real problems with the regulators. The shutting down of the Merchant Bank was prudent. I'm very happy that the sale of Hoare Govett and McIntosh has been set into motion. There are other parts and pieces we'd like to jettison. As for asset projections, I'm actively discussing that with the San Francisco Fed."

I asked Dick if there had been any changes.

"Not since we last spoke. The information Frank Newman received is still correct. However, we're taking a hard look at your dividend and strongly considering asking that you reduce it to the Bank of America level in anticipation of the merger."

"Excellent." I was thrilled with the cooperative spirit of both organizations. "It should be easy to resolve any difficulties that arise."

▼

On September 19, I woke up to news of a frenzy that I could not explain. Wall Street had inexplicably been pelted with rumors that a renegotiation of the exchange ratio was imminent. Crossing the Reuters newswire I was stunned to read that "Several arbitragers said they had heard talk that the merger could be renegotiated based on concerns about California economy and Security Pacific's fundamentals."

The sources for these rumors were unidentified, and the level of analysis shallow. It was beyond belief that these articles crossed the wire on the veracity of hearsay.

Two unidentified arbitragers at Prudential were quoted, but the quotes were specious and unattributed:

"'I think that at worst the deal gets renegotiated," said one arb.'

"'I think the deal is fine," said another arb. "Bank of America has been saying the deal is OK.'"

That was the sum and substance of the story, but it had sent Wall Street into chaos.

By the following day, stories were popping up everywhere that the merger was in jeopardy.

San Francisco Chronicle: "Wall street was buzzing with rumors yesterday that loan problems at Security Pacific are worse than previously thought, and that Bank of America Corp might alter or even abandon its merger agreement with Security."

Our Media Department located one possible source for the rumors; apparently our old friend at Prudential, George Salem—a.k.a. Nostradamus—had downgraded his rating on Security Pacific due to personal "doubts about the merger." Salem couldn't be located to confirm, to deny, or to relate the source of his terror—classic George Salem. We issued a statement to allay fears that renegotiations were imminent or that the merger was falling apart.

Early in the afternoon of Friday, September 20, Nick Binkley and John Kooken stopped by my office to inform me that Mike Rossi and Frank Newman had concluded their assessment of our loan portfolio and relayed the findings to Rosenberg, who would call me with an estimate of the amount Frank thought we needed to reserve against future reclassification.

"What are you hearing?" I asked.

Nick sighed. "Frank said the credit review indicates the need for about $2 billion in additional reserves."

I winced. *$2 billion?* The number poured over me in a torrent. This was inconsistent with what Rosenberg and I had discussed. "What happened to $1.2 billion?"

"They *thought* it was $1.2 billion, but after a closer look they've upped the figure."

This number was difficult to accept. "That can't be right."

Kooken agreed. "Somebody up north is hallucinating."

Nick said he had heard the number from Frank Newman directly. "If the number came from anyone but Frank I would doubt it myself."

"Was there any discussion of renegotiating the exchange ratio?" I asked.

"Not that I'm aware."

▼

At five in the afternoon Rosenberg phoned me. "I want to discuss a couple of important matters. First, the rollup of the credit review indicates a need of $2.1 billion in additional reserves. $2.17 billion to be precise." This figure was based on the assumption that Security Pacific would write off $900 million of loans in the second half of 1991. "The $2.1 is in addition to that." He reminded me that our plan had called for only $573 million in charge-offs in the second half of 1991.

"So you calculate we have another $327 million more to charge off, and in addition to that we need $2.1 billion in reserve?"

"Right. Give or take $300 million."

"These numbers sound impossible," I said in disbelief.

"I was also surprised. I realize this is about $900 million more than the $1.2 billion we'd assumed as part of the transaction. On a present value basis, this means it will cost Bank of America $300 million more. Perhaps in lieu of this you might consider helping us out by not paying a dividend."

I quizzed Rosenberg further on the discrepancy and eventually ascribed it to a bifurcation in methodologies. "You reviewed these loans on a mark to market basis. You're asking yourselves, *what can we sell these properties for now on the current market*, instead of viewing these loans as viable, trackable, and payable." Rosenberg and his people were planning a fire sale of Security Pacific credits. They were preparing to liquidate loans on a tremendous segment of our portfolio.

I got right to my major concern and posed a couple of You-Never-Ask questions that because of our urgent situation I needed to ask. "Dick, is this disparity so large that it triggers the material adverse change clause?"

"No, no, it won't. This is still a good deal. Just not as good a deal."

Good, I thought. "Then my next question is, Are you still comfortable with the exchange ratio?"

Rosenberg paused. "Yes. Anyway, we said we would not renegotiate. The deal and ratio are fully intact as far as I'm concerned. We just have to be aware that Security Pacific won't be able to push as much capital into the combined operations as we earlier hoped."

I understood that Rosenberg might be seeking justification to pump as much of our capital into reserves as he possibly could as a means to buffet any future storms without harming future earnings. It made perfect sense to take a very hard look at the loan portfolio. Neither one of us wanted to have to face credit problems and the need for additional reserves after the merger was consummated.

I suggested that Rosenberg allow Nick, Jerry, and George Benter to sit down with Mike Rossi and thoroughly review the methodology by which they'd arrived at the $2.1 billion figure. "We have got to understand exactly what's going on."

"That's fine. Let's set it up."

The second question Rosenberg had revolved around Sequor, our very profitable securities-related Merchant Bank remnant. Sequor was just as large an enigma to him as it had been to George Moody. "This month-to-month rolling securities verifications method I don't understand. The amounts we are talking about are so consequential—several hundred billion dollars' worth of securities—that what I'd like you to do if possible is authorize a one-time count verification of the securities in all five vaults so we know for certain the assets are in there."

This was a legitimate request. "Sure."

This conversation gave me insight into Rosenberg's two key concerns: Sequor, and credit quality—the *Beautiful and the Damned* that would later turn into *The Sorrow and the Pity*.

▼

I alerted Kooken about the $2.1 billion figure. His face went quizzical. "That sounds preposterous."

"Their way of classifying these loans is harsh. I think they're being pessimistic, looking at liquidation values. But I also believe they're imagining a worse-case scenario and trying to preempt any disaster that could possibly hit the combined bank in the future."

Kooken shrugged. "Their valuation methodology is tougher than the one the regulators use."

"But from their perspective it makes sense. They have no incentive to overestimate the quality of these loans, or to underestimate the numbers involved."

The $2.1 number was also embarrassing. It made Security Pacific look like a feeble shell of what it had been in the late 1980s. It would be difficult and humiliating to shuffle $2 billion more into reserves before the deal closed, on top of taking another $900 million for the anticipated write-offs. But if mild to moderate humiliation was the price we had to pay for getting this deal, I would swallow as much as they could dish down my throat.

Kooken nodded. "But how can we rationalize this to our accountants and, ultimately, to the shareholders? Bob, we've been using our methodology for a long time. Do we just suddenly adopt Bank of America's Doomsday Methodology?"

"I guess we'll learn as we go. Ultimately, we will have to shift to their methodology."

"But in the meantime we have to keep capital levels up and maintain integrity with our accountants and shareholders."

"Not to mention the regulators," I added. "We have to make it very clear why we are doing this. Looking to the combined company, we should try to shift as much as we reasonably can into reserves."

That weekend we embarked on a crash-course in Bank of America credit methodology, to both understand it mechanically and pinpoint the source of the discrepancy between their reserve projection and our own. Undoubtedly, their calculations were based on the classification of our loans—but what had they done to the numbers? What factors had they applied? We eventually reconciled the difference and discovered that while their factors were smaller in our favor, their auditors had turned a harsh eye toward the way we'd classified our loans. Any benefit we derived from their factors were undercut by a deleterious interpretation of our loan classifications.

"It's still a huge number."

"Yeah, I know." I was concerned by the $2.1 billion figure, but in light of Rosenberg's continued enthusiasm and reassurance, I felt we could move forward.

On Sunday, September 22, Jerry Grundhofer and I flew to San Francisco to host Security Pacific customers at a Rams–49ers game at Candlestick Park. Also in attendance, seated in our box, was a contingent of bank customers, including executives from our San Francisco office. This was recreational, but also business, so Jerry and I wore ties and coats.

Jerry nudged me and pointed to the Bank of America box just west of ours. "Good God, do you see what I see?"

I squinted. "Is that Rossi? Nah, it can't be."

"It is."

Jerry and I were instantly struck by his attire. He was here ostensibly for the same reason we were: to entertain clients. But, dressed as he was in a red 49er jacket, a flashy gold medallion around his neck, open shirt, skipping around between clients.

I didn't know Rossi well. I'd met him during the preliminary due diligence and had seen him several times during the official examination. Some Security Pacific people had mentioned his name to me in a not too flattering context. But I knew I would be seeing a lot of Rossi from now on and suggested to Jerry that we journey over to his box and say hello. "Shall we?"

Jerry nodded.

We excused ourselves and negotiated a circuitous path to Rossi's circle.

"Michael!" we shouted.

"Boys!"

"How's it goin'?" I asked.

"Good."

"I understand the due diligence is nearly complete and you've got a final handle on that reserve number."

"Well, things are coming out as we'd hoped. It looks like we're about *$3 billion* off."

Jerry and I stared at each other. Jerry's pupils elongated, his extremities drained of blood, and he began to vibrate.

I turned back to Rossi as calmly as possible. "First it was $1.2 billion, then I heard $2.1 billion on Friday. Now it's Sunday and you're telling me it's $3 billion?"

Grundhofer was apoplectic. "That's crazy."

"Michael," I said. "I spoke to Rosenberg not thirty-six hours ago and he told me it was $2.1 billion."

"Oh, no, no, no. It's closer to $3 billion. I'll take care of it, though. I'll work it out."

"Well, that's good. Enjoy the game. Sure hope our Rams cream your 49ers."

Jerry and I repaired to a corner and caught our breath. "Did he say $3 billion? Holy cow. This can't be happening."

Jerry was trembling. "Do we have a problem? We have a problem, don't we?"

I hardly knew what to say. We limped back to the customers we were there to entertain. It was nearly impossible to put on a smile. We tried to be good sports. Jerry was solemn. I found it excruciating to sit through this football game, trying to feign joviality and conviviality.

On the flight back to Los Angeles, Jerry and I dropped any pretense of jollity. We simply could not believe the latest number, nor the crass manner in which Rossi had tossed it to us—almost as if delivering news of our deterioration brought him joy.

"What, really, is going on here?" I said. "I'm literally confused as to whether we are in deep shit or not."

"You've got Rosenberg's assurance that he wants to go forward, right?"

"As of Friday."

"Should we call him?"

"No, I think it's better if we don't bring it up."

Jerry's forehead glistened beneath his overhead light. "What do you think Rossi meant when he said, 'I'll take care of it'?"

"I have no idea, and I'm afraid to guess." It was a peculiar, unfathomable, and arrogant pronouncement that conjured more fear than it allayed.

Grundhofer wasn't sure he could withstand another twelve hours without knowing why the reserve number had advanced 50% in twenty-four hours. "The waiting is excruciating."

"Jerry, it's only been a couple hours. We just have to admit to ourselves we don't know what the hell is going on." Equally inexplicable was Rossi's leisurely, off-the-cuff delivery of such a supremely perilous revelation, almost as if he were asking us to join him for a hotdog. This deal was very important—it was life and death stuff to us.

As it turned out, we had to sweat for an entire week. Rosenberg and I next spoke the following Friday. "The reserve number is now down somewhere between $1 billion and $1.6 billion."

"Down to $1.6 billion?" I did not mention Rossi's $3 billion number.

"That's correct."

I thought, *What the hell is going on here?* Now I was really confused. But obviously I wasn't about to argue with a lower number. But I wondered if he knew what was going on around him.

"And we're continuing to work the number down."

Why on earth, I wondered, *would Rosenberg want to work the reserve number down? On the other hand, why look a gift horse in the mouth?*

After pausing in some confusion, I found my voice. "Dick, regardless of what the final number is, I *absolutely* have to understand Bank of America's methodology. We've tried to keep up with your analysis, but we're obviously missing the mark. Until I understand your equations, I'm at a real disadvantage."

"No problem. Let me set up a meeting between you and Michael Rossi."

Swell, I thought.

▼

Thoroughly perplexed—but utterly obsessed with running down the origin of wildly discrepant numbers—Kooken and I streamlined our own analysis, working and reworking the numbers. Each time, we came closer to their numbers, but never hit the mark. And we never found any numerical basis for the derivation of Rossi's $3 billion.

We questioned Rossi and ultimately concluded that the substantial difference was attributable to the fact that Bank of America was simultaneously using two incompatible methodologies. The accountants used the traditional and industry-accepted Markov reserve methodology, but Mike Rossi used Rossi's methodology—and this was the crux of the problem. While Markov celebrated the consistent application of realistic numbers, Rossi's methodology hinged on Rossi's application of "arbitrary management discretion adjustments." In other words, wherever Rossi saw a number he deemed low, he spontaneously made it bigger—a million here, a million there, a few zeroes at the end of this number. All told, there was at least a $1 billion difference between Markov's and Rossi's methodologies. The intellectual contortions necessary to understand what Rossi had done with our portfolio were beyond my capacity.

I told Jerry what I had discovered. He was dismayed. "Maybe they're playing Good Cop/Bad Cop. Rosenberg is the conciliatory voice of reason; Rossi is the tough guy."

I agreed that Rossi was difficult to get a fix on. "I can't honest to god tell if he's trying to play savior or what. I'm sure he wants us to believe he 'solved' our $3 billion problem."

"All he did was ruin a perfectly good football game."

12

High Anxiety

Fear entered the building.

Rosenberg and I had just disrupted the collective lives of nearly one hundred thousand people. Every one of them—along with their spouses, children, and anyone dependent upon them—knew what this deal meant: consolidation and lost jobs in the most weakened California economy in memory.

The month and a half following the press conference was a period of turmoil for employees.

I was devoted to the concept that displacement be equitable and logical. I also felt Rosenberg wanted to be and could be dispassionate, impartial, and objective throughout the process. At face value, what could possibly be simpler, more logical, and more fair? We'll both cut equally, we'll keep objectively the best people for the job. The ideal was honorable, the intent was sincere. And if we followed the rules, the displacement process would be fair and the burden of lost workers would be borne equally by both institutions.

Kathy Burke, our director of human resources, was responsible for making the transition period as tolerable as possible. An extraordinary woman, Burke pulled out all the stops to psychologically cushion employees during this period. She felt strongly that there should be no embargo of information and, in this spirit, suggested issuing a newsletter, *Connections*, whose sole purpose would be to dispense hard facts about personnel issues related to the pending merger as soon as they became available.

"We should expect unabated anxiety," she said. "What will go through our people's minds? First, obviously, will my job be here for me in the New Bank of America? Second, what is going on in the economy? How hard will it be to find a new job if I lose my current job?"

That year alone, Los Angeles had lost more than two hundred thousand jobs. Unemployment approached 10% generally, and was far worse in many urban sectors and low-income communities.

I mentioned to Burke, "My god, if the California economy is bad now, wait until one hundred thousand employees stop spending even a nickel for six months because they don't know if they're going to have a job. Our people are not going to be making big financial decisions or frivolous purchases. They're not going to move, they're not going to put a down payment on a house, they're going to hunker down and save every cent they can. Forget about the concept of disposable income."

Just below the top level of ten or so employees who knew their fate were the other eighty or so executive vice presidents—and many more senior vice presidents—who languished in uncertainty, not to mention the tens of thousands of managers, assistants, and branch employees.

By late September, my calendar was filled with visits from executives, managers, and employees.

My discussions with them were always the same. For the first minute or so we slapped each other on the back, congratulated ourselves on the merger, and contemplated the bright future of what would be an invincible organization. But the discussions always came down to one thing— *"Where do I fit in?"*

These were our senior people, some of whom I'd worked with for ten or twenty years.

I couldn't soothe them much. "I wish I could tell you exactly. The truth is we haven't decided yet. We are going to do everything we can to select the best people for each job. And it requires both Rosenberg's and my approval."

Silence. Lean forward. "Bob, privately, what do you think's gonna happen? You can tell me."

"I honestly don't know."

Beneath even the most stoic and stalwart faces I detected the anguish. Who in such a position could not worry for the future? I had expected this aspect to be difficult, but to understand something conceptually and face it directly were two different things.

Within a couple weeks of the announcement, employees started to shut down, freeze up, and stop working. This wasn't to screw up the company, and it wasn't to make a statement— it was the symptom of primal fear; crippling anxiety that no displacement package, rally, or pep speech in the world could overcome. Even George Moody's golden-throat oratory could not have dissipated the cold-steel fog that seized our headquarters, branch offices, and satellite operations.

For a time, the rumor mill became more lethal than FIRREA, our loan portfolio, and a deal promoter's "great idea" combined. I was hearing things that had no basis in fact whatsoever, and they were scaring our people into abject paralysis.

With the aid of Kathy Burke and human resources, we tried to get people to focus on their jobs. Now we issued not only *Connections* but also *Communications*, a weekly leaflet devoted to the dissemination of merger information as soon as it became available that also effectively squashed the Rumor of The Week.

We also quickly inaugurated a number of promotions at the branch level—contests, deposit promos, and loan promos. These diversions were created to give employees something new to learn, think about, and work on—somewhere for them to channel the wayward energy.

▼

A month and a half after Security Pacific signed the agreement to merge with Bank of America, Ronald Smart, senior national bank examiner, and Jimmy Barton of the Office of the Comptroller of the Currency, issued the most shocking report on Security Pacific Bank to date.

It was brutal. In his summation of his review through midyear 1991, Barton stated that because the overall condition of the bank continued to deteriorate, Security Pacific was now considered *unsatisfactory*—a genteel way of declaring our bank a piece of junk. Problem assets had proliferated, with nonaccrual loans and other real estate owned climbing to historic levels. Furthermore, he noted that asset quality was poor and that criticized assets approached inordinate levels. Barton felt management had been reactive rather than taking a proactive approach to the problems. Six weeks hence, the Federal Reserve would convey a similar sentiment.

While there was ample reason to criticize Security Pacific, the flavor of the new reports was pejorative and unnecessarily divisive. *My God*, I thought, *we have solved so many of these concerns with our merger. Don't they understand what we've just done and why we did it? They can't possibly be this stupid.*

And rather than provide guidance for the fulfillment of our merger, they had written us off and were building a case for our burial. If these reports were paradigms for our destruction rather than strategies for our recovery, it was because both Security Pacific and the regulators had a personal stake in their disposition. Naturally, Security Pacific wanted to continue to be viewed as a robust and healthy organization; regulators wanted to protect their autonomy and scuttle any allegations that they had not detected our problems as early as they should have.

The inevitable net result of these clashing self-interests was an adversarial relationship. During this period, when regulators decided that a bank was in trouble, they wanted it sold or recapitalized at once, no matter what the cost. This ultimatum incited regulators to issue reports whose purpose was to make a bank look—and feel—as feeble and sickly as possible. The praise we received for our attempts to comply and fix our problems was begrudging, sparse, and feeble. In annual reports, the reader looks to the small print and footnotes for the bad news; in regulatory reports we had to consult the small print with a magnifying glass for any good news—what we had done right.

By late September, I finally began to understand the enormous implications of this merger. It went beyond the two corporations involved, their shareholders, employees, customers, and even beyond the economic stasis of California. The ramifications were social, judicial, and constitutional. At the end of September the House Banking Committee convened two days of hearings on the repercussions of large-scale bank consolidations. The purpose of the hearings was ostensibly to allow citizens to voice their fears, concerns, and reservations.

On October 3, Rosenberg called to inform me that Bank of America had concluded its due diligence to his satisfaction. "Everything is within our levels based on our standards. That previously mentioned number of $2.1 billion is down to $1.4 billion, or slightly larger than the number I gave my board."

I was relieved at the reconciliation but bewildered by the convoluted, frightening, and ultimately unnecessary roller coaster ride we'd all taken in order to arrive at this conclusion. Rosenberg was now very nervous about Sequor. Although Sequor was earning about $60 million a year after taxes, he found it unfathomably complex and was worried that it was run by people who'd been given an appalling amount of autonomy.

"Too independent," he said. "I'm going to send someone to have a closer look."

Rosenberg knew I had authorized his one-time vault inventory of Sequor and the result had been a success; all securities were accounted for and stowed safely in our vaults. He thanked me for the vault count. "But, Bob, I need a much more thorough understanding of what Sequor is and how it works. Hopefully, we can install rigid controls on what appears to be a very uninhibited organization."

"Dick, I know Sequor does look that way to outsiders. The business is difficult and specialized; we've made it very profitable by installing first-class management and we generally leave them alone because they're good. This is entrepreneurship at its best."

But the closer Dick Rosenberg looked at Sequor, the more terror he had *of* it, and the more questions he had *about* it. "It looks to me like this cash items in the process of collection (CIPC) system is really pushing the envelope of what is allowed by the regulators."

CIPC was a complex process by which Sequor took legal advantage of a provision of banking law which permitted the retention of undeployed reserves which we then invested rather than holding with the Fed as deposit reserves. This was unorthodox, but it was legal, acceptable to the Federal Reserve, and pretty shrewd—it was another reason why Sequor remained a successful yet misunderstood operation.

"Are Sequor's methods acceptable to the regulators?"

"Dick, I've personally discussed that issue with Jerry Corrigan until I was blue in the face." Corrigan was the president of the New York Federal Reserve. "I've told him that it is our intent always to operate within the letter and spirit of the law. Corrigan and his staff watch Sequor closely and he's agreed to let us know if we cross the line and so far that has never been the case. The CIPC generates about $5 million a year for our shareholders."

"And the Fed likes it?"

"Well, no, Dick, the Fed doesn't *like* it—they are not over-joyed about it—but there is no law on the books prohibiting it. All I can tell you is that Caggiano and his people are brilliant and dependable. Everything is on the up and up, and the organization is a huge success."

"Oh, I don't doubt that for a second. You have very smart individuals running that function. But if we can impose Bank of America *controls* and *fail-safes* we could eliminate the potential for future disruptions or concerns. I don't want to find out in the next few years that some process I don't understand carries a potential liability. My way, we could go forward without worrying."

His oddly phrased misgivings were just forthright enough to engender alarm and too unspecific with which to take issue. It sounded to me that because he didn't understand Sequor, his impulse was to rein it in, compress it into something he could control. Anything he could control, he could understand.

"I have a man in mind to work with your people at Sequor to identify areas of concern, evaluate their importance to the continued operation, and develop solutions that will eliminate or minimize any existing exposure."

I told Rosenberg we would cooperate, but implored him to look deeper into Sequor before approving radical changes.

"We'll have a look-see before we make a move. Be that as it may, I would like us to sit down with the man I have in mind to send to New York. He is a good man. I'll trust his opinion of the situation."

▼

Some analysts simply didn't believe the deal would survive. While attending a meeting of the American Bankers Association in San Francisco I was cornered by rapacious reporters. A reporter from Reuters tailed me to the water fountain. "Mr. Smith, Bank of America is not a dumb organization. They are conservative."

"You got that right."

"Well, are Security Pacific's problems so severe that Bank of America will back out of the deal? It's the question on everybody's mind."

A lump formed in my throat. Her question was my fear. I regurgitated the answer Rosenberg had given me throughout negotiations. "Bank of America knows our status as well as we do and the feeling is that although there may be continued deterioration—largely due to recession—it will not be dire enough to trigger the material adverse clause." I couldn't answer her any more directly, and she seemed satisfied. She lowered her pen and looked me straight in the eye.

"Mr. Smith, is the merger what you really want?"

The lump in my throat doubled. "Yes. Definitely. It will fulfill a lot of ideals I've had for a long time."

The next day, I again met with Rosenberg. I showed him projections of our third-quarter results and reserves. The earnings were low and the reserves were high. "Dick, you'll be asked by analysts what you think about these numbers and I'd hope that you would endorse them and be prepared to make some kind of statement."

"Yes, we'll be prepared."

We set a tentative close date for the merger: February 29, 1992.

Then Rosenberg brought in the individual who would whip Sequor into shape.

"The perfect man for the job," Rosenberg proclaimed.

I was disappointed. The person Rosenberg introduced me to was Dick Griffith. He was an ex-Federal Reserve Bank officer, apparent control freak, and one of Mike Rossi's protégés.

Rosenberg had the utmost confidence in Griffith. "What I intend to do, assuming you agree, is send Dick out to New York to get a fix on Sequor, assess its risk, and report back with his plan."

"I'll go back East and patch this mess up," Griffith said to me blandly.

"I don't know that there's any 'mess,'" I said. "Sequor is one of our cash cows, a star performer." I tried to tell him a little bit about Sequor. Griffith smiled, sluffed his hand. "You don't have to tell me too much; I'm an old ex-Fed officer myself. In a gut-way—a hunch way—I probably understand Sequor better than you or even the people who run it. I'll fly back to New York, see for myself, and make my determination."

What I didn't get to tell Griffith before he departed for New York was that the entrepreneurs who ran Sequor despised head office and had little tolerance for renegade pomposity.

On the afternoon of October 10 I was to meet with Mike Rossi to discuss our loan portfolio. I'd not yet had a substantive conversation with him and didn't know what to expect. I had made no judgments about his character based on the bizarre $3 billion fiasco. Admittedly, I was irritated by the needless panic Rossi's accounting methodology had produced, and I was dumbfounded by the manner in which he positioned himself as the hero of its resolution. "I'll take care of it" had become a sardonic mantra around the office.

I sat down with Rossi for what I anticipated would be a civilized meeting. We both wore suits, drank coffee, carried notebooks, and hauled binders cluttered with material. But then Rossi opened his mouth. "Hard times, buddy. Security Pacific is in hard times."

Immediately it was clear that some of the social graces eluded him. Rather than discuss loan issues in a straightforward manner, Rossi began with a hardcore slam. As we reviewed classified loans and discussed Credit Department personnel, Rossi sucked in the air, pursed his lips, clacked his binder, and thumped his fist against the surface of the table.

Maybe he was bored, but at some point the conversation took a perverse turn. "Bob," he grinned, "last year our corporate bank outgrew you guys three to one."

Minutes later he asked, "How much did Security Pacific make last year versus Bank of America?"

"Christ, Mike, the numbers are right in front of you. I think you know the answer to that question. We had a very rough year."

"Rough ain't the word for it."

"Our people aren't that stupid. I promise you we are able to distinguish greenbacks from subway tokens."

"Let's hope."

"Hopefully," he continued, "experience teaches you to recognize a mistake once you've made it."

I found myself in a Zen-like quotation contest with Rossi. "Mike, the trouble with using experience as a guide is that the final exam always comes before the lesson."

"That is a problem: good judgment comes from experience, and your loan portfolio comes from bad judgment." Rossi found his own comment hilarious and wise. Later, in an offhand but perceptive manner, Rossi compared the comingling of our respective banks to Charles Dickens's subtextually abundant portrait of the French Revolution. "You know the book *A Tale of Two Cities?* Our situation here is really *A Tale of Two Banks.*" I was intensely curious to know which aspect of this merger summoned to Rossi's mind that particular novel. Was it simply the irresistible title? Or maybe it was that spectacular opening sentence, which perfectly articulated the paradox of the merger: "It was the best of times, it was the worst of times, it was the age of wisdom, it was the age of foolishness, it was the epoch of belief, it was the epoch of incredulity, it was the season of Light, it was the season of Darkness, it was the spring of hope, it was the winter of despair, we had everything before us, we had nothing before us. . . . " Or, was it perhaps that the famous story culminates in such enormous tragedy?

In any event, when this meeting terminated, I felt like the recipient of forty lashes. If there had been one moment of substance it had eluded me; I felt that I'd wasted a plane ride and the better part of a day. Unfortunately, this was only the first in an unpleasant succession of what Binkley and I would refer to as "woodshed sessions."

As I drove back to the airport, I tried to understand what I had just seen. Like a remote-control sledgehammer, Rossi had made it his vocation to remind us that Security Pacific was in trouble. I was worried that he might be speaking badly about Security Pacific to his colleagues and, in so doing, poisoning the well. Finally, I wondered if Rosenberg knew the way Rossi felt about Security Pacific and, if so, what he thought about it.

▼

Around this time an unforeseen development added new complications to the enterprise. His name was Joseph E. Vaez. Vaez was Bank of America's assigned OCC examiner; his mandate had been expanded to include Security Pacific and he was now our primary OCC examiner in charge, concurrently fulfilling that same role for Bank of America.

I felt this was a peculiar move—to widen a San Francisco bank detective's jurisdiction to include our major southern California bank, particularly at a time when we were involved in a gigantic deal with the other preeminent bank over which he had oversight. While this may not technically have constituted a conflict of interest, I felt joint-purview might color the way Vaez dealt with Security Pacific.

In short order, my fears were realized.

His current examination of Security Pacific had commenced. Vaez was young and ambitious. He labored to convey his desire to help us and facilitate the merger in an orderly way. But following early encounters he quickly began to castigate upper management, ridicule our loan portfolio, and criticize the morale of our employees. Of course morale was low; his observations were hardly late-breaking news. He seemed not to comprehend that our precarious financial state was our prevailing concern. Wasn't this obvious? How could he not understand that these factors had precipitated the merger?

Vaez behaved as if Security Pacific had no idea it was in trouble, and that upper management had done nothing about it. He ignored the fact of the merger, and made no attempt to conceal the fact he had arbitrarily decided it was time to slam the door on Security Pacific. He sailed in like a knight prepared to slay the dragon and, finding the dragon already slayed, wanted to take credit for its demise. Without the knowledge and compassion a working history with Security Pacific might have engendered, he consigned and imputed recklessness to our organization from the top down.

Was Vaez a self-aggrandizing opportunist who wanted to make a splash in regulatory circles by piggybacking on the deterioration of Security Pacific? Was he trying, at this late date, to make himself look like the regulator who'd pressured Security Pacific to merge with Bank of America? Or perhaps he was merely executing orders from superiors in Washington. Damned if we knew. All we knew for sure was that a man called Vaez had swept into prominence, positioned himself like a cow pie between Security Pacific and Bank of America, and that it was our job not to step in the mess he was prepared to make.

13

By Whatever Means Available

On Friday, October 11, Jerry Grundhofer, Nick Binkley, John Kooken, Russ Freeman, and Dick Heilman, executive vice president of Risk, Compliance, Control, and Valuation, and myself flew to San Francisco aboard the Citation II for a joint meeting with the Federal Reserve Board and members of the OCC.

We arrived in San Francisco around noon for the 3:30 meeting with Federal Reserve officials for a scheduled review of the holding company and all of its subsidiaries, including the bank.

In light of our merger, I felt the meeting was probably unnecessary. I concluded that its purpose had to be for us to update federal regulators on the dynamics of the merger and expected them to be delighted by the fortuitous turn of events and to congratulate us on the consummation of a deal that would save them enormous time and anguish.

When we arrived at the Federal Reserve from the airport squeezed into taxi cabs, I was amazed to see a regulator named Don Chapman spying out at us through the ground floor window, shading his eyes. It was quite obvious to me what this was all about. He hungered to see if we would arrive in deluxe limousines amid extravagant fanfare; this would be incontrovertible evidence that we were not in touch with the reality of our situation and were living high on the hog in utter denial.

As we entered the lobby, Chapman greeted us and probably scanned our wrists for Rolex watches. Chapman was short, pleasant, and intelligent, but I felt he was wound too tight, even for banking. In the numerous visits I'd made to the Fed, I'd never in my life had a ground floor greeting. I felt a lump in my throat as we rose in the elevator; we were in for trouble. There would be no congratulations; no warm handshakes, back-slaps, or joyful accolades.

In the conference room we were met by a Napoleonic phalanx of regulators. We took our seats with six or seven Federal Reserve staff, including not only Chapman but Robert Parry, Tom Thompson, Gene Thomas, Terri Schwapkopf, and Mike Smith. Also present were Joe Vaez from the OCC and Wayne Hall from the FDIC. The mood was initially cordial but quickly turned dour, more appropriate to the viewing of a dignitary lying in state than to a regulatory review. After perfunctory introductions the meeting began.

We'd prepared a presentation, but before we could begin, Don Chapman began to speak and, in so doing, set the tone. "Mr. Smith, we've painstakingly reviewed and rereviewed your bank and have come to the conclusion that your bank continues to deteriorate."

No shit, I thought. *Good detective work, Ace Ventura!*

Chapman continued. "Your deterioration continues such that we now feel that you absolutely must make a concerted effort to increase the level of your capital to support these increasingly criticized loans."

Good God, I thought, as the meeting took on the absurdity of a Flannery O'Connor story. Did this man live in a cave? Didn't he read the newspapers or watch TV? Hadn't he heard the news? We had signed a definitive agreement to merge with Bank of America less than two months ago. With some wonderment I said, "Mr. Chapman, we just did raise capital."

"You just raised capital?"

I felt like saying, *Sure, you dipshit, about $6 billion*, but I held my tongue. "As I'm sure you are aware, we have a merger agreement with the Bank of America."

"The merger?"

Wait a minute, I thought, *these guys can't possibly be this stupid*. Something else had to be going on here. "Yes, Don, *the merger*. Capital is the point of the merger agreement. We want to merge with Bank of America, an institution that has a lot of capital. That is my solution to our capital weakness. We intend to combine a company without a lot of capital with a company with a lot of capital and, consequently, enhance our capital."

"I understand that," Chapman said, "but what if the merger doesn't take place for some reason or another?"

"We have an agreement that can only be broken in the event of a material adverse change. Bank of America has thoroughly reviewed our assets. Believe me, they've seen everything. I feel relatively safe in saying that, barring some Act of God, we have successfully raised capital by merging with the best-capitalized bank around."

Chapman glanced at his associates at the Fed. Then he returned his gaze to me. "Merger aside, we still believe Security Pacific has to raise capital."

I glanced at my team in dismay, then looked back at Chapman. "Maybe I'm missing something. I don't understand the logic." Capital was hard to come by. If I could have plucked capital out of my asshole like violets out of a bouquet I would have done so. "Don, can you give me one solid reason why the merger won't happen?"

"Because you don't have enough capital."

I felt like I was trying to explain trigonometry to a turnip. "That is why we're doing the merger—to get capital. Bank of America fully recognizes our financial status and they want to go forward."

The humidity in the room seemed to levitate in direct proportion to the rising tension. Don's neck turned bright red, as it often did when he became irritated. "Mr. Smith, what if there are complications?"

"I can't imagine what could go wrong under the circumstances, but *if* that should occur then we will raise capital, and you probably won't have me to kick around anymore because I'll be gone. Let me add parenthetically, if you want to kill this merger deal, force us to raise capital. I don't think you want to be responsible for the collapse of this deal, do you?" I looked around the table for some inkling of recognition, some comprehension of the truth I was speaking. I saw nothing.

Chapman sighed; his neck continued to brighten, approaching the hue of a Jalapeño pepper. "If the deal falls through, then what will you do about capital?"

"If the merger doesn't happen, and I have every reason to believe it will, then we'll *raise* capital."

"How?"

"We'll create a contingency strategy so that, in the event the deal falls apart, we have a plan to raise capital. Will that alleviate your concerns?"

Chapman looked at his superiors, then turned back to the Security Pacific team. "Sounds good." Then he threw us another curve. "Notwithstanding the fact we accept your plan to give us a plan on how you would raise capital if this deal falls through, we feel you should further augment your loan loss reserves."

"Pardon me?" I cocked my head in disbelief. I thought I heard one of my associates gasp.

"Mr. Smith, we feel it is essential that you significantly increase your reserve for loan losses in view of the continuing deterioration of your loan portfolio and the increases in your criticized assets."

Once again, he was making no sense. Binkley shook his head, stared down at the table. Jerry Grundhofer was staring at Chapman as if bewildered by an apparition. I hardly knew what to say. "Mr. Chapman, let me get this straight. You want me to arbitrarily move a large amount of money into reserves, at *this* point? After we've signed a merger agreement?"

Chapman nodded.

"If I don't increase capital, and our protection is the capital on the reserves, what honest-to-god difference does it make whether the money is in the capital account or the reserve account? The net result is exactly the same."

"Well, I know, but we want to see it in the reserve account."

"You want me to shuffle money into reserves so that you can remind the world what a big problem we have. This is a regulator-sanctioned exercise in self-humiliation, is that right?"

Chapman shrugged.

"You recognize, I'm sure, that Security Pacific is a public corporation and, as such, is a regulated institution that reports its financial status on an ongoing basis and whose reserve adequacy methodologies were long ago blessed not only by our accountants but by you and other regulators. Now, for me to arbitrarily move funds from the capital account to the reserve for loan losses account could make it look like we are publicly misrepresenting the status of the company."

"We want considerably more reserves, in case the deal falls through."

That's not what he wants, I thought. *He wants me to look like a bumbling idiot.* I carefully tried to articulate the paradox of what they were asking me to do. "Respectfully, this makes no sense. You're asking me to take money out of my right-hand pocket and put it into my left-hand pocket."

"Will you do as we ask?"

"I will promise only that we will review our methodologies. Rest assured, we will do only what is appropriate to maintain the integrity and accurate reporting of the balance sheet of our corporation."

One of the federal regulators piped up: "What do you mean by that?"

"I mean, honest to god, we have an adequate level of reserves based on our methodology. To shift that kind of money arbitrarily will bring a lawsuit."

"What do you mean, *lawsuit?*"

"The shareholders will think we've been dishonest. And you know Wall Street has ears. An analyst like George Salem reads that we've suddenly slid a billion dollars into reserves, he goes to Bank of America and says, 'What the hell are you doing, are you crazy, buying a piece of shit like Security Pacific?' The rumor mill starts churning and then Bank of America's stock drops. This will have huge repercussions. There has to be some rationale to your madness. I have to be intellectually honest with the investors on the street who are going to wonder why in the hell I would put one nickel more into reserves than our methodology requires. It's going to be mighty hard to explain why I'm mindlessly shoving a big hunk of money into reserves after I've cut a merger deal with one of the best-capitalized banks in the world. If we go along with you on this, any fallout is your responsibility."

The meeting concluded with my promise to the Federal Reserve to come up with a plan to raise capital in the event that the merger should fall through.

Their message was loud and clear: *Mr. Smith, you have screwed up this bank and now you must pay.*

▼

The next day, I huddled with Binkley, Grundhofer, Kooken, and Freeman to review our third-quarter numbers. They were awful.

"This," I said, forsaking understatement, "is as bad a quarter as I've ever seen."

Nick's expression intensified. "We have to follow the advice of Abraham Lincoln: 'Among your troops walk without fear.' We must not let them see the whites of our eyes."

Binkley was tough, Freeman was steady, and Kooken was a tank; I believed that come what may, they could put forward the steadied serenity of reason. Even Jerry Grundhofer, who on occasion became agitated during periods of uncertainty, was committed to keeping a positive face.

Following this triad of events—Fed meeting, third-quarter results, and doomsday session—my view had darkened. I sensed that the momentum was so fiercely against Security Pacific—not just the autonomy of the organization but against its independence—that we had to do this deal, even if it meant acquiescing to Rosenberg and his bank on nearly every decision. If the deal was to collapse, the confluence of opinion and action alone made it inconceivable that I could ever find another merger partner. In order to get this deal done, we were crippling ourselves. The transaction was devouring our capital as there was a greater and greater demand for reserves. Once recalibrated, our loan portfolio could not be uncalibrated.

We also had the added exposure of Bank of America's bleak view of our credit portfolio. This was a one-ton block of granite balanced on the backbone of an emaciated mule— bad PR that no disinformation campaign could achieve. If the deal collapsed, we would be living under that cloud, that stigma of failure.

This deal *had* to go through.

Over the weekend, I rethought what had transpired at our meeting with the Federal Reserve, and reconsidered the validity of their insistence that we further append our reserves. My personal irritation at Don Chapman was largely responsible for my refusal to accede with his suggestions. I realized that I—all of us—would have to be very careful not to let emotion be our guide in the heat of the moment. What I had done at that meeting was yield to irritation. Like a drunken picador waving a red veronica at a furious bull, I had tempted fate, angered the very people who most needed to be appeased.

I'd screwed up.

In the calm light of day I thought it was probably wise to review our methodology with an eye toward increasing our reserves and positioning ourselves more in line with Bank of America. Our banks were like two airplanes trying to dock in the sky. Security Pacific had to get up to speed.

While it was true that I had an obligation to the shareholders and the public, because of the impending merger, I also had an obligation to Bank of America. An abrupt shift in methodology was not something a bank undertook overnight, or lightly, but if any institution ever had good cause to change its reserve methodology, it was Security Pacific.

▼

I met with John Kooken and our accountants to discuss the Federal Reserve's request. "It sounds like a sick joke, but they're not kidding around. By the same token, we have to be straight with the public. We have to review our reserving methodology. What I suggest is that we establish a methodology to gradually adopt Bank of America's way and, in the natural course of events, bolster our reserves. Then the Fed is happy, Rosenberg is happy, and the transition and systems coordination will be that much easier."

Kooken didn't believe this would be difficult. "It doesn't have to be all or nothing. We can do this in increments and move in the direction of a methodology that is consistent with that of Bank of America."

"It's the rational thing to do. Ultimately, we are going to be part of that organization. And even if we aren't, it isn't a bad idea insofar as it sets exceedingly high standards for credit classifications."

"The only downside," Kooken believed, "is that an abrupt switch will result in the appearance that we anticipate a lot of losses."

"Well, John, we *will* have a lot of losses."

Nick said, "I think Stephen King once wrote, 'You can't polish a turd.'"

"We've already done a lot of the groundwork," I said. "Let's hold our nose and make the changeover."

Using the revised methodology, we reported a third-quarter net loss of $4.10 per common share, compared to net income of $1.05 reported for the same period the year prior. In the accompanying press release, I expressed our disappointment with the numbers but stressed the need to bolster reserves for anticipated adverse economic conditions. "Our ratio of the reserve to nonperforming loans now ranks third highest of the ten largest bank holding companies."

That same day I issued a board-approved statement announcing, in conjunction with our poor third-quarter results, that we would, accordingly—and in order to conserve capital and intelligently leverage our resources—eliminate the dividend on common stock. The dividend suspension was an especially sensitive issue with enormous symbolic and historical significance; for shareholders—and those who measured those intangible signals of decay—it was perhaps the single most ominous beacon of forthcoming change. All Security Pacific common shareholders would, however, receive dividends following the merger with Bank of America and the conversion of their stock to Bank of America common stock.

For nearly one solid year we had struggled with a handful of core issues; asset quality improvement, reduced credit approval authorities, risk culture retraining, resolution of problem credits, and tracking of regulatory compliance measures.

And yet, we were just barely keeping our head above water. I was disappointed that we had so little to show for our efforts.

▼

I phoned Rosenberg to report on our board's response to the new pre-Vaez OCC report critical of Security Pacific's management. "Dick, I had a fruitful discussion yesterday with our board about the report. In spite of the ongoing credit deterioration, individually our bank operations continue to be fairly well regarded. But you won't see many kind words when you read the cover report, which is very critical of management and our board." I assured him we were taking steps to resolve problems exposed in the report. "But frankly I was surprised by its negative tone and flavor."

"How did your meeting last Friday with the San Francisco Fed go?"

I told him the meeting had been somewhat contradictory. "They believe our holding company performance this year is not as good as in previous periods. This overview, however, is in some conflict with the pre-Vaez OCC bank report we just received. Joe Vaez," I went on, "noted during the meeting that he sees Security Pacific somewhat differently. His view is much bleaker and this is where he diverges from the recent report. Joe admitted that his opinion doesn't necessarily echo the view of his superiors."

So as not to unduly alarm Rosenberg, I did not mention the prolonged discussion on capital shuffling.

▼

Richard Flamson III died at 1:00 P.M. on October 17. His wife and family were with him when he died. Although Dick had been ailing for years, it was difficult to accept that his valiant battle was over. He had fought so hard for so long, and there were moments when I simply did not think anything could kill that man. We all knew this moment would come, but no amount of mental preparation could assuage the loss. Not only had I lost a confidant and mentor, but an important ally. I would miss the comfort of his advice and sharp wit in the months ahead.

Flamson was the one who put Security Pacific on the map. Under his guidance we had pushed the walls of the bank away from the vault and for one brief moment captured the imagination of the corporate world.

I would miss the braggadocio, the irreverence, the candor, and the guts. I thought his epitaph should read: "Hell, we coulda bought Bank of America if we really wanted—but *nah.*"

▼

In New York a pathetic melodrama began to unfold.

Dick Griffith arrived spry and eager for a shakeup with his team of ace pathologists and immediately went to work dissecting Sequor. Michael Caggiano had taken a disability leave due to a heart condition, and in his absence Tom Connaghan and Sal Ricca continued to operate Sequor on high octane; they knew of the merger but had no reason to suspect that the operation was a candidate for complete renovation.

Griffith and his squad culled through files, probed computer hard drives, examined the operations, and fired off questions. Within days, Sequor's executives were calling Los Angeles to complain. Sal Ricca was fit to be tied. "This fellow Griffith is not performing a due diligence; he's issuing pompous proclamations on how we should run our business. He is in waters way, way over his head."

Connaghan was sickened. "Griffith is a full-blown jerk. Everything we do here that makes money, he wants to kick out of the equation. They're gonna kill it."

"Head office horseshit," said Connaghan. "If Griffith is going to interject himself into the running of Sequor we can basically kiss the success of this operation good night."

▼

Nevertheless, Griffith returned from his fact-finding mission with a pot of ideas. Rosenberg and I sat down with him. Nick Binkley was in attendance because I had transferred jurisdiction of Sequor to him.

"I believe," Griffith said, "that I've located the core problem and it revolves around two issues, two centralities: the people, and the procedures."

"Is that all?" I asked.

"We need to de-entrepreneurize Sequor, slam on the brakes, put more controls on it, change what they do and how they do it."

"That doesn't make a whole lot of sense," I said. "You can only install so many rules and so much oversight before you kill the spirit and profit of the thing. Sequor is a high-volume, low-risk operation. As for personnel, the people who run Sequor *are* Sequor. Without them you don't get a safer operation; you get an empty building."

Rosenberg lifted his hands, palms out, and scuttled them. "I don't think we intend to *kill* Sequor. We want to compress it and bring it within Bank of America's parameters, its framework, its policies and culture."

Griffith sat forward. "What we really don't want is problems with the regulators. Sequor pushes the envelope too far."

"Yes, Sequor pushes the envelope. I told you Sequor pushes the envelope; that's the business, that's what they do. That is what's *special* about it. Caggiano, Ricca, Connaghan—these guys are entrepreneurs. They're experts at what they do."

Griffith winced. "The regulators squint at Sequor."

"Sure the regulators squint at Sequor—if regulators aren't watching Sequor, then Sequor is probably not running on all cylinders."

"So you're admitting that they are kind of wild," Griffith said with a silly wink.

"I'm admitting nothing of the sort. They're just smart businesspeople. They're enormously successful, they make a lot of money, and they know when to get in and out of a business. It's a hunch and gut operation—timing, networking, personal relationships. Who are you going to find to replace them? You can't just nab that kind of intuition off any street corner. They created this business."

"That may be so, but we feel Sequor is out—way out—on a limb."

I listened with sad nostalgia as Griffith described his "vision" for a postmerger Sequor. He painted with words a Normal Rockwell portrait of a "safe and sane" lending operation populated with short-hairs and white-shirts. "By the books, in the spirit of the law, no weird things."

When he was finished, my stomach growled. In my mind's eye I watched the sun set behind Sequor. I sensed that Bank of America had an aversion to anything it could not understand, and by definition the unknown posed risk—and Bank of America hated anything having to do with risk. Unfortunately, Sequor epitomized all of the above.

Rosenberg asked me what I thought. "Don't you find his argument compelling?"

He left a silence for me to fill; I hardly knew where to begin. "Frankly, it sounds like the objective is to scrub Sequor."

Griffith disagreed. "No, not scrub it. Just remove the elements of risk and the practices that stretch regulatory law."

"The people will leave."

"If the people leave, that's their decision."

In other words, scrub Sequor.

I probably sighed. "Naturally, you can do what you want. But Sequor makes $60 million for us after-tax. It's the goose that laid the golden egg. You're valuing it at approximately half a billion dollars. You want to nebulize it. It's one thing for you to come in and run Sequor by your standards—and they may be tougher and safer than ours—but my advice to you is not to bother, because you'll just destroy the business. And if your new standards are going to destroy Sequor, I would rather that we sell it. What's the use of taking a profitable operation and turning it into an unprofitable operation? It would be just another clearing house. Let's at least get value out of it for the sake of the company going forward."

Rosenberg rocked back and forth in his chair. "Of course I'll take that into consideration."

▼

Outside the Bank of America headquarters, Nick and I paused near a 15-foot, pitch-black sculpture in the shape of a human heart. The cement sculpture was known in the financial district as "The Banker's Heart."

Nick shook his head. "Without Sequor, I'll have one less thing to worry about."

"No guts," I lamented. "No one could ever accuse Bank of America of having a spare pair of *cajones*."

It reminded me of an unpublished poem, a raunchy ode Hemingway had written to one of his contemporaries. The apt title of the poem made its point: *Lines To Be Read at the Casting of Scott Fitzgerald's Balls into The Sea.* This adequately captured what most frustrated me about Bank of America. Its fear was going to kill our stars.

"It's such a risk-averse, committee-laden bureaucracy," I complained.

"Bob, perhaps I'm painting with too broad a brush, but at times it seems Rosenberg is unwilling to draw any distinction between operations that are a little unique or offbeat and operations that are genuinely risky; if it is too complex for him to understand it has to be risky and therefore had to be jettisoned. It's a false tautology."

▼

The November cover of *Banker's Monthly* resembled a tombstone: *The Curtain Comes DOWN on Security Pacific.* The article, authored by Los Angeles Times staff writer Tom Furlong, was an elaboration of his previous article for the

Los Angeles Times. It was elegiac in its acknowledgment of Security Pacific's past but relentless in its pursuit of blame. This was one in a series of mainstream analyses that began to rip the veneer of equality off the merger.

Furlong began, "The past year will likely rank as the saddest and concluding chapter in the history of Security Pacific, the once-noble banking house that has been an establishment mainstay in Los Angeles throughout much of the twentieth century. . . . " Furlong likened the merger to a "takeover or rescue operation" and lamented the disappearance of the Security Pacific name.

"Security Pacific officials strongly deny that the merger amounts to a rescue operation by Bank of America. 'We did not have a gun at our head,' said Richard Flamson, a Security Pacific director and retired chief executive. 'We did not do this because we had to.' According to Flamson, Security Pacific had been searching for a merger partner for several years and had held talks with several financial institutions."

Like the article in its embryonic form, the feature relied on unattributed sources—"some say . . . "—to paint a merciless portrait of an organization out of control.

Business reporters understood that Bank of America and the regulatory community kept abreast of such views. The accumulative effect would be continued pressure on Security Pacific and myself to resolve our problems the Bank of America way.

▼

That afternoon I phoned Rosenberg, who wanted to hear the details of my morning meeting with Mayor Bradley and Councilman Ridley-Thomas. "They are concerned, naturally, about the impact the merger will have on South Central. There's a lot of emotionalism attached to this issue that has nothing to do with the reality of the impact a bank merger has on people. The hyperbole is as much to blame: mega-merger, consolidation, layoffs. The words are loaded with subtext and the people are scared. I assured Bradley we wouldn't abandon our communities. But I think there will be angry people."

We agreed we should prepare ourselves for the eventuality of citizen groups politicizing the deal.

"Dick, the Fed is going to take its time with this deal because it is so huge and there are so many concerns. I'm beginning to doubt we can close the deal by the end of February."

"Maybc not, but let's keep that as our target."

14

Brinksmanship

Every morning I thanked God that I at least had the merger deal in my pocket, but I was haunted by the knowledge that if the California economy fell into the Pacific Ocean— or if local or national government stepped forward with any more legislative "quick fixes" that were lethal injections in disguise—Dick Rosenberg might have second thoughts and try to break the engagement. For this reason—and because the market gyrations I was seeing were precursive of a broader economic disaster—I continued to seek the recognition and assistance of anyone in a position to help stabilize California. Strangely, I wasn't sure our politicians understood what was happening. And I wasn't alone.

I was a member of the California Business Roundtable, an association of the one hundred largest companies in the state. We met routinely to discuss the kaleidoscope of issues that faced California. As fate would have it, I was the chairperson of the public policy subcommittee, which dealt directly with state government policy.

The Roundtable arrived at a consensus: we had to face Governor Pete Wilson head on. Wilson's staff had predicted 3% job growth for 1991. Who was he kidding?

How could he lead this state or even decide what was best for California business if he didn't understand or, worse, ignored the realistic, front-line outlook of the very people in the best position to know?

As chairman of the subcommittee, I was chosen to meet with Governor Wilson and his staff, along with other members of the committee. Our goal: encourage the governor to implore business to remain in California and to actively solicit new business to move to California. We would urge Wilson to mount a counteroffensive against governors from the south and states as nearby as Oregon and Utah who sought to entice business away from California.

We arrived at this crucial meeting prepared. Our attitude was upbeat, our agenda ambitious, and our case solid. We felt our recommendations were logical, achievable, and in everyone's best interest.

Wilson entered. Before the first word had been spoken, he seemed impatient to leave. He sat on the corner of his chair, knee gyrating, one foot pointed at the door and his eye fixed on the wall clock behind me. "Morning, gentlemen."

Governor Wilson is not like a Keating or a Trump. He could slump past you on a street corner without you ever knowing you'd been in the proximity of leadership. His posture is feeble and no one will ever accuse Wilson of speaking with great conviction.

But what we had going for us, we thought, was common sense and the greater interest of California.

We introduced ourselves. Governor Wilson was familiar with the Roundtable but our presence did not appear to exhilarate him. Perhaps we had caught him at an inopportune time. Animated by his impatience, I rapidly explained our concerns and proposed our solutions. Wilson squinted at me as if through dense fog.

When I alluded to his participation in our plan, he abruptly interrupted me. His cheeks puffed and his face went red as he addressed us in a peremptory tone, almost as if he was censuring pet dogs that had yipped at a head of state. "You don't even need to tell me. I am very well aware of all that," he said in a condescending rasp. "What you probably *don't* realize is that the real culprit here is not the governor's office, it's not even the economy. You know who it is? It's Willie Brown," he revealed. Mr. Brown was the Speaker of the Assembly, an entrenched and powerful African-American Democratic legislator with a vociferous share of supporters and detractors. "Willie Brown, with his distinctly strong liberal bias, is at constant odds with me."

For the next fifteen minutes it was *Willie Brown this* and *Willie Brown that.* "It's all Willie Brown's fault," Wilson continued. "He holds the key to all our problems in the palm of his hand and he will not let go." To believe Wilson's lament, all that had ever gone wrong in the state of California was directly traceable to the nefarious designs of Willie Brown.

Governor Wilson's tirade handily filled the time he'd allotted for our meeting. Rather than discuss the impact of a wan economy on state business, we watched as Governor Wilson raised his voice, cleared his throat, hemmed and hawed, screwed up his face, and damned everything there was to damn about Willie Brown. "He's the villain in this sad charade. Now if you'll excuse me."

"Governor, one more moment of your time, if I may." Innocently believing there was no problem that could not be solved by reasonable people who put their minds to it, I foolishly suggested we include Willie Brown in our discussions. "If Mr. Brown is the obstacle, let's sit down with him and calmly hash out these problems. Certainly we can agree on some reasonable steps. Liberal or Conservative, it's in no one's best interest—not even Willie Brown's—for the state economy to collapse."

"You don't know Willie Brown." Again, Wilson shot for the exit.

"Governor, why on earth would anyone stand in the way of a plan whose purpose is to keep jobs in California? Certainly there are partial solutions—trim redundancy, streamline government, a stimulus package?"

"You don't understand," Wilson bellowed. "You have no idea who Willie Brown is or what he's capable of. That man is impossible. There's no talking to him. There's nothing you can do, nothing I can do, nothing *anybody* can do about Willie Brown." Again, the door. "It was a real pleasure speaking with you gentlemen."

Wilson spun around like a wind-up toy when I made a final appeal. "Governor, forgetting about Willie Brown for one second, we think you should make a visible effort to get behind the business community. Would you consider personal involvement in a program to keep jobs in California, or perhaps establish a staff operation whose aim is to attract new employers to the state?"

Wilson shook his head. "The economy, according to my staff, is certainly on the mend, and we have that to look forward to. And I've got too many other initiatives to fight right now."

Well. We thanked him, and he pushed us out of the room as quickly as he could without appearing rude.

My colleagues and I briefly lamented the time and effort we'd put into our presentation. I felt we had wasted our time.

▼

That afternoon we mailed a proxy statement and prospectus to shareholders of both corporations describing the rationale for the merger and urging them to consider and vote for the deal. Shareholders were to return their ballots by mail or bring them in person to special meetings of the shareholders to be held by both companies on December 19.

What most frightened me was the adamantine posture the regulators had assumed; they stood in direct opposition to Security Pacific's continued viability as a sovereign and self-reliant corporation. Between the lines, Don Chapman and his colleagues had made it clear not only in our October meeting but in further discussions that Security Pacific should perish, and that because I was at the helm when it sank, I should perish with it. They wanted a scalp, someone to blame.

I knew I had to go straight to the board of directors and tell them what I felt was going on, and convince them—if they needed convincing—that if anything crushed the merger, they would absolutely have to do something I really didn't want to contemplate.

At our November 19 board meeting, following a solemn tribute to Dick Flamson, I brought directors up to date and apprised them of Jimmy Barton's departure and Joe Vaez's instatement as our new OCC examiner.

The implorations of regulators and Bank of America that we shuffle more and more money into reserves had damaged and would continue to damage Security Pacific's earnings substantially more than any economy could. I laid our financial state out on the table.

"The California economy, as we know, has not stabilized and continues to slide. We are projecting an increase in non-performing loans to $2.7 billion at the end of this quarter, with a potential slide to $3.5 billion by the end of first quarter 1992." I cleared my throat before discussing criticized assets. "Our classified assets are $15 billion on a portfolio of $55 billion."

"Wow," Boswell said. "Those are some ugly numbers."

"I know it."

"Where do we stand with the OCC and the Fed?"

"Jim, the regulators are sending very mixed signals. While as far as I can tell they support the merger, they are not supportive of Security Pacific. You've seen the reports and what is clear is that they want to send us out with a bang. They are not giving us Brownie points for our diligence, and nothing we do seems to appease them. Their view seems to be that we cannot possibly survive without the merger, but by no stretch of the imagination are they making the road any easier. They've chosen, for whatever reason, to tighten the screws. I would say that a couple of regulators are overtly hostile to management. We will naturally do everything we can to address their concerns, but our immediate goal, pure and simple, has to be the consummation of this deal."

Boswell grunted. "Can the deal be blown? What could blow the deal?"

"Only something I don't now see and can't imagine."

Another director looked befuddled. "Did you say the regulatory oversight has intensified *since* the agreement to merge was announced?"

"It's worse than ever. Every time a regulator slips on a banana peel, we get dinged for it. And I'm really feeling the pressure. With each loan we write off I appear to have less and less credibility with them as a person who can solve our problems. The most critical issue I have on my plate is to keep this deal alive—to get it done. I think we have the deal. And I feel almost certain that if for some unforeseen reason the deal doesn't go through, it won't be a result of credit deterioration—and that was at one time my chief fear. But we have continued to deteriorate. This deal is chewing up a lot of our capital, and we're down to the wire.

"The truth is that if the merger falls through, we, you, all of us, have a lot bigger problem than simply that a deal fell apart.

"The point I'm getting to is that our state is so tenuous, and the regulators are taking such a bleak view of me, personally, that should this deal fail to close by April, you—this board—will have no alternative but to fire me and bring in someone new. You'll have no choice. You'll *have* to fire me. Even if it's to sell assets and turn out the lights."

Their faces were serious and somber. The board was not

hearing anything from me that they didn't already know, but to hear it from the horse's mouth was a shock even to directors who knew me well.

"With someone else at the helm, Security Pacific will have a much better chance of navigating the stormy waters ahead. The media, the regulators, the Street—they could take a step back to catch their breath. This bank, or what is left of it, could, I think, go forward and do what it has to do to survive with new leadership."

Boswell scowled. "Who would we bring in?"

"Somebody with a track record. Somebody who maybe has the reputation as a bailout man. Somebody that Wall Street and the regulators trust."

"Somebody who can raise the dead," said another director.

"Most important, somebody who can raise capital and protect our ability to fund ourselves."

While no one said his name, I knew who some of them were pondering: Frank Cahouet. An obvious choice, Frank was intimately familiar with the nuts and bolts of our corporation. Like the Ghost of Hamlet's father—or, more aptly, Christmas Past, Present, and Future—that name had stalked me for ten years. He was either my superior, my competitor, my possible replacement, or my successor.

To a lesser degree, Frank would be like our Tom Clausen. We could 'bring the old man back,' so to speak, like Bank of America did, and spin it that way to the regulators and to Wall Street.

The meeting ended with each board member walking out of the room fully cognizant of the importance of completing the deal and directly facing issues of survival they never really wanted to contemplate. For my part, I felt I had laid it all on the table and drawn a line in the sand.

▼

On Monday, November 25, a bomb dropped in my lap, but didn't go off—yet.

"We'd better investigate this. The last thing we need now is to find out we are breaking the law," I told Maurice DeWolff, who along with Russ Freeman, had just arrived in my office to inform me that they had grave misgivings about the discovery of a potential, very complicated violation of law at Sequor.

What had happened?

In August of 1991, just before the signing of the merger agreement, Security Pacific completed an exhaustive internal audit of our securities lending operations at Sequor. One area of contention that arose from this audit was the suggestion that because we were running one of our securities lending armatures like a mutual fund, we may have been in violation of laws that restrict banks from operating mutual funds. Our auditors examined the transactions more closely and concluded that, while in all likelihood we were doing nothing unlawful, to be on the safe side it merited further attention.

In September, Sequor hired New York based attorneys to review the issue and resolve its legality once and for all. They issued their findings in October. They felt it was neither a violation of law nor a problem warranting further investigation.

I thought the issue had been put to bed. I was mistaken.

Trouble of a much greater magnitude emerged when Maurice DeWolff, chief counsel for our banking operations, grew distrustful of the opinion rendered by the attorneys. He found it superficial, shallow, and vague. DeWolff turned around and hired a another law firm based in New York—Millbank Tweed—that was a specialist in the area of securities law. Millbank Tweed promptly turned their attention to Sequor. Throughout October they conducted their examination and in November we received their findings. They concurred that the mutual fund issue was not a problem; however, in the course of their investigation they uncovered what may well have been a violation of Employee Retirement Income Security Act (ERISA) regulations.

ERISA is a law that defines the parameters for use of pension funds. It is designed to prevent the abuse of pension plan monies by the entities that manage or service them. Pension plans are regarded as sacred; penalties leveled against abusers are uniquely the domain of the Internal Revenue Service, and are swift and harsh. ERISA law is particularly averse to "self-dealing," described as any transaction in which the holder of the funds deploys them to his own financial benefit.

What Millbank Tweed was concerned with was a practice utilized by Sequor in its securities lending arm. Sequor had a number of pension accounts whose contents it used in overnight transactions for which it had not obtained the pension account administrator's authorization.

We were, in effect, taking loans we originated to other customers within Sequor and selling or lending them overnight to the pension accounts. These were transactions involving millions of dollars, and so habitual and second-nature to how Sequor operated that they were executed by employees far down in the Sequor hierarchy who perhaps did not even realize what they were doing. It is only a slight exaggeration to characterize them as administrative assistants.

In a typical example, Sequor would make a loan to finance Salomon Brothers overnight with Sequor funds secured by U.S. government securities. We would then sell or lend this loan to a pension account.

The logic behind this practice was sound. Ideally, customers want their money working for them twenty-four hours a day. This investment provided a safe and certain return to the pension account and, at the same time, allowed us to serve our borrowing customers at no risk. This was as good an investment as we could make on a short-term basis with the excess funds we held in the pension accounts.

Now, however, Maurice—a paunchy, vigilant, and relentlessly scrupulous attorney—sounded a cautionary alarm. "Millbank Tweed's assertion is that these transactions constitute self-dealing insofar as we took our own loans and sold them to our own pension account customers. Because the accounts in question are under the purview of ERISA—and because we did not obtain the explicit consent of the account holder—these might be construed as prohibited transactions and therefore very serious violations."

"Should we worry?" I asked him.

"I don't think we should worry, but I think we should be very, very concerned."

"What does that mean, Russ?"

"If this is a violation it can probably be resolved without overriding damage to the bank, and it might not jeopardize the merger."

This explanation did not reassure me. I immediately alerted our auditors and requested that they investigate the matter. I asked Maurice to contact me the second he or his legal staff concluded whether or not the transactions were ERISA violations, and what it meant for the merger.

▼

It was now December 5. We were two weeks away from the shareholder vote on the transaction. Attorneys Russ Freeman and Mike Halloran drafted a memo warning members of both corporate management committees to refrain from making any statements about the merger between now and December 19—the scheduled day of the vote—that could be construed as proxy solicitation statements. "The SEC could take action against the corporation and the individuals responsible for the statements. Among other things, the SEC might insist that the meeting be delayed."

Meanwhile, in preparation for the physical transition, Rosenberg and I widened the circle of managers who met regularly as a single team. This new cooperative was christened the combined joint management committee and included top executives and managers who would meet monthly in San Francisco.

We convened our first joint management committee meeting.

Binkley, Grundhofer, Kathy Burke, and I represented Security Pacific, with Rosenberg, Coleman, Newman, Rossi, and

Marty Stein representing Bank of America. Participants on both sides began to twist apart the nuts and bolts of Security Pacific and deliberate on the future of particular divisions and operations.

Rosenberg, Binkley, and I discussed FSS.

Rosenberg was pleased by the continuity shown by the FSS earnings stream and was inclined to keep it organizationally intact, with one reservation: in two decades of rampant activity, the only instance in which FSS had stumbled was in the United Kingdom, in the late 1980s when, at the behest of Flamson, one of its Eurofinance subsidiaries originated a flurry of third-tier pub and restaurant loans.

But this was not what most concerned Rosenberg, who then voiced the opinion that he disliked Manufactured Housing as a business. Manufactured Housing is the financing of the building and development of mobile homes. "I don't like it," Rosenberg announced. "Manufactured Housing is for the birds."

I discharged a small laugh. Security Pacific's Manufactured Housing operation was making $30 million a year after tax with a miniscule number of employees and very little capital. It had a 2% plus return on assets. "Dick, why don't you like Manufactured Housing?"

"Just don't. Never liked Manufactured Housing."

Binkley spoke. "As a point of interest, Manufactured Housing consistently makes a lot of money, is run by a very small group of people, requires low overhead, and generates strong returns you can depend on."

"I know, but I think we should get rid of it."

Rosenberg's answer didn't make sense. "Richard, just out of curiosity, why would you want to get rid of it?"

Rosenberg shrugged. He said he just hated that business. Couldn't stand it.

I looked at Nick and wondered if he was thinking the same thing I was: *Rosenberg's full of shit.*

Rather than sit and argue with him—Manufactured Housing had been a successful part of our business for years—we acquiesced. We had to change our psychological approach. We had to get into the spirit. We had to stop drawing lines in the sand, thinking *This is our business and it goes forward with the New Bank of America.* "Okay," I said, "If you don't like it, that's a right you have. We need to have a collection of activities that we all feel comfortable with going forward."

Binkley nodded. "Sell it, okay. But for god's sake, let's not kill it."

"Right," I said. "Let's not get angry at Manufactured Housing because it's no longer something we like. I feel confident that we can find a buyer who will pay up."

Rosenberg said he would give this serious thought.

Later, the joint committee meeting took an embarrassing turn when we introduced key executives to Bank of America management. The expressed purpose was a "meet and greet," but it was soon apparent that Mike Rossi, who did the bulk of the questioning, had another agenda in mind.

R. Harold Owens, chief executive officer of our Consumer Finance Company, was the first raw steak tossed into Rossi's pen. Moments after Harold took a seat, Rossi descended on Owens like a furious tornado, firing questions at him like a federal prosecutor trying to shed doubt on the credibility of a star witness. Rossi would ask for numbers and facts, spurring Owens to scan furiously through a binder clotted with statistics.

Rossi rushed him along. "I'm trying to pin you down on numbers."

"I'm trying to answer your questions, Michael."

"I asked you a simple question. Can't you give me that number?"

"I'm trying to find your numbers."

"Did you not come to this meeting prepared?"

"I'm entirely prepared, but I'm not a mind reader. Give me a moment." Owens rifled through a pack of papers, found whatever Rossi was looking for, and showed him a number highlighted in yellow. "Here are your numbers."

Rossi glanced at the figures. "Why is that number so high? Why is it higher than it should be? It's astronomical." Rossi exhaled. "Show me the loans from the first quarter of 1989. Let's compare. We here at Bank of America would never have a number like this, I can assure you."

More paper shuffling. Harold's composure began to fracture. His hand now trembling, he brought forth a list of loans. "Michael, these are the latest classifieds. Take it, find what you want."

Rossi snapped it up, gave it a cursory read-over. "Why on earth were you making loans to these people? Why are you making loans to this group? It doesn't make any sense. Where are the business loans?"

Under such pressure, Harold's customary eloquence gave way to halting and reluctant locution. He stammered, blinked, and shook his head in dismay. "They are handled by a different subsidiary."

"What subsidiary? Why are those loans handled by a different sub?"

"Michael, they just are. We have different operations to generate different types of loans." Owens's forehead glistened with perspiration; Rossi smelled panic and intensified his attack. Harold grew more and more traumatized. Rossi had nearly reduced the man to tears.

"You still haven't given me a clear answer," Rossi pummeled.

"Michael, I just run my own division. I can't tell you why other subsidiaries do this or that."

On and on it went. "How could you? How could you make this loan?"

Flustered and beleaguered, Owens gave up. Despondent, he stopped talking. His eyes fuzzed on a quadrant of numbers on the table between his hands.

I'd had it. "Time out," I said. "Mike, what are you doing?"

He seemed not to know what I referred to.

"You're ripping Harold apart."

Invoking the escape hatch of "Tough Love," he said, "I'm just being direct. My intent is not to harm."

I asked that the interview be terminated. Owens gathered his paperwork, took a deep breath, and left the conference room.

"Mike, this has got to stop. Harold doesn't work for you; he works for me. This is uncalled for. If you don't like Consumer Finance, we can discuss that. But you don't have the right to tell Harold what to do or how to do it. That's our business. We can adjust it as we move forward."

Rossi shrugged and looked at Rosenberg.

I looked at Rosenberg. "Dick, I'm not going to tolerate this. Harold Owens doesn't deserve this treatment. Harold has done a great job for us, is expected to do a fine job for the New Bank of America going forward, and what we don't need right now is to have him become discouraged and quit in disgust."

Rosenberg nodded, but my appeal fell on deaf ears. We took a short break. Rosenberg's admonitions to Rossi—if there were in fact any—had fleeting, but insufficient, effect. Like a naughty Doberman pinscher slapped on the nose, he would demure just long enough for it to be noticed by his master. His voice would soften, his criticism would abate, he'd suck his chest in and pay lip service to team spirit. Then, inevitably, he'd start to bark again.

The next bite-victim was Dick Madresh, chief executive officer of our Business Credit subsidiary. With slightly diminished intensity, Rossi heaped hyperbole and shame on one of our most diligent and productive managers. Gathering steam, Rossi leveled him with a shrill desecration of the loan portfolio. "You are looking at a high percentage of bad loans."

"That is yet to be decided."

"Oh? And who is going to decide it?"

"We'll decide it."

"Madresh, I've got to be honest with you: I don't understand Business Credit, but I do understand these numbers, and I've got to ask you how you can ever hope to generate profits?"

"Mr. Rossi, we generate profits every day."

Madresh hunched over his paperwork in the manner of a human fortress as Rossi censured, upbraided, and reprimanded him.

Right in front of everybody—peers, colleagues, and superiors. The casual "meet and greet" had transmuted into a Machiavellian monstrosity. And Rosenberg just sat there and watched; I did not understand how Rosenberg could tolerate it, or what this revealed about the relationship between Bank of America and Security Pacific, in the present and, most ominously, in the future.

Afterward, I was sick to my stomach. Nick and I grabbed a cup of coffee at a nearby bistro. I sighed. "So much for the spirit of bringing two families together. Rosenberg allows Rossi to get away with psychological homicide."

Binkley stirred his coffee. His take on Rossi was that Rossi was being protected. "He's Coleman's boy. Coleman was instrumental in luring Rossi from Wells Fargo. I think Coleman protects him. Rosenberg may want Rossi to say these things, create this environment. He articulates the things Rosenberg can't because of his position."

"To what possible purpose?"

"The more he breaks us down, the more concessions we'll make during the course of bringing our two companies together—because it's too painful to argue."

"But Rosenberg wants the deal."

"Yeah, but we *need* the deal. And he's aware of that."

▼

Late that afternoon I met separately with Rosenberg and told him that if he didn't like Consumer Finance, Manufactured Housing, or Business Credit, or couldn't tolerate the risk associated with them, we should sell them now, before the franchises were irreparably damaged, demoralized, or withered.

Rosenberg agreed.

"Second, we have to discuss the treatment of my people by Michael Rossi."

"What do you want me to do?"

"Put a muzzle on that pop-off. Humiliation is not the purpose of the joint committee meetings. Consumer Finance is still a Security Pacific business, and Harold Owens runs it, and I'm pleased with his performance. Rossi's got neither the cause nor the authority to denounce Harold Owens. It's obvious from Rossi's line of questioning that he doesn't even understand Consumer Finance. Now, if you guys don't like that business, we can discuss that separately; that's a business issue. But assailing my employees is far beyond the purview of this committee. And, Dick, if this doesn't stop, I'm simply not going to bring my people into these meetings."

"Did you think his explanation had merit—that he did not intend to hurt feelings?"

"Rossi apologized, and thirty minutes later he mauled Dick Madresh."

"I'll concede that his questioning was combative."

"Dick, refresh my memory if there is some provision in the agreement to merge that provides for the systematic abuse of our VPs." I appealed to Rosenberg's self-interest, pointing out that Security Pacific's managers would be of little use to him if they were all clinically depressed.

"Bob, I hear what you're saying. I agree with you on your point of view. But Michael Rossi is his own person. I don't know what I can do, or why I should curtail him in what he sees as his effort to do his job."

What a load of crap, I thought. The Rossi's-his-own-man excuse didn't fly with me. I didn't know how Bank of America worked, but at Security Pacific I was responsible for the conduct of my people.

On my way out of the building, I found a moment alone with Frank Newman. "Honest to god, Frank, how can you put up with this guy? He's intolerable."

Newman, who knew who I was referring to, just shook his head. He refused to say an unkind word about Rossi. "Bob, we know, but there's nothing much we can do about it. He's Rosenberg's guy."

But one thing was clear: I now understood the magnitude of difference between the cultures of our organizations. And it gave me insight into Rosenberg. Perhaps the most apt descriptions of Rosenberg came to me from analysts on the street who'd felt his pulse. I'd heard him characterized as "cherubic," "childlike," and "mischievous." He was pleasant enough to transact business with, but also reticent, reserved, and unwilling to lay his cards on the table. He never let the mask drop, even for a second. I found it impossible to discuss the passion of banking with him. Emotional issues were off limits. And *innovation* was not a word in his vocabulary. Neither was the phrase *individual autonomy*. On the Bank of America organizational chart you would not find diagrammed lines leading to individuals—you would see chains and chains of committees all reporting to Dick Rosenberg. No man or woman was referred to as an entrepreneur, unless it was in a pejorative context. No individual was given discretion to undertake change without the consent of a myriad of boards, auditors, and senior executives. The notion that a single person might be entrusted to use his or her own street smarts to run a Bank of America subsidiary or conscript individual talent was anathema to its corporate philosophy. When I spoke to Rosenberg about certain of our operations like Sequor and securities lending, or how I'd realized the value of allowing creative individuals to operate their subsidiaries and, within reasonable constraints, to do as they saw fit, it was as if I was speaking Croatian. Of that expressed thought he would have recognized perhaps one word: *constraints*.

▼

The detrimental effects of Rossi were such that Binkley, Grundhofer, and I realized we would do well to have a strategy exclusively to cope with these corporate mind-games, and we held a meeting solely to address this dilemma.

"This process is going to be rough—not logistically, but psychologically," I told Nick and Jerry. "There are a million ways this deal could collapse. Deals like this don't implode because of numbers; they crumble because of indiscreet slips of the tongue and harsh words spoken in the heat of the battle. It's the social matters, the psychological friction; it's panic and ego. And we're only human, and Rossi—or someone else—is bound to trigger some kind of explosion unless we swear an oath—a covenant—among ourselves to put up with it."

"Sometimes it is excruciating," Nick said.

"I know. It's humiliating."

"It's Rossi," said Jerry.

I didn't disagree. "But the bottom line is: Bank of America has to win. They've gotta win. We are on the edge. We cannot risk blowing this deal. It's hard, because we are in discussions all day long with these people on a multitude of issues. We are in discussions twelve hours a day on how our company looks, how it will combine, how it looks going forward."

"Security Pacific," Nick realized aloud, "will look to them the way they want it to look."

"Unfortunately, it is in our self-interest that we look just as bad as they want us to." I suggested we adopt a philosophy of passive acquiescence. "Our interests are synergistic but *not* identical. We are the weaker of the two parties. This process is embarrassing, and it hurts your feelings, and it's sometimes unfair." My point: we had to take the high road. We had to choose the long-term benefits of general solicitude over the transient gratification of a wisecrack or fistfight. "Never lose sight of the desired goal."

"We need capital," said Nick, "and this is a way to get it that has almost no downside."

"Jerry—we must absorb this bad feeling because the deal has to go through."

"But," Jerry said with emotion, "this is no longer a merger of equals; it's a sale, it's an acquisition. We've lost our footing."

But I still believed—I wanted desperately to believe—that following this merger Security Pacific would exist as a force in the forward momentum of Bank of America. But were we deluding ourselves? "We'll have to give up some things, but if Security Pacific still has a voice when this is complete—equal board representation, a handful of our best subs and executives in high places—I'll feel that it was a merger of equals."

Jerry was not appeased. "We have to sit there and take it? I mean, can we *never* question *anything* they say?"

"No. I think we should disagree openly. Be plainspoken and firm. Challenge them, debate them with the facts, make your case. But if they disagree, then at the end of the day Bank of America has got to win these disputes. If they start *losing* arguments they may grow skittish and take a harder look at us in an effort to find some rationale for sidestepping the transaction."

Nick made a good point. "The way I look at it, if we can keep Bank of America busy with the divestiture of subsidiaries, we can keep their minds off the credit difficulties."

Jerry was now on board. "Our goal: the tremendous value that is created."

"Let Rossi laugh at us," I concluded, snapping shut my binder. "Big deal. With an appropriate amount of humility and a little luck, our shareholders might have the last laugh."

▼

This decision marked a juncture: this was the point at which the mask of equality slipped off the face of the deal. No longer was it possible to characterize this marriage as a merger of equals. Although at a distance the merger looked and waddled and quacked like two big ducks it was, more accurately, one big duck sneaking up behind one shrinking duck.

Merger of equals? No. And to pretend it was—or negotiate in the hope it would become so—could imperil the deal by pitting ego against ego in a contest which by virtue of our size and instability we could not possibly win. This had become the unspoken truth of the merger.

15

Esprit de Corps

The Covenant of Serenity I made with my key guys, Binkley and Grundhofer, to swallow as much guff as Bank of America could slam down our throats was now to be tested, more strenuously than we could possibly have imagined.

Now, Rosenberg reflected on my recent concerns about the unspoken caste system that stigmatized Security Pacific employees and made them feel unwelcome. He informed me that Mike Rossi had an idea—a *brainstorm*—for an orientation program that would not only prepare Security Pacific personnel for a transition to a stricter credit process, but lay the groundwork for a more nurturing and cooperative environment. All Security Pacific managers would be required to attend a one-day seminar on credit culture. "Bob, I'd like to baptize, as it were, the Security Pacific people in the Bank of America culture. If you agree, we'll bring each and every one of Security's managers into a one-day session whose purpose is to introduce and orient them, get that *good-fellow feeling* flowing, make them feel comfortable, ease them into the new organization, soften the landing."

Sounded like a solid, rational idea. "Great. How can I say no to that?"

▼

Rossi convened these summits in northern California, gathering Security Pacific managers, executives, and employees in clusters of about two hundred. The sessions came to be known as "Camp Rossi" and raised the eyebrows and blood pressure of a number of my top executives, many of whom—like eyewitnesses at My Lai—seemed at a loss even to describe what they had experienced.

Without going into details, one vice president phoned and left an ominous message on my voice mail. "Bob, you gotta check out this Rossi symposium. You'll be *astounded*."

I was not required to attend but I decided it was vital to see what my managers were learning; I felt that my attendance might encourage other executives for whom the seminar was optional to attend.

I flew up to Oakland, hopped in a rental car, and drove out to Bank of America's credit and technology facility in the East Bay. I was totally by myself and had no idea what to expect.

I grabbed a cup of coffee and entered a dim training room where Security Pacific managers lingered in apprehensive silence, as if waiting for an apparition of the Virgin Mary.

And then Rossi—attired in Alligator shirt, short pants, crisp white tennies, and swinging coin medallion—ambled through a side entrance like he had come to teach us how to mix cocktails. He entered stage-left with a giant Styrofoam cup and a satchel crammed with handouts. The only fashion accessory missing from Rossi's apparel was a coach's whistle. I thought he was going to begin the day by ordering us to do forty push-ups. "'Morning," he muttered.

Following an obligatory welcome speech and an abstruse introduction, Rossi postured himself in a professorial manner and began to wander around the stage in front of his large audience. In lieu of a more sociable approach, he ordered us to follow his instructions. "I want everybody in this room to raise his hand," Rossi commanded. "Raise your hands! Do it! Raise up your hands!"

With the proficiency of circus animals, we reluctantly raised our hands. A hand here, a hand there. Then ten, then forty, then two hundred. Feeling like an idiot I raised my hand.

"You know what that is? That is you waving goodbye to your customers. Because the key to your success at Bank of America is having customers who do business with us in strict adherence to our credit policy. And my gut tells me you may have to wave goodbye to a lot of your customers."

Jesus, I thought, *what sort of a routing are we in for?*

Immediately, Rossi tore into Security Pacific's credit methodology. "It doesn't take a John Kenneth Galbraith to see that Security Pacific is in big-time trouble. Your numbers take my breath away. I've never seen so many classified loans in my life. It's chilling."

I listened in dismay to what I hoped was a joke.

"The answer: The B of A Way. And the B of A Way is the *only* way, because it holds the secret to how we got out of our difficulties. You are all going to learn the B of A Way—no exceptions. You're going to learn a new credit culture, or you're not going to be here."

A real winning approach, I thought facetiously. *He wants none of our customers and none of our employees.*

"Bank of America was in the same boat as you before I came over. Remember 1986? Yep—we've been there, done that, but I came in and we triumphed. We *revitalized.* And you know why? Because Bank of America is a survivor. Always has been, always will be. But now times have changed, and Security Pacific is Humpty Dumpty. You've had a great fall. All the king's horses and all the king's men can't put you back together again. But I will, and Bank of America will. And if Humpty Dumpty doesn't go back together again, you're not going to work here."

An absurd chuckle from the rear of the auditorium broke the rhythm of his consciousness-raising patter.

More speeches, more insults. The orientation groaned on. Minutes flattened into hours. The second hand on my watch seemed to stop as Rossi continued: "Is there anybody here who is opposed to the Bank of America Way? I want to hear it. Anybody?"

No one said a word.

Didn't Rossi get it? Didn't he understand how desperately willing Security Pacific employees were to fit in? My god, we had transformed ourselves so many times, through so many permutations and strategies. Had we not demonstrated our cultural plasticity? This was like watching Wilt Chamberlain admonish Trappist monks on the topic of promiscuity.

About midway through the ordeal, I grew restless. My eyes drifted to a man in an adjacent chair. I recognized him as one of our managers—perhaps eight levels down—but I couldn't place the name. I couldn't restrain myself; I leaned over and whispered, "Can you believe this crock of shit?"

He recognized me and was surprised to hear this critique coming from the chief executive officer. "Yeah, it's pretty gruesome."

"It's a fucking disgrace," I whispered.

"The gap between our culture and theirs is simply not this gigantic, is it? I mean, isn't he exaggerating?"

"He's full of crap. How is this supposed to bring solidarity to these two organizations? How is this supposed to make us feel welcome?"

When Rossi finally dismissed us, I ran. I could not get out of that room fast enough. The seminar had been interminable, the longest day of my life. When twilight descended on northern California, and the prison gates opened, I thought I would have to be airlifted out by a crack team of paramedics who specialized in boredom-induced comas.

Over the next two months, some two thousand Security Pacific employees were subjected to Camp Rossi. My heart went out to them. This was so far above and beyond the call of duty that I was sorry we could not pay them some kind of emotional distress gratuity.

▼

In preparation for the watershed meetings at which shareholders would vote for or against the transaction, Rossi had pulled together a list of Bank of America's classified credits.

I received it with some wonder.

Mike Rossi had been unrelentingly critical of Security Pacific's classified loans. I found it revealing to see a list of their nonaccruals.

Bank of America's exposure to lesser developed nations was considerable. Brazil still owed them nearly $700 million; Argentina, $186 million; Ecuador, $173 million; and Panama $123.

A familiar name leapt to my eyes: *Campeau.* I distinctly remembered how I'd virtually tossed that clown out of my office. Bank of America had lent him $74 million, which they now had to eat. I wondered by what moral authority Rossi felt comfortable upbraiding our credit culture at the haunting spectacle of Camp Rossi. At least it had been an ideal—California real estate—that got us into trouble. If Rossi was making loans to the likes of Campeau, this was not an example I wished my credit officers to emulate.

Bank of America also had their fair share of higher-risk textile, real estate, electronics, and entertainment loans. With private glee, I showed the list to Nick.

"Interesting," he said. "I think a wise man once said, 'He who live in glass house ought not throw stones.'"

▼

A special meeting of shareholders was scheduled for Wednesday, December 19, at the Sheraton Grand in Los Angeles. At that time the owners of Security Pacific would consider and vote on the proposal to approve and adopt the agreement and plan of merger. The meeting would begin at 10:00 A.M.; a prospectus and proxy card were enclosed with each invitation so all shareholders could vote whether they attended the meeting or not.

Our shareholder meetings had traditionally been attended largely by retirees. I was aware of this and suspected many of them were emotionally involved in the company after having witnessed the passing of the torch from Fritz Larken to Flamson to me.

I wanted them to feel welcome to express their feelings and pour out their hearts. But the media would undoubtedly cover the official shareholder meeting, and I didn't want it to in any way degenerate into a spectacle. For this reason, we arranged to have a luncheon—a pre-shareholder shareholder meeting—exclusively for the retirees and to be held the day prior to the official meeting. The retiree luncheon would be held at the Bonnaventure Hotel in downtown Los Angeles.

Meticulously orchestrated as both an opportunity for free expression and as a dress rehearsal, the format was to be the same as that of the following day's official shareholder meeting.

The retirees began to trickle in around 10:30 A.M. Availing themselves of the open cocktail bar, many of them ordered their usual martinis, Manhattans, and Bloody Marys. This luncheon would set the Bonnaventure's house record for the most liquor consumed at a function.

As expected, it was exceedingly emotional.

In the style of an open-mike night at city hall, retirees poured their hearts out.

Sentimentality operated on all cylinders. Memories, poignancies, bank-haiku, poems, and recollections. Kind words about Flamson. Reminiscences of Carl Hartnack and George Moody. Some of them even resurrected remembrances from the Great Depression. The meeting took on the aura of a memorial service. Many of the retirees spoke with a power and passion that nearly brought tears to *my* eyes. Some felt that with the passing of the Security Pacific name, so passed their own history. The issue was very personal. Few of them were sympathetic to the merger, even though they would financially benefit from it if they owned our stock. It didn't matter to them that shareholders were the first priority in the thought process leading to the merger. Many didn't care about the good exchange ratio or the insured dividends; to some of them it was as if an old friend had passed away.

Some retirees were complimentary, others were heartbroken and choked with emotion: "My company is going away; my bank is going away; my friends are going away. Where is George Moody? Richard Flamson is dead. Dick Rosenberg is taking over. Bob Smith won't have as much say in our future. This just won't be the same company. I know it won't be."

Some of them funneled their upset into single issues that, to them, had enormous symbolic value:

"When they send me my retirement check, will it still say 'Security Pacific' on it?"

"I think the merger is the best solution to the problem, but I don't want the Security Pacific name to go away. Can't the company keep its name?"

"I don't care if it's a good deal. What I care about is Security Pacific; my pride in this particular bank, this particular name. By the way, will the new organization—I refuse to call it Bank of America—have a Retirees Club?"

I assured them that we would have a retirees club going forward, and tried my best to sound enthusiastic when I told them, "Now you'll be part of the Bank of America Retirees Club."

"I don't want to be part of the Bank of America Retirees Club. I want to be part of the Security Pacific Retirees Club."

No matter how much detail I went into, how meticulously I took them through the thought process that had led to the merger, I could not repeal their unhappiness.

"I know Security Pacific had had a rough year, but are things so bad we have to resort to *this?*"

By the end of the luncheon, I was emotionally drenched in regret. I felt like crawling out of the Bonnaventure.

▼

The official shareholder meeting was serious but nowhere near as gut-wrenching as the retiree luncheon. There were fewer in attendance than we'd anticipated; many proxies had already been received by mail.

The meeting, though tense, was productive.

I opened up by asking those present to pause for a moment in the memory of the passing of Richard Flamson. "He served you, the shareholders, for thirty-seven years, the last eleven of which were as the chairman of the board. His accomplishments over this period provided the foundation for this proposed *murder* with Bank of America."

I didn't realize I'd misspoken until the entire audience broke up in hysterical laughter.

I inserted an unscripted line: "Ooops. Well, I guess that's what many of you were thinking anyway." This embarrassing misstatement had a salutary effect—the tense atmosphere was broken and the meeting proceeded without a glitch.

I introduced key executives and a number of people who'd been instrumental in merger negotiations, including Dick Thornburgh.

In the first moments of my speech I reflected on the history of Security Pacific. "Without previous mergers, acquisitions, and consolidations, Security Pacific would not be what it is today." I took them back to April 10, 1871, when Isaias Hellman opened his safe to a Los Angeles of only seven thousand residents. I retraced Sartori's ascent and Security Bank's expansion, took shareholders through the logarithmic growth of the corporation's assets, and brought them up to the important decision they had to make today. "This historic step surpasses the dreams, ideals, and expectations of all previous directors and the six leaders who preceded me and who directed our company through so many challenges and changes."

Optimistically, I added, "Let me assure you that the spirit

and history of Security Pacific is far from over. Each of the many smaller and several larger banks that helped Security Pacific become the fifth largest bank holding company in the United States lives within the fabric of our company. The legacy of our founders and the company's many leaders continues. Our history does not disappear. It becomes part of the New Bank of America, where our two histories and cultures merge to live on in a new greatness."

I summarized the events of the 1980s, describing the regulatory environment, sluggish economy, credit crunch, absence of banking reform, and unforeseen competition. I took shareholders through the process that led to the merger, and emphasized the impact a sliding economy would continue to have on the corporation unless we pursued this option with haste. I talked about the overcapacity of the market and the partial answer to be found in consolidation.

I took shareholders through the exchange ratio and stock conversion process. "The board of directors of Security Pacific believe the merger is in the best interest of Security Pacific and its shareholders and unanimously recommends that you vote for the approval and adoption of the agreement."

I opened the floor to questions pertaining to the merger.

The questions were germane and on point. There were no tears, no speeches, and no strolls down Memory Lane.

In response to an angry query about the recent suspension of the dividend, I said, "I recognize that the suspension of our common stock dividend is especially painful to shareholders who depend on it for income, and I would just implore you to take into account the uncertainty of the economic future and our need to maximize corporate strength, especially at this time."

I expressed the hope that I would not have to "pull" my parachute. On the contrary, I felt a duty to stick with the combined company and would do so as long as there was a meaningful role for me to play in the merged organization. Why would any banker in his right mind turn down an opportunity to help run what would be the most powerful bank in the United States?

After the Q&A, we handed out ballots. We adjourned the meeting for ten minutes while a final vote was counted and verified. When we reconvened, the secretary reported on the results of the vote.

Shareholders approved the merger, by an overwhelming 98%.

▼

Meanwhile, in northern California, Rosenberg went through an identical tango with his shareholders. They too had approved the merger by 98%. Echoing discussions we'd had, Rosenberg said, "The inescapable truth is that there are just too many banks in this country chasing too few customers" and pointed out that both Security Pacific and Bank of America would save an estimated annual $1.2 billion by uniting.

▼

The following day, Maurice DeWolff hurtled into my office. "It has to do with ERISA." The truncated alarm in DeWolff's nasal voice told me this could be traumatic. With no time to decompress from the prior day's shareholder meeting, I tightened the grip of my hand on the armrest.

"Bob, perhaps you should get hold of either Mike Caggiano or Sal Ricca and see if either of them can provide an explanation for what happened, mechanically. Get more details. We have to begin to construct our *legal defense*."

"Whoa, Maurice. Do me a favor and take three giant steps back. Start at the beginning."

I'd pressed the ERISA matter into the far recesses of my mind and it took me a moment to remember the subject at hand. As of November 25, we suspected we had an ERISA violation, but we didn't know the magnitude of the violation or whether the transactions were subject to penalties. The analysis was incomplete. But Maurice was closing in; he pulled no punches, and it was not his style to sweeten bad news.

Maurice had a twangy Bronx style of articulation and a subtle way of expressing emotion. "Bob, with respect to Sequor, there are two possible interpretations we can give to this matter."

"First, Maurice, how serious is the violation?"

"That depends on which interpretation is deemed accurate. First of all, these *are* potentially prohibited transactions. If in fact they are prohibited—understanding that we didn't obtain our customers' consent, but admitting that it was the best investment we could get for them, and they did in fact benefit—"

"Didn't we benefit by reducing our corporate assets?"

"That was the only benefit we derived from the transactions. We removed assets from the balance sheet, yes."

"In exchange for that, we gave our customers a good investment. I mean, these transactions were fully secured by U.S. government securities, so there was no risk attached."

"Correct. And let's hope the Department of Labor and the IRS see it that way." DeWolff explained the possible interpretations. "One: we *sold* these loans to the plan. Two: the transaction is really a *loan* disguised as a sale. In other words, it was a transient and strategic overnight *use* of loans to maximize benefits."

"So it boils down to a definition."

"The definition means everything in the world. The difference in penalties between the two definitions is proportional to the distance between our moon and Alpha Centauri. If the IRS decides these are sales, the penalties rise exponentially, they proliferate, they smash through the skylight."

"Maurice, how many transactions are we talking about?"

"Many. We're talking about many, many transactions. I can't give you an exact number. We're still attempting to reconstruct the calendar, but it appears the transactions go back as far as 1985."

My eyes glazed over. "Maurice, please find out what the penalties could be and get back to me as soon as you can."

"We'll work on it, but I do know that with the wrong interpretation ERISA would mandate a penality of 5% of the transactions."

Shit, I thought. That meant that if we hypothetically had a billion dollars of these transactions, our fine could be upwards of $50 million.

That afternoon, this unsigned pièce de résistence was circulated corporate-wide:

THE NIGHT BEFORE MERGER

'Twas the night before Merger and all throughout SPAC
Not a person was working, prepared for attack.
The pink slips were hung by the guard shack with care
In hopes that displacements soon would be there.
The employees were restless, awake in their beds,
While visions of unemployment danced in their heads;
And Bob in his tower, and Dick in his suite,
Had just settled in for a long Merger's sleep.
When down in the ranks there arose such a clatter,
One level down and the rest just don't matter.
"Away with our jobs," the news spread like a flash
To support the three stooges took $13 million in cash
The staff, under stress of the new fallen bank,
Could not believe how the promises stank
When what to our wondering eyes should appear
But an org chart of eight, with no one else near.
With two little drivers, so sneaky and slick
The one in control could be only Dick
Now Marty! Now Jerry! Now Frankie! Now Lou!
On Tommy! On Nicky! On Mikey! Okay, Kathy,
we need one of you too!
To the top of the lists, before you all fall
Now cash away, cash away, cash away all!

16

This Can't
Be Happening

New Year's Day 1992 passed beneath a cloud of concern. I still had not heard back from Maurice on potential ERISA penalties.

As we moved closer to the activation of the agreement, there were many issues still to be resolved. I thought we would have to push the closing date back at least a month, if not more.

The Justice Department now observed the merger closely. They had to study the impact of the merger on commerce and guide us in the disposition of branches prior to approving the deal. Their predominant concern was that the conjunction of two such large banks would impede fair competition in the markets they served.

For the New Bank of America, by virtue of its marriage with Security Pacific, to have too many branches in one district would exert too much dominance and thereby force a divestiture. We knew this and had concluded some time ago that disposition of branches would be necessary.

There was a litany of issues to confront and decide related to the Justice Department's review of the merger.

Reams of analysis were produced—market share data, computer runs. We inventoried and alphabetized files, labeled and numbered boxes, and, ultimately, produced nine hundred boxes of information whose destination was the Justice Department in Washington, D.C.

Kooken was aghast at the amount of paper we had produced. "Who the hell is going to review all that information?"

"Who knows? I don't know if our efforts are another example of bureaucracy, or if a team of officials is going to pore over that material with a fine-tooth comb, but it's got to be done."

At dawn one morning on an Oakland International tarmac, baggage handlers jammed these crates into every nook and cranny of a chartered 737—from the cargo hold to the first-class lounge.

Justice Department approval hinged on their review of this material.

▼

I'd tried to maintain open, two-way communication with the regulators, particularly Joe Vaez, or *Pal Joey* as I now thought of him.

In phone conversations, Vaez accused us of being unresponsive to regulatory criticism. He continued to insinuate that the deterioration of Security Pacific was of greater moment to him than the pending merger, and seemed not to comprehend how the two were connected.

"Joe, don't you see how Number Two solves Number One?"

"Unresponsive," he repeated, like a mantra.

I could have strangled him.

Vaez snorted. "These matters of accountability can be easily and readily decided by a special study."

When Vaez suggested that in order to settle issues of culpability for the decline of Security Pacific we commission a special committee of the board to review financial decision making and analyze the sequence of events that drowned Security Pacific in hardship, I was relieved and offered to consider such an undertaking. I felt it might have a cooling effect on what had become an incendiary regulatory stance.

You got it, Joey. "I like that. I'll take it to the board. We could establish a committee and bring in some experts and outside consultants to review the actions, decisions, and the rationale behind them."

"Good, then."

I took Vaez at his word that the results, whether they acquitted or condemned us, would be of interest to him.

▼

Dick Rosenberg and I arranged a conference call on January 13.

He said he was vexed by the Federal Reserve's extension of Community Reinvestment Act hearings and anxious about his upcoming personal appearance at one such Los Angeles forum.

I tried to reassure him. Both banks had excellent records with, and mutual concern for, the community. In fact, it was one area where Bank of America and Security Pacific found common ground. Just as we were devoted to that aspect of Sartori's vision, Bank of America was enormously loyal to founder A.P. Giannini's ideal that banks serve the common good wherever possible. "Bank of America has a tremendous record of community involvement."

We turned our attention to the Justice Department. They'd begun to look at our data and consider our relative sizes and the impact of our consolidation on fair competition. They believed that our anticipated saturation of particular jurisdictions—Washington State, Nevada, Arizona, and portions of California—could overwhelm market share.

"Frank Newman told me about your intent to divest a significant number of branches in Washington. Is that going to affect the closing of the deal?"

"No," said Rosenberg, "The deal is still good. I'd much rather auction off these branches than sell a separate bank." Rosenberg asked if we had amassed our year-end numbers yet.

"Not completely, but I do know that last-quarter loan losses will be about $525 million, the provision about $725 million, and that the nonperforming loans will increase by about $400 million."

"That's within our expectations." Once more, he mentioned his having to fly down to Los Angeles the following day for the hearing. "I hate these damned things."

▼

On Tuesday, January 14, God began to distribute the humiliation more equally between myself and Rosenberg.

At the first of four public forums held by the Federal Reserve to grant citizens, politicians, and special interest groups a venue to voice opinions, Rosenberg came under fire—unfairly, I thought—from community-based minority groups and Los Angeles city officials who feared the New Bank of America would not pay satisfactory attention to the needs of southern California's inner cities.

According to eyewitnesses, the event became rather crazy at times. At one point, activists and outspoken city council members irrationally urged Rosenberg to "promise" banking and credit services to Los Angeles' minority communities, holding Rosenberg's word of honor as hostage in exchange for their "approval" of the merger.

South Central Congressperson Maxine Waters thought the merger did not bode well for the South Central community she served: "The sting of redlining and discrimination is not easily erased." She told Federal Reserve board members that the merger should be permitted only if the New Bank of America made an extensive effort to find jobs for those laid off and promise not to close branches in low-income and minority neighborhoods.

Rosenberg defended the track records of both banks and pointed out that the new Bank of America's pledge to provide $12 billion in loans over ten years to low-income minority customers exceeded the prior combined goals of the banks independently by 33%. "Our programs are comprehensive and we are absolutely committed to providing broad services in all areas—rich and poor, urban and rural. A larger bank can be a larger help for all its customers."

I gave our board of directors and Rosenberg a heads up on the January 16 release of our fourth-quarter earnings, in conjunction with the release by Bank of America of their concurrent earnings report. Security Pacific had incurred a net loss of $409.2 million, or $649.2 million worse than our mid-year target number. The causes were numerous, but the ordinate factors in this slippage were the provision for credit losses, the write-down of assets in Hoare Govett, EuroFinance, the perpetual floating rate note portfolio, and other real estate owned (OREO) expenditures. For all of 1991, the net loss totaled $774.5 million, or $1.3 billion below plan.

That afternoon I met with Russ Freeman and Maurice DeWolff on the ERISA matter. Both attorneys now believed they had a full grasp of the ERISA violations and the potential penalties. I had spoken only briefly with DeWolff since our last meeting. He had mentioned no numbers, but something in his voice did not evoke my confidence.

DeWolff and Freeman cascaded into my office, each man hauling tons of documents, files, folders, and reports. Freeman had to make a second trip.

Halfway kidding, I said, "So what are the penalties? Are 45,000 people going to be out on the street with empty soup cans?"

Seriously, DeWolff answered, "That depends, and I do mean that literally. Your question is rhetorical, but there is more truth there than you could possibly know."

The attorneys were in no mood for frivolity.

We sat down. Freeman lit a cigarette, paused to enjoy the prick of smoke in his lungs, and gazed out the window at a nearby skyscraper. "That could be decided relative not to the amount of the transactions but also the number of the transactions."

"Yes, but what does that mean in *dollars?*" I'd prepared myself mentally for the possibility of a $50 million penalty. But that was a worse-case scenario.

Freeman waved his cigarette. It was his style to deliver bad news with the warm smile and engaging countenance of a favorite grandfather. "Bob, this potential misuse of pension funds is not something that Sequor just thought up this year. The records reflect that this process began nearly seven years ago."

"Oh my god! Well, wait. Is that one seven-year transaction?"

DeWolff gave a sick laugh.

"No," Freeman said, "this constitutes, unfortunately, not one seven-year transaction. This is hundreds and thousands of one-night transactions."

"I want to make sure I understand," I gulped. "Not only are we potentially liable for what we did in 1991, we are theoretically liable for every overnight transaction dating all the way back to 1985?"

"That's about the size of it," said Freeman.

I thought, *This can't possibly be happening*. My customary optimism gave way to a siege of negative thoughts, visions, and nightmare hallucinations. It felt unreal. "So this is a problem and not my imagination?" I shook my head. "Christ, that could be billions."

Freeman exhaled smoke and said calmly, "It's a potential catastrophe."

The fact that these practices were now in question, but had been been routine since 1985 begged the question: Where was everybody? Not only had our internal accountants and auditors missed it, but the Federal Reserve, who'd audited Sequor a number of times, had never mentioned, flagged, or even questioned the transactions. As recently as August, the Federal Reserve had reviewed this function and given us a clean bill of health.

DeWolff referred to some attorney work product. "We conducted a full analysis from 1985 to May of 1991, when Sequor ceased this practice. There was a cumulative $570 billion of these transactions."

"Of that amount," I asked, "what was the involvement of pension account participation?"

"Roughly $12.7 billion."

Russ interjected. "We now estimate the potential penalty or excise tax to be approximately $672 million if the transactions are held to be prohibitive sales, or are determined to be within the definition of self-dealing."

I didn't even register that number—it flew into my head and right out again. "Are they sales? Are we positive they were sales?"

"You see," said Freeman, "you've put your finger on the crux of the problem. How these transactions are defined is the single most important determinant factor on how badly we are penalized. The transactions might be sales, or loans, or use of funds."

"What kind of penalties are we talking about?"

Freeman went into a sort of free association. "In the best of all possible worlds, these transactions were rudimentary, nearly automated, short-term use or loans of funds. In that case, the penalty may be in the $300,000 range. But Bob, if in fact these transactions are deemed to be overnight sales, the potential ERISA penalty is much higher. The total penalty would be about a billion dollars, including the accumulative interest costs and potential excise tax."

"You mean a million-dollar penalty."

DeWolff slapped his belly. "No, billion—with a *B.*"

"Shit. That can't be right. *A billion dollars?* Guys, that's about 25% of our capital! *A billion dollars?* What for? We didn't benefit from the transactions, the customer received the benefit. I'm sure we didn't do it on purpose. It's technical, it's complex, it was an oversight. . . . "

I still didn't really believe what I had just heard. *Naw*, I thought, *can't be right. He means a million.*

Good good god.

Freeman motioned for calm. "Bolstering our assertion that we didn't engage in these transactions intentionally is the fact that there were two separate operations utilizing pension accounts in the transaction of overnight funds; one of them did it perfectly correctly, obtained all the necessary approvals. The other function did it wrong. If the unauthorized bunch of transactions are defined as sales, this is a flat-out disaster!" Freeman had an unusual quality of voice; if I wasn't looking at him, I'd have thought he was jolly.

I asked DeWolff how we had defined these transactions to our customers.

"In our accounting statements, we characterized these transactions—in writing—as sales, not as a loan or a use of funds."

"You mean, Maurice, if I'm hearing you correctly, if these transactions are deemed to be individual sales, we essentially violated ERISA gazillions of times every single day for several hundred weeks?"

"Yes."

I said nothing for a minute or two. "We have to present our case. Who do we make our case to?"

Freeman answered with a diplomatic serenity that was beginning to irritate me. "The OCC, the Fed, Department of

Labor and, really, the Internal Revenue Service has jurisdiction over the penalties. The IRS calls the shots, but we have to play to all these constituents."

"So our best shot is to persuade the IRS that this was a loan or use of funds?"

"That would keep the penalty down to a very understandable $300,000. You see, the 5% formula in ERISA law will apply in the event these are deemed sales. That's where we really get whacked."

Still doubting the billion-dollar figure, I mentally applied the 5% penalty formula to $12.7 billion. "If these are deemed to be sales, by my calculation the penalty would be $672 million."

"You got it," said Freeman. "You see now that this is a veritable disaster. Now add to that number a litany of interest charges and ancillary penalties." Freeman balanced his cigarette on the armrest and showed me the matrix that confirmed the numbers.

Instantaneously three words flashed in my mind: *material adverse change.*

Dick Rosenberg was no fool. *He might want Security Pacific, he might even want it badly—but not this badly.* No friggin' way. For all the happy-go-lucky lip service he paid to our deteriorated credit, high reserves, and quarterly losses, he would have to be brain-dead or a masochist to go forward with us knowing we faced a billion-dollar penalty.

Freeman added, "There is another way that this ERISA business could screw us up. We have to make our case to four bureaucracies, and the facts at issue are exceedingly complex and could take months and months to interpret. Now, Bob, our close date is just a month or two away. In all likelihood, the hashing out of this predicament could take at least six months, maybe a year. Our deterioration will continue. And as you know, Rosenberg has the option to pull out of the deal in September."

My mind flashed on the bravado-filled speech I'd given to the board, demanding that they *can* me if the deal did not close by the end of April.

I had a pounding headache.

"So," Russ continued, "this could unseat the merger like nothing else we could have imagined."

A potential billion-dollar violation? A six-month dick dance with the Internal Revenue Service? Our stock price dropping to $4 a share? Rosenberg pulling out of the deal in disgust? The shareholders would hunt me down with spears and axes; they would hoist me from a Security Pacific sign.

"What do you think of this, Bob?" DeWolff asked. "What is your plan?"

"My plan? I'm going to drop by the magic shop, get a fake goatee and mustache, withdraw several hundred dollars from the bank, and purchase a one-way ticket to Israel where there's no extradition."

Freeman lifted his hands. "Let's not panic."

"Why not?" I asked seriously.

"I'm going to talk to the regulators and see if they have any ideas on how we can push this through the obstacle course. It's the IRS I'm most concerned about."

All right, I thought, *don't panic*. "We need to gather all the information."

Maurice also thought he saw a possible escape hatch. "I'm going to sit down and write a comprehensible and compelling argument that these transactions were not sales but a reasonable and logical use of funds—even though we have typified them on the documentation as sales—and solicit third-party opinions to validate that conclusion."

Freeman agreed. "We'll augment our support as we go. If we can convince the OCC, they'll speak up for us and help convince the Fed, and the Fed will support us with the Department of Labor. It's a daisy chain of hope and conviction."

"But," I said, "springboarding off what you said, this could take aeons."

"Well, it could but it *can't*," said Freeman. "We won't allow it." Like a mysterious magician he stood up, gathered his papers, and walked out of the office. He made a phone call to Price Waterhouse; he wanted them to prepare an independent review and opinion on the definition of our transactions.

With a little less confidence, DeWolff assured me he would do his best and hurtled across the executive floor to get to work.

I now brought Kooken into the loop. He had to know what we faced. He was in the process of finalizing our year-end numbers. Freeman, Kooken, and I sat down with our external lawyers and outside accountants and concluded that a special reserve had to be set aside as a contingency against these penalties.

We debated over whether a billion-dollar penalty was possible.

"It's definitely possible," said Freeman. "Now whether it's realistic or not is another matter."

We knew that if we took a billion-dollar reserve, a delay of the merger became an equally great possibility. We grabbed a number out of the sky and fixed the reserve at an optimistic $10 million.

▼

This was no longer small potatoes, and I promptly phoned Dick Rosenberg. The hardest part was not to sound agitated, or as if I'd just made a mess in my pants. I had to keep the deal on track. What I didn't want to do was call Rosenberg in a blind panic: *Jesus H. Christ, Dick, we're facing a billion-dollar catastrophe.*

I was loathe even to broach the subject, and we spoke for what felt like a week about totally unrelated issues. Knowing what I knew about this gargantuan development, all else seemed incredibly trivial. Thankfully, Rosenberg was preoccupied with obtaining the approval of the Department of Justice—how many and which branches would we have to sell?

How will various community groups react to the merger?

"Dick, I understand our Community Redevelopment Act hearings went well."

"Yeah, well, they went okay." He griped about some of the comments made at the hearing, and expressed his relief that it was over and his desire that the Federal Reserve shut off the period for comments so that we could move forward with the deal.

Then we discussed Security Pacific's quarterly results.

"The only concern I have is that the nonperforming loan numbers should, in our view, be higher." Rosenberg went on and on; all I could think about was ERISA. When the issue came to the tip of my tongue, I pulled it back. It was very hard to talk about.

I managed to sound like I was listening: "How much higher?"

"$100, $150 million."

"That's not out of the question."

"Bob, how is your review of credit ratings proceeding? Are you using Bank of America methodologies?"

"We are certainly learning and studying your methodologies. For the time being, we are using our own judgment on credit ratings and other items relative to quarterly results."

"Anything else?"

"Dick, we've taken a number of charges in addition to the loan provision and OREO write-downs which adversely impacted our quarterlies, significantly. We've written down by $20 million some potential floating rate note bonds and our Hoare Govett tax asset as well as some of our offshore losses. This was the result of the Peat Marwick interpretation. And there are some other small provisions and write-downs." Then I slipped in, "We added $10 million to our reserve for regulation and litigation, particularly pertaining to one Sequor-related matter."

"Really? What brings that about?"

Now we were getting perilously close to the real issue at hand. "Well, Dick, this stems from a further exploration of our securities lending operation by outside attorneys."

"I thought those issues had been resolved."

"Indeed, most of them have. But one or two linger." I thought: *A billion dollars?*

He was about to sign off when I said, "Oh, Dick, by the way, just a bit more on that issue so you're up to date."

"Yes?"

"One of the issues brought to the forefront by the review of securities lending appears to indicate, appears . . . it appears that we could have an ERISA violation."

"ERISA?"

"This goes to a very technical and somewhat obscure part of Sequor."

"No, I know what ERISA is. ERISA can be a real problem. What's the violation?"

I paraphrased the problem but tried to suggest by the tone of my voice that it was no big deal.

"Bob, don't some rather severe penalties go along with an ERISA violation?"

"That's what I've heard. Our attorneys feel it is reasonable to assume that on the very outside a penalty of $4 to $6 million is a real possibility and, taking into account the legal costs, that's why I've placed an additional $10 million in reserves."

"Oh, that's what the reserve is about. Good, good. $4 to $6 million, huh? That's a hefty gouge, but it could have been a lot worse."

I began to spin like crazy. "Well, no decision has been made on the penalties. Of course there's an outside, *outside* chance—a potential, in the event the ERISA matter is viewed very harshly—for a larger penalty. Now of course, a big penalty is unlikely, but you could take it at its harshest terms, and it could potentially get up to a billion dollars." I laughed as if this was an impossibly unlikely exaggeration on my part. I smoothed out my voice, sounding like the most laid-back CEO ever to occupy a chair in a bank. "Now, of course, that would be illogical. Our attorneys feel that our interpretation is right on point. All the logic is on our side, all the facts are on our side. I just wanted to make you aware of this. Of course, like all of these legal issues, if the IRS was to give it the harshest possible interpretation—and no one here believes they will—the math works out to a billion-dollar fine, including penalties and interest."

There followed a brief pause at the other end of the line. "Should we get involved?"

"Sure, Dick, if you feel you should, but we've got plenty of horses working on it, both internally and outside, with the best legal and accounting firms."

I didn't want him to obsess, didn't want him to fixate, and didn't want him to open the contract and reread the material adverse change clause.

▼

But of course Rosenberg understood. It was like trying to conceal the eruption of a volcano from the people who lived on its rim. The issue was humongous, it was a potential disaster, and for that reason nobody really wanted to talk about it.

Despite my cool inference, Rosenberg promptly involved Bank of America's accountants, lawyers, experts, and auditors in the investigation. Now we had two sets of accountants, lawyers, and auditors, not to mention Millbank Tweed and Price Waterhouse. Sequor must have looked like an after-market party at Harry's Bar as this army pored over its documentation, ransacked its computer hard drives, turned the place upside down.

The involvement of Bank of America's troops filled me with apprehension. I was fairly certain that despite our characterization of these transactions as sales, they were in fact overnight loans or use of funds. But Bank of America had an uncanny ability to interpret our financial predicaments to our disadvantage. I prayed that they still wanted this deal as badly as we did, and that they would come to a similar conclusion.

But that would only be the first hurdle. Then we would, en masse, have to convince the entirety of Washington—from the regulators on up. And we would have to do it in a matter of weeks.

I thought this would be impossible. We would have to drill through four layers of bureaucracy in the time it normally takes just one bureaucracy to return a phone call. Anyone who's ever been audited knows that the IRS moves like a glacier. Babies are born, marry, reproduce, ripen, and die of old age before the IRS replies to even the simplest of inquiries. I was worried that even if the evidence fell on our side, it would take so long to garner the approval and consent of each constituent that the deal would linger in oblivion.

What we had going for us was the following: we'd uncovered the problem ourselves, we'd disclosed it, Security Pacific didn't benefit from the oversight, the customer did, and the violations in question were submerged, obscure, and highly technical. Moreover, there was no intention to do anything illegal or illicit and, thank God, no customer had been hurt or financially damaged by the error. Finally, as far as I could determine, the OCC, Federal Reserve, and Bank of America all wanted the merger to succeed. They *needed* it to succeed. If there was a unified motive to place this issue on a greased rail to resolution, it was the personal interest at least three of the parties directly concerned had in the execution of the merger agreement.

The predilections of the Department of Labor and the IRS were the two most onerous unknowns. The burden of proof was on us, they had no stake in the merger, and the verdict was theirs to decide.

All of our attorneys concluded in truthful conscience that a fair interpretation of what we had done was to lend or provide a use of the funds on an overnight basis. They conceded that there existed facts that did not support this conclusion, but that these facts boiled down largely to the lax use of a single word—in other words, the fate of the merger rested largely on an issue of semantics. We'd called the transactions *sales*. Now the burden was on us to prove the opposite.

▼

The one thing we didn't need right now was the headache of the special study.

Joe Vaez and Jimmy Barton had now formally requested that our board go forward with the study and that a committee investigate the causal chain of events leading to Security Pacific's deterioration.

"What we want," Vaez explained, repeating virtually word for word what I'd suggested, "is a special study committee. This would be an independent collection of observers who can conduct a fact-finding mission and issue a report to your Board and to us enumerating the causes and factors contributing to the decline of your bank. Why the deterioration? *What, or who, was to blame?*"

I was supportive of the investigation, but the timing and subtext put me under additional pressure. I had no idea how long such an investigation would take, or how it could impact the merger. The inference—that blame had to be located and apportioned—was unfriendly. Nevertheless, it was important to play ball with the regulators. If the results were what I anticipated, I hoped this would be an opportunity for me to clean the slate with the regulators, personally. "I see no problem," I told them. "I meet with our board of directors next Tuesday and at that time I'll broach the subject, get their ideas and obtain their approval to move forward. What sort of time frame are we talking about?"

"Don't you think a month or two would be sufficient?"

I didn't know. An investigation like this—examining events that occurred years before—was potentially open-ended. The pressure was on to do it quickly, and this made me nervous.

17

Working the Maze

The ERISA crisis had probably not opened Rosenberg's heart to Sequor, nor imbued him with warm and fuzzy affection for Caggiano and his crew. Rosenberg now decided to go forward with the radical changes ordained by Dick Griffith.

At this point, there was little incentive to fight Rosenberg on Sequor.

Because Rossi had so poisoned the atmosphere, to suggest that Rosenberg adopt any of our riskier operations de facto was almost certainly to provoke the admonition that it was divisions like Sequor that got us into trouble in the first place—even though that was not the case. Why should they listen to us? What credibility could we possibly have in their eyes, in light of our tarnished credit and reserve predicament? The good track record, a lauded international strategy, star performers, access to California real estate developers that had few historical antecedents, sky-rocket stock, and the unprecedented growth of earnings between 1971 and 1990—none of that mattered anymore. We were only as good as our last OCC review. Rossi appeared to have little respect for Security Pacific.

Bank of America wanted Sequor, but apparently in name only. Refuting my belief we ought to sell the operation, they suggested the installation of new procedures and the removal of controversial or creative maneuvers that made it a shining star.

Bank of America's plan was to decimate its pieces and parts.

Sequor, an all-star by any measure, was being gutted.

▼

I met with the board of directors and informed them of the regulators' request that we undertake an unbiased investigation of the events contributing to the deterioration of Security Pacific. "They want it and, unfortunately, we have to get this thing underway as quickly as possible."

Boswell was bemused by the timing and quizzical about the intent. "Is the purpose of the report diagnostic, or are they on a scalp-hunt?"

"I don't know and at this point I don't care." My focus was the merger, and my prevailing concern was ERISA.

We discussed the timing of—and motivation behind—the investigation. Some directors found the notion of a regulator-sanctioned quest to scapegoat individuals distasteful, but agreed that an honest look at the cause and effect of the bank's problems had real merit. "Could be beneficial," muttered Boswell. "An educational tool. A roadmap for management and this board."

I shrugged. "I think the investigation will reveal systemic weaknesses in our credit culture and some poor decision making in the past, but on the upside it might derail any effort by Vaez to point the finger at me, my management team, or this board. If Vaez is indeed looking for scalps, this report could dull his hatchet."

Anyway, we had to do it.

The board authorized the investigation and immediately

assembled a special study committee to be headed by Cal Knudsen, a trustworthy director who also sat on our Washington State Bank board.

By week's end, the committee would swing into action, assembling a geo-economic map of our past five years, tracing the strike-slip faultlines that had given way to cause our present earthquake.

▼

Resignations now proliferated at Sequor. I called Dick Rosenberg to discuss my fear that without the knowledgeable people our level of risk increased mightily. "Dick, I hate to see these people go. We need their know-how and experience."

Rosenberg pledged Bank of America people to fill the gaps if necessary.

How kind of him, I thought. *How convenient.*

Rosenberg had bigger concerns. He was antsy about the length of time it was taking to implement expense reductions. "I want to accelerate this process to get the savings faster. I want to accurately identify the Day One saves." He intended to raise these issues at a joint management committee meeting to be held on January 30, and I told him I would support him at the meeting.

"Second, Bob, I'm thinking that we should not immediately merge our leasing operations because your key officer and my key officer are each unwilling to work for the other."

"Uh-oh, what's going on?"

"It's your fellow Norm Chapman. He's very distraught about the merger, and he's not cooperating with my people."

This was news to me. Both banks had leasing operations. Bank of America's leasing division was indirectly under the auspices of David Coulter, at the time a relative unknown who later would come to play an enormous role in Bank of America's future. Security Pacific Leasing was run by Norm Chapman. Chapman had been one of Nick Binkley's brightest stars.

Rosenberg continued. "The conflict surprises me, because Coulter and the leasing team are eminently reasonable men. I've never known them to become caught up in these social dramas."

I had little doubt where the trouble lay. "Unfortunately, Norm Chapman has never been the corporate type. I'll speak to him."

▼

When we were not working on the ERISA problem, we were scrambling for capital. We were selling our corporate airplanes, buildings, collecting nickels and dimes off the floor. I learned that for some reason Bank of America had put the brakes on the sale of a number of our operations, including our bank in Chile, whose sale was an important component in our quest for capital. I phoned Frank Newman to find out why.

"Frank, why has Bank of America put a stop to the sale of our Chilean bank?"

"I wasn't aware we had."

"This interference—if it is true—will potentially keep a $50 million gain from being realized. You know we need all the capital we can get."

"I understand, and I think it should be discussed on Thursday."

Nobody knew anything. I was becoming tense, more tense than usual.

▼

On Thursday, January 30, we received word that a European bank had offered to pay $80 million for Hoare Govett. This was music to our ears; maybe the operation would finally be sold.

But, always, ERISA hovered in my thoughts like an unwanted obsession; I ate, drank, and slept ERISA. At Thursday's joint management committee meeting, I had to exercise uncanny mental discipline to focus on the agenda.

Bank of America planned to make a move on a medium-size S&L in Texas called Gibraltar Savings. Because of the stipulations set forth in our agreement to merge, the transaction had to have the approval of both managements. Rosenberg's team, looking into the viability of the acquisition, presented their arguments to the joint management committee:

"Because it is a thrift, and because of our market share in Texas—and what we are paying—we are getting a strategic base of business in the third largest state. . . . "

Nick and I glanced at each other.

The analysis was pitiful. The presentation was so poor, so feeble. There were no meaningful numbers to analyze, no binders replete with rationale, no extrapolations and even less logic. This was a sizable acquisition that begged for comprehensive analysis. At Security Pacific, our analysis of even the smallest bank acquisition was twenty times more sophisticated than the analysis of this impulsive grab for Gibraltar.

When Rosenberg opened the meeting up to discussion on the acquisition, no one said a word.

I thought, *Am I missing something?* With some hesitation I said, "It appears to me there is no way this deal could ever be financially justified. I don't see any shred of economic evidence that supports the acquisition of this thrift. You won't pay for this acquisition in one hundred years. From the financial perspective, it makes no sense. Am I right in assuming this is purely a strategic decision?"

Rosenberg said, "It's costing us less than we earn in a month."

"Be that as it may, that still doesn't sound like a rock-hard argument. We're buying a market share in Texas."

Rosenberg nodded. "We can rationalize it on that basis."

"But that's a very slender argument. There's so little financial justification."

"The strategy is the thing—the strategy is important."

I blinked hard. "You're buying a fourth-place position in Texas for less than a month's earnings." I simply didn't understand the reasoning; and no one had an answer.

During a break, I spoke to Frank Newman. "Frank, correct me if I'm wrong: this acquisition makes absolutely no sense."

He nodded. "Yeah, I know. But it's what Dick wants."

Next I discussed the deal with Lew Coleman. "Where is the value to the shareholder? Where is the value to this corporation?"

"The deal makes no sense," said Coleman.

"Then we don't have to do it."

"Well, Dick wants to do it."

I shook my head. "Lew, this atmosphere is just so strange to me."

"I know," Coleman said. "We are so different. We are dominated by followers and Security Pacific is dominated by leaders. We have a bunch of people who follow the rules and sit in their offices; you have creative people. We're a bunch of clerks; you're a bunch of entrepreneurs."

I didn't know whether to be flattered or wary. I was blown away by his candor, but stunned by its implications. Were our banks really so incompatible? Was there no room for the entrepreneur—the "creative" person—in the New Bank of America? A clear pattern had emerged: no one challenged Rosenberg. It was true with personnel issues—Rossi—and it was true with strategic moves and deals. Anything he said was universally accepted as unassailable orthodoxy.

And what did this say about Rosenberg? He was smart; so were Coleman and Newman. Why surround yourself with such aptitude and fail to solicit opinions? What good was it to blunder into a deal for which your two top guys can find no rationale? Why waste their skills like this?

This was how Bank of America really worked, how it functioned—hierarchical, staff-driven, and laconic. I had begun to find these meetings vaguely oppressive. The atmosphere here was nothing like it had been at Security Pacific. There was no freewheeling debate, no confrontation, no Devil's Advocate, and little humor.

▼

The massive task of trying to calibrate our risk ratings with those of Bank of America was still unresolved. I received a report from Dick Heilman informing me that reconciliation of our California real estate portfolio—without a doubt the key area of concern—had yet to be completed. The numbers thus identified were enormous, and the issues of discrepancy complex. Bank of America had so far identified $677 million in accounts they deemed to be losses. This number dwarfed the $268 million figure proffered by the Federal Reserve.

▼

The unwillingness of Norm Chapman to cooperate with Bank of America's leasing operation now came to a head. I'd spoken to him on the phone the week prior but it had apparently done no good. Chapman had fired off an inflammatory fax that found its way into Rosenberg's hands. As he read it aloud over the phone, I wilted in embarrassment.

"Bob, we've talked a lot about solidarity, and I must candidly express doubt that Chapman's faxes are conducive to a spirit of cooperation within the framework of the merger."

Although, in light of Rossi, this admonition was less potent and more ironic than it otherwise would have been, I had to agree. Two wrongs didn't make a right. "I'll speak to him in person."

▼

I set up a meeting with Norm for early February.

"Norm, what the hell is going on?"

Norm poured forth. The merger sucked. Bank of America stank. It's leasing unit was on a frenzied power-grab and had covert designs on Norm's operation. "I won't be able to run things my way anymore." It would all be ruined, *ruined.*

As Norm explained what he was up to, he used words like "We" and "They," "Us" and "Them." It was symptomatic of a mentality that had become troubling but inevitable, and which I felt had been exacerbated by the conduct of people like Rossi. Turf fighting, I thought; there had been so little of it at Security Pacific. If I privately admired Chapman's recalcitrance, it was because we'd taught our people to be protective of their work and their divisions—but also to respect the autonomy of other divisions. This attitude was one unfortunate outgrowth of the entrepreneurial spirit we'd encouraged and that had made us different.

"Okay. No more faxes, Norm."

"Bullshit! I can say what I feel!"

"Sure, you can say what you feel; you just can't say it in such a public way."

"I didn't intend for it to get to Rosenberg."

"Norm, do you understand why we can't have things like this going on? I'm trying to build a little esprit de corps, and when you tell Bank of America to shove it up their ass, that is just not in the spirit of congeniality. I don't want any personal intrigue injecting itself between me and Rosenberg while this deal is pending. And ideally, it would be nice if you and them would kiss and make up."

Norm's face reddened. "Nobody tells me what to do with Leasing—I mean, *you* can tell me—but those B of A guys don't get it. Bob, how can you be so naïve? They've got a secret agenda."

I cautioned Chapman that if he continued to badmouth the merger and foment disharmony, I would have no choice but to fire him. "Let's move forward. These differences will all be resolved at the appropriate time."

"By then it will be too late!"

"Norm, get hold of yourself! Bank of America is not the enemy. You have to make this work."

"We don't see eye to eye on core issues."

"Anything can be accomplished with a little patience, and if you *want* to get it accomplished."

"Bob, I've run Leasing for decades. Bank of America is a babe in the woods. They ought to be asking *me* questions and seeking my wisdom, not telling *me*."

Chapman and I were now just short of coming to blows. I called a time-out. "Norm, you've gone too far. You take a rest. Go home."

Chapman frowned and walked out.

▼

I phoned Rosenberg immediately. "Dick, unless you can think of a compelling reason to keep Chapman, I'm inclined to remove him as CEO of Leasing."

"Will he remain with the company?"

"My feeling at this point would be no. I think we've had our fill."

"That's fine. But I have an issue to discuss." Rosenberg was upset because I'd recommended that one of his employees report to one of mine.

"I just learned that you suggested that Dick Fulp report to Nick Binkley rather than Lew Coleman. Is that a fact?" Dick Fulp was the head of Bank of America's Trust Department.

Office drama, I thought. I surmised that Lew Coleman, fearing a loss of "power," had gone behind my back over this trivial issue.

"That wasn't a judicial mandate, Dick, it was merely a suggestion, and I fully intended to discuss it with you. It's not a problem. I'll talk to Nick." It was clear Rosenberg didn't want me farting around with anything. I switched discussion to a more important topic. "I heard the meeting Russ Freeman and Mike Halloran had with the Justice Department was disturbing."

"It was. Halloran told me that the Justice Department would formally talk to him and Freeman next Thursday about what they, the Justice Department, *want* from the transaction."

"That's ominous," I said.

"It is. Very upsetting. Mike's view has always been that southern California would require no significant adjustments, but that is clearly not the DOJ's view. He also said that if the meeting doesn't go well, or if the Justice Department appears

to be unreasonable, he will go to Secretary Brady on the matter and ask for prompt intervention."
Good to have friends in high places, I thought.

▼

Late in the day I received a copy of a press release out of Washington State concerning a proposed banking market share limitation: BANK AMERICA-SECURITY PACIFIC MERGER JEOPARDIZED. Carried by United Press International, and dated February 6, the release read, in part:

> A state committee's approval of an anti-trust bill that could block a multi-billion-dollar merger between Bank of America and Security Pacific led to a halt in trading for Security Pacific's stock Friday.

> Bank of America lobbyist Joe Brennon told the (State) House Commerce and Labor Committee the whole merger, which would create the second-largest bank in the United States, "could fall apart" if the bill becomes law. . . .

> Critics of the merger also have pointed out that Security Pacific has been a better "corporate citizen" in Washington State, sponsoring more community related projects than its chief competitor.

I was startled. And there was more: Lobbyist Joe Brennon, after telling the House Panel that the measure "Could kill the merger . . . this whole thing could fall apart," went on to assert that the intention of the measure was purely to harass Bank of America. He angered politicians and citizens alike by declaring that the state of Washington had no authority to block the merger. "It's strictly up to the Federal Reserve Board."
He also refused to provide an estimate on how many people would be laid off in Washington and dismissed House

Panel estimates of one thousand as a number plucked out of a hat.

The implications were uncertain, and its ramifications had yet to be evaluated, but the thrust of the story was that, if approved, this legislation could capsize the merger. News of the pending measure shocked Wall Street. The business wires were flooded with dire speculation. Because of the fear and momentum it engendered, speculation that caught fire could be as deadly as a material adverse change. My immediate concern was not the proposed legislation itself but the reaction on the street, particularly in response to the comments made by Brennon; renewed skepticism about the completion of the deal could result in an immediate drop in our stock price.

Russ Freeman reviewed the press release. "The statements made by Brennon were totally inappropriate."

I agreed. "He's pissed off a lot of important people. And we've tried to be so careful about divestiture and the sale of branches."

That night on the evening news reporters speculated on the repercussions of the proposed bill and went so far as to say it posed an imminent threat to the merger.

Rosenberg took the ball and issued a resoundingly confident statement downplaying the importance of the proposed law and ensuring that both corporations would comply with all anti-trust edicts.

▼

On February 7, the Washington State problem intensified. As a result of veiled threats issued by Bank of America the prior day, the House Commerce and Labor Committee unanimously voted to support a bill preventing any single bank from controlling more than 30% of deposits in the state.

Cutting to the heart of the matter, journalist Jim Simon wrote in the *Seattle Times* that "the law would make Bank of America's proposed purchase of Security Pacific Bank—the

largest bank takeover deal in U.S. history—illegal in this
state because the two would have a 50% market share here."
    All trading in Security Pacific stock was promptly halted
on the New York Stock Exchange.
▼

Three days later, at a joint management committee meeting,
we focused on what was transpiring in Washington State and
how we could appease the people behind the legislation.
Bank of America had hired a new public relations firm to
soothe tempers in Washington State. Both corporations were
being bombarded by phone calls from rating agencies concerned about the impact of the legislation on the merger. We
reviewed a chilling press release issued by CreditWire:
"Should the merger not be consummated, Standard & Poors
anticipates that Security Pacific's ratings would likely be
lowered to the low-investment grade range given the substantial asset quality deterioration since the merger was announced, the continuing sharp slide in California real estate
markets, and a reduction in capital levels."
▼

On February 12, Cal Knudsen, the chairman of our special
study committee of the board, and I met with OCC representatives Jimmy Barton, from Washington, D.C., and Vaez.
"The board," I explained, "has begun the special study under
Mr. Knudsen's leadership but would like you to clarify the
purpose and parameters of the investigation."
    Vaez took the position that the findings, regardless of
whether they were positive or negative, should be shared
with the new combined Bank of America board should the
merger go through.
    "I have no problem with that whatsoever. Joe, the facts are
the facts. If the report is critical of me, I'll accept it."
    "It will be out in the open," Vaez volunteered.

"Fine. But in the best of all possible worlds, the report will clear management of blame, and I would want that finding out in the open too."

In contrast to vibes given off by Vaez, Barton maintained that the purpose of the report was not that it might be used as ammunition for punitive measures against the bank or management. "You already have a fall-back contingency plan in the event of no merger, and we accept that. But our future recommendations with regards to Security Pacific depend in part on our timely receipt of the analysis. We think this is part of the contingency plan and will be an emergency roadmap in a no-merger-stand-alone scenario."

Vaez wanted the final report before the deal closed. "I would like to target a completion date of, let's say, March 31 of this year." This deadline gave the special study committee only six weeks to research five years of Security Pacific history, and to trace the origin and source of every major decision, as well as its outcome—and to prepare a report.

"And they are to answer what questions?"

"Who is responsible? Who is accountable? Is it you and your team? Is it the board? As for the impetus of the investigation, it is a search for the truth."

Because of the timing and the tenor of my discussions with Vaez, I thought the proffered motive was transparent and the desire behind it more disingenuous: Vaez wanted to get to the board. And he wanted to get to me.

▼

The very same day, in Olympia, Washington, House Bill 2891—whose unabashed purpose was to demolish the merger—had gravitated officially from the slate of doomed legislation to proposed law. To quote an article from the *Seattle Post Intelligencer*, House Bill 2891 "overnight blew from a candle flicker to a firestorm." The issues at the core of this legislation were concerns over community neglect and restraint of trade;

the goal was to maneuver Bank of America into selling Sea-First to a local buyer, or to ambush the merger altogether.

The issue had become enormously animated, with lobbyists and politicians battling each other for television coverage. Luke Helms, the chairman of Bank of America's Seafirst Bank in Washington, got caught in the crossfire. Under heat, he made some foolish statements to Senator Dwight Pelz, an extreme opponent of the merger and a chief proponent of the suggestion that Bank of America was unresponsive to community concerns. Luke Helms then participated in a meeting of the editorial board of the *Post-Intelligencer* and told them in light of this pressure Bank of America might "abandon the merger."

"That's exactly what we want," responded Senator Janice Niemi of Seattle.

Bank of America's handlers ran to Luke's assistance and clarified his point: "He meant to say that in light of legal delays, Bank of America might have to continue on with the merger without Washington State's Security Pacific branches."

The following day, an army of bank analysts stepped forward to express doubt that Washington legislation's effort to derail the merger would bear fruit, and agreed that the combined corporation would not be greatly damaged if it had to sell off Security Pacific's Washington operation.

Luke Helms had by now got his story straight and told the *Seattle Post Intelligencer* that were the bill to pass, Bank of America would go forward with the merger and simply make due without Security Pacific's Washington State branches.

Bill Virgin, in an article appearing in the *Seattle Post-Intelligencer,* quoted a Wall Street trader as saying, "There's an unbelievable institutional push behind this deal" and went on to write: "Regulators in particular want a deal because Security Pacific has been weakened by bad California real estate and international loans, and they'd like to merge it into the healthier bank before Security Pacific gets any weaker."

This was an important point, and I was gratified to see it in print. Many of the regulators I'd dealt with refused to acknowledge how important this merger was, not only to Security Pacific and Bank of America, but to the Federal Reserve and the OCC. The fact of the matter was: the regulators needed this merger as badly as we did, but were too pugnacious to admit it, congratulate us, or assume a more constructive or encouraging role in its effectuation.

▼

On February 14 I wished Rosenberg a Happy Valentine's Day and told him I was increasingly concerned about the number of good people who were resigning, quitting, or flirting with the overtures of corporate head hunters. "My people are beginning to look around. Some good people are flowing out."

Rosenberg said he too was losing some people, mostly in technology. "On the other hand, these are people we won't have to displace."

"That's the only good thing about it. Some of these people are reasonably valuable and it would be nice to keep them in the organization."

What I was thinking but did not say was that, should something happen to blow the deal, Security Pacific would be left with a skeleton crew—a handful of janitors and a bank teller. Many of our top people would have departed. And while I wished them well and prayed they would be able to navigate their way through the disastrous California economy to a safe landing pad, I was tense about losing so many people in the event the deal shredded.

Personnel had become a hot-button issue. Days before, I'd received a displacement breakdown that shattered the parameters Rosenberg and I had set forth regarding parallel displacement. Our pledge of equilibrium had evaporated; the numbers revealed a disparity impossible to deny. The evolving one-sidedness of the deal was nowhere more evident than in these displacement statistics. The stated ambition that lay-offs be equalized had taken a back seat to expediency and, possibly, factors of which I was unaware.

Rosenberg and I identified 642 senior officers in the separate companies. These 642 positions were combined to 438 as the companies joined and redundant positions were eliminated. In the final analysis, these 438 positions were to be filled by 187 (43%) Bank of America employees and 251 (57%) of Security Pacific employees. Sounded good. But statistics are deceptive: displaced were only 19 Bank of America senior employees, while 177 Security Pacific senior officers were sent to file for unemployment insurance or find new jobs. In other words, all but a handful of Bank of America's senior employees were retained in senior positions, while nearly 70% of our senior officers were displaced. Of the total 196 senior officers displaced, 90% were Security Pacific employees. With each man and woman sent away went a little piece of Security Pacific.

Admittedly, exigent factors sometimes contributed to this disparity. Because Bank of America's headquarters was located in San Francisco, most of the senior positions were now in northern California. Many Security Pacific officers simply didn't want to move. Second, as the consolidation process moved forward, some senior officers grew disenchanted with what they saw as the imposition of Bank of America's culture over Security Pacific's. They felt there were more appealing opportunities elsewhere and were unafraid to seek them. Lastly, the choice of senior officers was part of the negotiating process; if Rosenberg was fiercely adamant about the selection of a Bank of America employee over a Security Pacific employee, I let him win in order to guarantee that the deal stay on track. I had grown somewhat weary, and with the ERISA problem hanging over my head like a pendulum, I was losing my ability to say no; both my negotiating power and my credibility were in doubt as a result of the growing strife with regulators. A feeling ran very deep within the organizations that was difficult to combat: *Bank of America is bigger and Security Pacific is smaller*; *Bank of America is smarter and Security Pacific is dumber.*

Increasingly, Rosenberg was calling the shots. I knew this was part of the strategy, appreciated it as such, but could not deny it was intensely annoying. The side-effects were injurious: morale, dignity, and sense of purpose flagged among Secury Pacific employees, and even on the management team. Bank of America was winning nearly all of the personnel debates. As he picked apart subsidiaries like Manufactured Housing and Sequor, I felt I had been tied up and forced to watch the execution of my bank.

▼

On the afternoon of Friday, February 14, Rosenberg's attorneys met with the Justice Department regarding divestiture issues in Washington and Nevada and Dick called me back to say he was not happy with the results. Apparently, it had been a Valentine's Day Massacre. "We explained our rationale but they still want more damned divestitures."

"How many?" I asked.

"Thirty-five more branches in Washington State and ten branches in other states. This amounts to $3 billion more."

"Retail branches?"

"Generally business offices servicing the business community."

"Jesus. They want to clean us out."

"The Justice Department says they are open-minded and willing to listen, but I have yet to see an inkling of receptivity. Mike Halloran believes we can work this out on our own with Justice and should stop short of involving U.S. cabinet members in the mix, at least for now. They have got to resolve these issues by February 28 and they know that."

"These delays are driving me crazy. I'm going to phone

Bob Parry and let him know that even a month or two could kill us."

"Good idea."

Bob Parry had idolized Dick Flamson and remained friendly to Security Pacific and supported the merger. Parry was sympathetic to our plight and it was fair and wise to seek his support if possible.

"We are getting down to the wire and everyone is concerned over the delays in the approval process," I told Parry. "We are turning out the lights at Security Pacific. My staff is declining, people are resigning in many crucial areas; technology, real estate, corporate, and Sequor. We are beginning to see a loss of business and, pending the merger with Bank of America, Rosenberg has told us to put the brakes on the disposition of some of our key operations and we need those sales to bolster our capital and improve funding in case something happens to the deal."

"Okay, I hear you."

"Even a delay of a month or two could be very serious to Security Pacific."

"I'm behind you. Let me talk to some people and get the Federal Reserve behind you in completing this transaction."

▼

A few days later I phoned Dick Rosenberg to see if he'd heard anything new from Justice.

"They told us to go ahead with the sale of southern California branches to Union Bank. As soon as Nevada is resolved we will consummate the sale of northern California and Nevada branches to U.S. Bank out of Portland, Oregon. Arizona is not a problem, but we don't have many buyers. There is one group headed by Peter Ueberroth that has indicated a strong interest."

Wow, I thought, *wouldn't that be ironic*. I told Rosenberg that I was less worried about finding buyers than about the debacle in Washington State.

"That's also my main concern. I can't believe the Senate will pass that legislation. We are meeting with Justice this Wednesday to attempt to finalize this matter so that they can submit their official view to the Federal Reserve by February 28."

Good, I thought. "The faster we get the federal government on board, the less likely the Washington State legislation is to become a reality."

▼

Rosenberg, too, was incensed by the delays. "The Federal Reserve's umpteenth thirty-day extension and the complexities it creates for us, notwithstanding the cost to our franchises and our people, are becoming ludicrous."

He was also upset that the meeting between his people and the Justice Department had fallen through at the last minute. "I think we've been patient and gracious. We will submit our proposal this Friday and ask them to expedite their decision, by next week." I identified with his frustration. His people were spread thin, all over the map. "Yesterday we testified at hearings in the Arizona House and now we have to go before the Senate in Washington. I'm going to meet with the attorney generals of Washington and California this week."

"Dick, I hear you. There's no justification for any more delays."

"Meanwhile the economy goes from bad to worse. We are projecting more layoffs in aerospace."

"We are also hearing that," I said.

"We are rereviewing our own real estate portfolio in light of the continued slide. The future doesn't look very bright, especially in land."

▼

After more than a year of uncertainty, Security Pacific finally signed a letter of intent to sell Hoare Govett. Although the deal wouldn't close until the second quarter of the year, I was delighted.

Emboldened by the good news, I phoned Steve Steinbrink, acting comptroller of the currency, to emphasize the risk to our transaction posed by the endless delays, which by now had impacted capital, funding, customers, the peace of mind of our employees, and Wall Street analysts. "We are a severely weakened institution and we can't shoulder too many more delays."

"Yes, I agree. I think the delays are nearly over. Let's get the Fed hearings out of the way and move forward. No more extensions."

▼

I flew to San Francisco, where we tore through a myriad of issues at a joint management committee meeting. Loan reconciliation continued at a breakneck pace; our numbers were now nearly in line with Bank of America's.

Binkley, just back from the United Kingdom where he'd overseen the planned transition of EuroFinance to Bank of America Europe, had hired First Boston to independently review Manufactured Housing and explore its sale or alternatives. Binkley would now turn his attention to the stabilization of Sequor, an institution now in such disarray that Marty Stein of Bank of America Automation and Bill Czerniewicz of Security Pacific's technology operation had been furiously dispatched to manage and monitor its systems staff.

Mike Halloran was to meet with the attorney general of Washington State, who in the wake of Senate hearings had upped its request for divestiture from 69 to 85 branches, not including an additional 13 Security Pacific Business Centers servicing small business. From our perspective, that state's politicians were trying to choke every percentage point they could out of our market share. From their perspective, their demands were generous, and they were giving us "slack" in order to speed the deal.

▼

On February 25 I encountered a pissed-off Russ Freeman as he recounted the stubbornness of Washington State's attorney general. "There's not an ounce of give in that SOB. Halloran is at wit's end. Washington State doesn't care what the Federal Reserve says and they are threatening litigation if an agreement is not reached."

"This is getting ridiculous, Russ. We have made so many concessions."

"Every state wants total control of our divestiture issues within their borders, above and beyond the concessions we have already made. Washington is stubborn and fastidious and they want to ordain how many and exactly which branches we sell. One tactic we might try is to threaten to release a memorandum to the press citing Washington State's resistance as a key obstacle to the closing of the deal. This might expedite the process."

I attempted to call the attorney general of Washington State myself but instead got hold of a senior official. I told him that because of their obstinacy, I really had no alternative but to issue a public statement placing blame for the delays and uncertainty at their doorstep. "I have to provide an explanation to all our banking people in Washington State whose futures and interests hang in the balance. I just wanted to give you a heads up on the public statement."

"What will be the substance of the press release?"

"I'm going to reiterate your attorney general's hard position on divestiture, and why this massive transaction must now be postponed."

A few sentences later, the official softened his perspective. "Let's think this thing through carefully," he said. "I've received Michael Halloran's outline but we haven't had the opportunity to review it. Maybe I ought to. We were prepared to object and litigate the matter only in the event we were unsatisfied with the plan."

"Who mentioned the possibility of litigation?" I asked. "Where did that come from?"

"Litigation was a possibility only if the Federal Reserve did not listen to our objections."

"What are your objections, specifically?"

"We have no hard or fast objections. We have taken no definite position. We've neither agreed nor disagreed."

It sounded pretty flimsy. "On that basis you're going to hold up the biggest bank merger in history and threaten us with litigation?"

"Well now, hold on, Mr. Smith." He told me he would confer with others in the office and call me back. He phoned back later in the day to say the attorney general had backed down and would accept the agreement.

▼

Frank Newman called to relay that his meeting with the Department of Justice had been spectacular. "Very few areas of concern remain. They are prepared to commit their support for the merger in writing and forward it to the Federal Reserve."

Newman had heard about Washington State's change of heart and was delighted.

I informed our directors that the Department of Justice had finally accepted our proposed divestiture plan to resolve competition concerns and had recommended that Washington State's attorney general advise the regulators that he would no longer impede the merger.

18

Dead Bank Walking

The ERISA issue continued to loom beneath the deal like a toothed chasm.

On February 26 I met with Russ Freeman to review our legal argument with respect to the ERISA violation. Freeman, with DeWolff, had completed what he felt was a truthful and believable legal argument in defense of the transactions not as sales but as loans or use of funds.

"Bob, one bit of good news. I spoke with Mike Halloran and he agrees with our position. Not only is that one hurdle down, but I think Bank of America's belief in our viewpoint can be helpful to us with the Washington, D.C. power-maze."

"Good. We need Bank of America on our side. That's one down and four to go."

Freeman explained the argument he would use with the regulators to convince them our oversight was a million—not a billion—dollar mistake. But would it work?

He was ambivalent: "The fact remains, our customers did not approve, nor were they aware, of these transactions."

"Is our best defense then that these were not prohibited transactions?"

Freeman shrugged. "No. Our best defense is The Truth, without distortions: it was an honest mistake. We could argue that we had an implied authorization to use the funds insofar as we were co-investors, acting as an implied agent in the strategic deployment of riskless principal."

"But those arguments are either unsupported by the facts—"

"Right, or insufficient to prevent the transactions from being subject to the ERISA prohibitions. Mary's little lamb could have made these transactions; they are still legally prohibited."

"So there is no question that we face some penalties?"

DeWolff joined us. "I've scrutinized law books for legal precedents and can find no authority construing transactions of this type under Section 4975 whatsoever. This is uncharted terrain; the transactions are exceedingly complex, and the amounts are so enormous and stretch so far back that we can only present a ballpark estimate. I think we can make a reasonable argument that these transactions should be treated as loans or use of funds."

"How?" was my question.

"They were similar to repurchase transactions and have attributes of both sales and loans, but lean toward a use-of definition. The Catch-22 here is that if in fact we sustain the argument that these are loans or use of, we would have to carry them on our balance sheet and, therefore, have filed years of incorrect Fed and OCC reports. The regulators will surely zing us for that."

"But, guys, the OCC wants this merger completed."

Freeman nodded. "And that could be a tremendous advantage when we face off the Department of Labor and Internal Revenue. But once we bring the violations to the forefront and place them before the OCC, we will effectively lose whatever control we have over its resolution."

"Russ, that may be true, but I don't see that we have any choice. We want to do the right thing."

Freeman nodded. "I think so."

"Then," I said, "we have to be very careful how we present it to the OCC, because they in all likelihood will present it to the Federal Reserve."

"That is key," said Freeman. "I think we should approach them this way. Step up to the plate, accept full responsibility for the transactions, and concede that limited penalties are in order. We remind them that the transactions were inadvertent and resulted in no damage to the accounts."

"They probably *helped* the accounts."

"And on an aggregate basis, Security Pacific realized no profits or gains; in fact, transfers resulted in a net loss for our own affiliates and benefits to our customers. Obviously, we discovered them ourselves and were tenacious in bringing them forward to the regulators. The investments were eminently logical, fairly priced, and collateralized by U.S. government securities. You can't get any safer than that."

"If we can convince the OCC and the Federal Reserve," I noted, "perhaps they will intercede on our behalf with the Labor Department and IRS. That would be a huge relief."

"Right. We'll work our way up the ladder, rung by rung, and agree to pay a limited excise tax, plus penalties, in order to gain closure on this issue once and for all. The IRS is the biggest hump."

▼

Rosenberg phoned me on February 27 to discuss his meeting with California's attorney general. "California is still a problem. They are concerned about Fresno."

"Dick, who did you speak to?"

"Some guy I know only as 'Marcum' wants $200 million additional divestiture in Fresno."

"Who the hell is Marcum?"

"Bob, I have no damned idea. All I know is that he works at the AG and is weighing our savings and loans at 25%, which is a problem."

I called a senior officer at the California attorney general's office by the name of Rod Walston. I told him that I felt we had been more than cooperative and responsive to all of his concerns, and that squabbling over branches at this point was unproductive.

Walston sounded surprised to hear from me. "We do not oppose the merger and we will not oppose the merger. We see no adverse impact. The only snag is Fresno." He said he felt it could be quickly resolved and agreed to talk again to Rosenberg.

Rosenberg called a few hours later. "California looks okay. Washington is fine. So is Arizona. The Department of Justice has issued a press release—the same letter they fired off to the Fed. They are on board."

▼

During the merger negotiations I was interviewed by a reporter who wanted to know if I was sleeping. "I'm sleeping very well," I confessed. Even during high stress, I always slept well. "It's my wife and kids who aren't sleeping."

The following morning about 4 A.M. I heard Loretta stirring. She'd risen and brewed a pot of coffee. I followed. With some amusement I told her I couldn't understand why she was more agitated than I was.

"Aren't you concerned?" she asked.

"I'm very concerned, but I restrict my concern to the daylight hours."

"Have you forgotten, or do I need to remind you that our own personal financial situation is potentially as desperate as Security Pacific's?"

"What do you mean?"

"I'm no expert in banking, but Bob, didn't you buy a lot of Security Pacific stock?"

"Yeah, we own a lot of it."

"And didn't you borrow against it?"

"Yes, it's pretty highly leveraged."

"Very *highly* leveraged?" she asked.

"Quite leveraged."

"Well, maybe I'm mixed up—I hope I am—but if that stock isn't worth anything, then aren't we in a whole lot of trouble?"

"Er, it's possible."

"And aren't we involved in a pretty awful real estate deal?"

Loretta was dead on. Half our own capital was deeply sunk in a bad real estate development in Glendale—land that we could not develop, build on, or give away to homeless people.

"I mean, Bob, if this deal falls, you would lose your job, the bank and the stock will deteriorate to the point that it's nearly worthless. We have quite a few loans, don't we? Who is worse off, your bank or *our* bank? What will you do for a living? Will you be able to get another big job in banking?"

"I don't know." This was something I didn't want to contemplate.

"We would owe a million dollars, I think."

"Closer to two," I corrected. "I don't want to think about it."

"And this ERISA thing. I don't really understand it, but it sounds like a huge mess that could kill the deal."

"It is and it could." *Material adverse change*, I thought. Yes, it had the power to take out the deal like the very Finger of God.

"Well, Bob! I hope I'm wrong, and tell me if I am, but if this merger doesn't happen, aren't we going to be *bankrupt?* And from what you've been saying, about the regulators and all, it sounds like you could be potentially unemployable."

"I'm not going to think about it."

The next day, at work, it was *all* I could think about.

I had numerous loans totaling just short of $2 million, including five trust deeds on my house. I had financed stock purchases, a bad real estate venture that sounded like something out of Keating's portfolio—*Linda Vista*.

Whether out of blind ignorance, repression, or blissful denial, I had managed to delete personal finance from my memory banks. But Loretta had fixed that; I could no longer pretend I would not be personally devastated by the failure of the merger to materialize: I would be *nailed*.

Whether fired by the board of directors or ousted by the regulators, I stood to lose everything. There would be no golden parachute, no job at the New Bank of America and no income. I'd be persona non grata in banking. As for my Security Pacific stock, forget it. The bank would be destroyed. The stock price would collapse, most likely to the humiliating $4 range—the bank stock Hall of Shame. My loans would slide into default. My property, too, would be foreclosed on once my personal income was lost. I'd be bankrupt. My loans would end up on a classified list in a stack of papers on my successor's desk. Rosenberg would joke about me the way I'd joked about Campeau.

I could not professionally or financially survive the collapse of the deal. The smart thing to do was to borrow as much cash as possible now, before my life had a chance to cave in and take with it my creditworthiness.

I immediately made arrangements for a $400,000 loan on my house, and picked up the loan application on my way home from work. I walked in the door with the loan application in one hand and Loretta smiled—perhaps she thought I'd brought in the mail. The smile faded rapidly as she read the heading on the document. She put her hands up, one on either side of her face. "Oh, my dear. What is this about?"

"You put your finger on something last night. Our situation may not be so good. We could be in big-time trouble."

"Why didn't you think about this earlier?"

"I don't know," I said, and added with inappropriate understatement, "but now I'm beginning to focus on it. Sign this so we can get some cash—just in case."

Her fingers twitched as she signed. "Bob, what are we doing? What's going to happen?"

"We'll have to wait and see, won't we? I can always pump gas."

"Bob, be serious. This is *not* humorous."

"I know, but look at the bright side: it's probably funny to someone somewhere."

I continued to confide in Russ Freeman during this horrible period. I had probably convened with him fifty times on the ERISA commotion. When I wasn't on the phone to Russ, I was pacing back and forth in his office, wearing his carpet to tatters.

My imagination worked overtime, manufacturing nightmare scenarios in which this ERISA disaster would topple the merger deal. I would ruminate on its potential destruction, and phone Russ to bounce the latest fear off him, to verbally play out a theory, a scenario, or propose a legal solution to the problem. He indulged me, listened patiently to my fears, and tried to allay them.

"Don't worry, Bob." He was supremely cool under fire.

Russ had his hands full, dealing with in-house and outside counsel, accountants, with Bank of America's attorneys, with the regulatory authorities, and soon with the Internal Revenue Service. Like DeWolff, Freeman was on the go twenty-four hours a day, seven days a week, usually with a cigarette dangling from his yellowed fingertips, flicking ash every-which way, analyzing documents, running numbers, consulting case law.

"Russ, we have so much at stake. If this sonofabitch doesn't get resolved, we can kiss the merger deal goodbye."

The original closing date, a Leap Year Saturday as it turned out, came and went. The merger wasn't yet on the Federal Reserve Board calendar for official consideration. I felt we were still at least two months away from closure, as there was a thirty-day waiting period following Federal Reserve approval. The delay had one beneficial side-effect: it gave us time to deal with ERISA.

▼

I flew to Washington, D.C., on March 3 to meet in person with Jimmy Barton to solicit his views on how best to present the ERISA violation. I departed on a red eye, arriving at 5:30 A.M. for a 9 A.M. meeting at the OCC. I grabbed a couple hours of sleep on the plane, then had to pull myself together for a day of meetings.

I discovered at the Washington meeting that the ERISA issues were not well understood, even by the regulators, and pending a deeper understanding there was little Barton could offer beyond well-wishes and the promise to give our attorneys their undivided attention when it came time to lay ERISA on the table.

That afternoon I ran into Bill Seidman, the just-retired Chairman of the Federal Deposit Insurance Corporation, in the lobby of the Washington Ritz Carlton. When he stopped me I was surprised; I didn't even know that he would recognize me.

"I have to admire you, Bob," he said. "There is not one corporate president in a thousand who would have taken the unselfish approach that you are in solving this problem of your bank. You did it. You saved your shareholders and this country a lot of grief. You put your own reputation on the line to solve a problem, and we really appreciate it."

My first impulse was to reach out and pinch him to see if he was real; I thought perhaps I was hallucinating. I hardly knew what to say. "You mean that? Honestly?"

"Oh yeah. You saved the regulatory community a tidal wave of problems by stepping forward voluntarily. If the government had had to take over the institution, it would have traumatized investor confidence, maybe even sparked a nationwide panic."

"You think so?"

"Absolutely. People get concerned about their banks and the state of the world. The failure of Security Pacific would have been an economic liability that stretched beyond the four walls of your office. I think you saved the regulators' collective ass by being willing to merge with Bank of America, by not trying to fight the momentum, to addressing the problems and by finding a painful but ultimately intelligent solution."

This encomium, as no other, lifted my spirits. Here was one of the top regulators in the country, assuring me I had done the right thing. I left D.C. with a rare warm feeling in my gut.

▼

On March 11 Russ Freeman called me with an ERISA update. "I met with Millbank Tweed to strategize on how to present the ERISA issue to the OCC. Frank Newman thinks it would be a blunder to emphasize or, frankly, even articulate the potential fines involved. Naturally, we need to discuss this, but Newman's idea is to play the numbers down on the theory that out of sight is out of mind."

"Has the Fed been made aware of our strategy?"

"Yes, Frank talked to Tommy Thompson of the San Francisco Fed about the issue and provided Don Kline in Washington with a summary. Peter MacPherson at Bank of America is attempting to contact the Treasury Department and also Tim Ryan at the Fed."

Very late that night I received a phone call from Mike Halloran, Bank of America's chief legal counsel. He was working diligently on our behalf with Freeman and DeWolff. "Our presentation is going to be very strident, much more of an advocacy piece than simply a laying out of the facts. Time is so short that we think there's no reason not to go for the knock-out punch. I think a winning approach is to admit that a modest penalty is in order, but that both Bank of America and Security Pacific would hotly contest any fine in the hundred million to billion range."

"Damned right," I agreed.

"I'm going to remind them that you guys discovered and brought this issue forward on your own and that your investigation was not the result of any legal claims or regulatory pressure."

"I appreciate it, Mike. It's a great comfort to have Bank of America back us so strongly on this."

"Well, we both have the same goal."

▼

Piecing together several discussions, I concluded that Bank of America's outside attorneys had memorialized their opinion on the ERISA issue in the written form of a "comfort letter" to Rosenberg that could give him support for an emergency exit in the event the penalties exceeded the amount he was willing to tolerate.

Although our interests were synergistic—Rosenberg wanted the deal, the regulators wanted the deal, and I wanted the deal—Rosenberg was a smart man who knew how to wear a Happy Face while privately parlaying backdoors out of the deal.

With the supporting documentation of Price Waterhouse in hand, we produced a carefully argued advocacy paper and scheduled a fusillade of rapid-fire, one-after-another, life-and-death meetings with the OCC, Federal Reserve, Department of Labor, and IRS. Freeman and DeWolff would be joined by Bank of America's chief legal counsel, Mike Halloran, and CFO Frank Newman.

These four men would be our Dream Team.

▼

Our Dream Team met with the OCC on March 12.

Freeman opened with a grim recitation of facts.

"The key points are, one: ERISA client agreements did not authorize investment of their cash collateral in loan participations and did not authorize transactions with the bank or its affiliates.

"Point two: we had full investment discretion with respect to securities lending and associated cash investment and therefore were acting as a fiduciary.

"Point three: since October 1985, on an almost daily basis, cash collateral arising from stock loan transactions for ERISA accounts was used to acquire participations in broker loans from the bank's affiliates. A collateral purpose was to remove loans from our balance sheet. The participation agreements characterize these transactions as sales. During the period from October 1985 to May 1991, when the practice was discontinued, these transactions encompassed approximately $13.4 billion in ERISA account funds."

"My God," someone muttered.

Freeman continued, undaunted. "In our defense, the rates at which these transactions were executed was, as far as we know, superior to rates for comparable overnight investments. The loan participations were intended to be, and to our knowledge were, fully collateralized by U.S. government securities or other high quality Fed-wire eligible obligations."

"In other words, there was no risk?"

"Exactly. Now let me lay out our legal argument. May I smoke?"

"We'd rather you not."

"No problem," he said in a tortured voice. Russ continued, addressing the more technical underbelly of the transactions.

Freeman retained their undivided attention. He answered a number of questions and closed with a hard sell. "In the interest of expediting the merger, as well as pursuant to sound legal argument, I ask that you construe these transactions to be loans or use of funds and penalize us accordingly. There is no legal precedent whatsoever for the type of billion-dollar penalty that has been described as a possibility. Even knowing, malicious, and negligent abusers of pension funds have not been treated so harshly. Please keep in mind these transactions were not due to willful neglect and, as such, penalties levied should not be done so with an eye toward punishing Security Pacific."

Freeman called me as soon as the meeting concluded. "The OCC agrees that while we had transgressed our fiduciary rights with the accounts, these transgressions were the result not of ill-intended conspiracy but regrettable human oversight."

"Was there any discussion of penalties?"

"They will most likely fine us about $50,000 for improper reporting on our balance sheet numbers. They'll exact their pound of flesh, as it were, and prod us up the ladder to the Federal Reserve.

To successfully garner the support of the Office of the Comptroller of the Currency—this was good news.

The same day, Frank Newman led our Dream Team in a presentation before the Federal Reserve. He provided them with our legal arguments and encouraged them to reach a reasonable and speedy resolution.

Within hours, Freeman—who'd been with Newman at the Fed meeting—phoned from Washington to give me the results. "Bob, it went as well as could be expected. There was a greater lack of comprehension than I would have expected, but that could work to our advantage. I think by the meeting's conclusion they understood the issues and our position on the matter. But they were upset that the transactions dated back to 1985. I reminded them that they themselves had audited and reviewed these transactions a great many times since 1985 and missed the violations. We basically told them that if the IRS made a big deal out of this, it could take five years to litigate and Security Pacific would win it anyway but be destroyed in the process, and that should Bank of America make a claim of material adverse change, or activate its legal right to terminate the agreement on September 30 of this year, the Internal Revenue Service would bear some responsibility for the derailing of the merger."

"Did it seem to sink in?"

"I believe so. After the meeting Halloran met privately with the Fed staff and was assured that the ERISA violations would not stand in the way of the merger as far as they were concerned."

"Did he mention Fed approval?"

"Yes. The Federal Reserve is expected to grant tentative approval of the merger as early as Monday."

"Tremendous. Just maybe we've got this roller coaster going downhill."

"The Justice Department, as you know, has formally approved the merger and Halloran thinks they are going to waive the thirty-day option to reconsider."

"This is all good news."

"Bob, I've also learned that Joe Vaez contacted Frank Newman and told him the OCC understood the issues and would do everything it could to push the issue forward. So I think the regulators are lining up behind us."

"Hot dog! We're rocking and rolling."

"Well, the biggest obstacle is still ahead—the Internal Revenue Service."

"What about the Department of Labor?"

"No longer a concern." Freeman explained that ERISA issues are technically under the administrative purview of the Department of Labor. "But in the lawbooks, it falls to the IRS to litigate and settle perceived violations of ERISA."

In the days that followed, officers at the Department of Labor received our presentation, withheld judgement, wished us luck and passed us up Jacob's ladder to the Internal Revenue Service.

▼

Rosenberg phoned early on Friday the 13th. He was pleased by Halloran's upbeat reaction to the meetings with the OCC and Federal Reserve. "Bob, I think your interpretation will prevail. I had no idea how complex these transactions were." With a sly laugh he added, "Your guys are very innovative."

"Fortunately Freeman and DeWolff really jumped on this thing. And I appreciate the work of Halloran and Newman—

you have some pretty sharp guys too." I hoped we'd still be congratulating each other after Freeman's encounter with the IRS. "Have you heard anything from the OCC?"

Rosenberg said the only snag he'd encountered was in a conversation with Jimmy Barton, who confessed he was not yet comfortable enough with the facts to recommend the merger to the Fed, but that he would diligently review ERISA with labor experts and arrive at a conclusion as quickly as possible. Echoing Halloran's sentiment, Rosenberg said, "I wasn't thrilled with the manner in which Millbank Tweed presented the penalties so boldly in these meetings; it just lends credibility to what I feel are preposterous and impossible penalties."

"On the other hand, maybe seeing them with their own eyes, and hearing from Freeman that there is no legal precedent for that kind of number, drove home the outrageousness of the billion-dollar figure."

"All the same, I hope that isn't the tack they choose to take with the IRS. I have a feeling the IRS is a tough nut to crack."

I returned to what sounded like Jimmy Barton's reluctance to take a stand on the ERISA issue. "If we are going to war with the Internal Revenue Service, I want the OCC and the Federal Reserve not only to wish us well, but to back us with those organizations and, if possible, join us in pressing the IRS to resolve the issue immediately. The longer the issue lingers, the greater our exposure."

Later that day, Frank Newman got hold of Barton, persuaded him to place ERISA on the front burner, and strongly encouraged him, should he conclude that Security Pacific's legal position was the tenable one, to speak up in our behalf before the looming bureaucracy that remained to be convinced. Barton agreed.

Concurrently, the OCC and Federal Reserve conducted an updated audit of our Securities Lending unit. Freeman called to relay that our report card, to my relief, was outstanding. "Our audit performance blew them away. They verified that our alleged improper lending practices had been discontin-ued and that our presentation of the facts was accurate to the letter."

"How about our documentation, Russ?"

"Complete, scrupulous, detailed, and up to date. This writ-ten report will be useful in persuading the Internal Revenue Service that despite the ERISA error, the organization was competent and ethical, and took pains to record every trans-action and remedy mistakes."

Frank Newman was also excited. "I think it's a real possi-bility that the Fed could approve the merger on Monday, March 23."

Our spin department swung into high gear both in prepara-tion for federal approval and in response to a March 19 arti-cle in the *San Francisco Examiner* erroneously reporting that, all told, 20% of the combined Security Pacific/Bank of America workforce—or 18,500 employees—would lose their jobs. We distributed our own revised estimate via fax, electronic mail, and Federal Express to every major news source. Our figure was closer to 12,000, and these jobs were not—despite our initial fears—in imminent danger, but rather would erode gradually over a three-year period in a layoff of attrition.

▼

I spoke with Frank Newman that afternoon. He remained ec-static over the results of the joint OCC–Federal Reserve audit of our Securities Lending unit and felt the high marks we received would greatly heighten the odds that the Federal Reserve would approve the merger. "If they do indeed ap-prove the merger as scheduled on Monday, the merger will close on April 22."

Yes, I thought, *maybe I won't be standing in the soup lines after all.*

19

One Minute to Midnight

T hree hurdles were behind us, but unquestionably the last and most onerous lay ahead. We had not only to present but to *resolve* the ERISA issue with the IRS in two weeks, or the merger could be a dead duck. And with my self-imposed April "Fire Me" deadline just around the corner, so could I.

Although Freeman and DeWolff had been successful with the bank regulators—familiar turf—they were increasingly reluctant to enter the ring with an unfamiliar opponent like the Internal Revenue Service.

"I'm having second thoughts, Bob." Russ Freeman shook his head in a rare gesture of insecurity. "We've done well so far, we have honest to god momentum, but prodding the IRS to reach a decision on this complex an issue in two weeks is going to be harder than trying to get Vaez to be pleasant. I simply don't think I have the political ammunition to get them off their ass. Deadlines mean nothing to the IRS."

I was sympathetic to Russ's plight but had no solution. "I can't think of any alternative to just going in and making our case."

"There is one narrow but incandescent ray of hope."

"Don't keep me in suspense."

"My idea is to find some Washington-based attorney who knows his way around this thick-headed bureaucracy."

"I like it, Russ. Inject some beltway know-how into this. Shit, Russ, you have my carte blanche to do whatever—and I mean *whatever*—it takes to get this resolved."

Three days later Freeman phoned from Washington, D.C., to relay his success. "I think I've found The Man. His name is Gibbs."

That is how I would come to know him—only by the elusive moniker of "Gibbs." He was a person I never saw, never met, never spoke to on the phone. I didn't know if he was a she, White, Black, or Chinese. I didn't know his face, his voice, or his age. I didn't know if he wore a $1,000 suit or a sombrero. I never even asked his first name. But if he knew what he was doing, he was going to help us save the merger.

"Bob, Gibbs is a former commissioner of the Internal Revenue Service. He's going to bat for us."

"Wow." *Freeman is a genius*, I thought. "He can do all this in one week?"

"Gibbs believes he can. He's very well connected. And I'm told the IRS staff people trust him."

When I heard this, I was struck mute. How had Russ got him on our side? I didn't analyze how he'd done it, I just thanked God Freeman had come to work for Security Pacific.

There was more. "Bob, not only does Gibbs know his way around the IRS," Freeman told me, "but he honestly agrees 100% with our interpretation of the Sequor transactions."

"No question," I said. "Send him in there with my blessing."

▼

The special study committee looking into the causes of our deterioration was prepared to render its opinion. On March 21, Vaez, colleagues from the OCC, and members of our board gathered with the committee in Los Angeles.

Cal Knudsen presented the findings. "In accord with the direction of Security Pacific senior management and the regulatory agencies, we conducted a full investigation of the deterioration, its causes and origins. We have a pretty good understanding of what happened and why." Knudsen summarized roughly five years of our bank's activities, focusing in particular on the Merchant Bank and our lending practices. "Throughout this period, Security Pacific embarked on a very aggressive program to augment earnings. Prior to the recession, its credit culture was by all appearances aligned with successful policy. Ratings were strong until the fourth quarter of 1990. When the economy slumped, there was serious erosion in the real estate market. Compounded by the effects of FIRREA, the consequences to Security Pacific's loan portfolio were profound. Throughout this deterioration, executive management took substantial and vigorous actions to counteract these forces. The board backed these efforts. This process continued in spite of the planned merger. Further attempts to remedy the deterioration are ongoing.

"We found no instances of fraud, negligence, or abuse," Knudsen continued. "The corporation has a strong, entrepreneurial bent, and its scope is splintered, diversified, and broad. The strategy, while ambitious, has considerable drawbacks in hard economic times.

"While mistakes were made, no one at Security Pacific sat down one night and concocted a scheme to immerse the corporation in risk and jeopardize its future. This committee can pinpoint no specific action, individual, or instance and say, 'This was wrong, this was the cause of the fall.' Decline was due to an agglomeration of events. The reasons previously given for Security Pacific's hardship are in fact the reasons for its descent. There is no sleight of hand going on here. Furthermore, when problems were detected, the reaction was swift, proactive, and what would be expected from competent management and board. No one was asleep at the switch. Motives were above-board; there were no executives trying to figure out how to feather their nests at the expense of the larger corporation."

Thank God, I thought. This was what I had hoped and prayed for.

Knudsen concluded the formal portion of the report. "This predicament was the result of a complex series of circumstances, some within and some beyond the control of senior management. The bank had lower capital ratios, poor funding, depleted reserves. Of the California majors, Security Pacific was the bank most at risk. Remember, there was a lot going on in the outfield: Security Pacific was faced with the challenge of dismantling the Merchant Bank and bore the considerable cost of relinquishing large subsidiaries."

Knudsen set down his report. "The deterioration is symptomatic of what we saw in the 1980s, when all the banks followed each other. The actions senior management took were in general concordance with the culture and climate of the time. Questions? Comments?"

I waited.

Vaez seemed unusually dispirited by the good news. "But the board didn't change," he argued.

Knudsen paused. "What do you mean, sir?"

"The responsibility has to be shared with the board."

"What?"

Vaez lifted his voice. "I'm critical of the board."

Ted Gildred, a former U.S. ambassador and a director on the board, jumped in. "I have a different perspective. As a real estate developer, I've seen firsthand the living hell this economy has inflicted on California. I'm very happy this study was done—it is indispensable as it sheds light on what is becoming a New World. And while I'm saddened, I don't feel this board has any reason to feel ashamed."

Vaez sat far back in his chair, uncharacteristically silent.

I thanked Knudsen and the committee. "I appreciate this discussion a lot, and I think we've learned something from this report and hopefully we can apply these lessons and become a better organization. But I dislike the aspersions being cast around, particularly at the board. I'm the guy at the top and I'm accountable. I admit there was some arrogance on our part, particularly in the 1980s, but I don't feel it was personal or mean-spirited. As far as our current weakness, I think the merger is the solution. If all goes well we should have a very satisfactory outcome."

Then I turned to Vaez. "Joe, any comments?"

Vaez roused himself out of a melancholy stupor. "My conclusion remains the same. As I see it, the management team is inferior. Board oversight is insufficient. As for the merger, it is certainly the way out of this mess. But what do we have when it's over? Management walks away with clean hands."

"Whoa, whoa. I don't intend to walk away from anything." On the contrary, I saw myself as walking from one storm into a very challenging atmosphere.

Vaez didn't hear me. "And the board walks away clean; their jobs go on, their careers go on."

Joe had apparently not heard what he wanted to hear. I hoped—but doubted—this report would soften the approach Vaez would take going forward and dissuade or at least neutralize his criticism of Security Pacific at our pending March 31 OCC review.

The press release arrived via fax on Monday, March 23, on Federal Reserve letterhead: FOR IMMEDIATE RELEASE.

THE FEDERAL RESERVE BOARD TODAY CONDITIONALLY APPROVED THE APPLICATION OF BANK AMERICA CORPORATION, SAN FRANCISCO, TO MERGE WITH SECURITY

PACIFIC CORPORATION, LOS ANGELES AND THEREBY
ACQUIRE SECURITY PACIFIC'S BANKING AND NONBANK-
ING SUBSIDIARIES.

Dick Rosenberg called. "Bob, congratulations. The vote was unanimous and the official order is ninety-five pages long. Naturally, the approval is contingent upon Community Reinvestment Act (CRA) and divestiture issues."

"And the outcome of ERISA."

"Incidentally, included in the packet is a transmittal letter from our attorneys articulating their belief that the ERISA exposure is most likely in the $800,000 range and that any penalty beyond $10 million is extremely remote."

Rosenberg had never mentioned obtaining such an opinion. By revealing its existence, he'd tipped his hand. The subtext of this transmittal letter was that, in the terrible event that ERISA penalties exceeded that optimistic pittance—$800,000—or edged nearer the $10 million mark, this most likely represented the threshold at which Bank of America would seek a renegotiation of the deal or pull out altogether. *What happens,* I thought to ask but couldn't bring myself to, *if the IRS decides to take a few months to review the situation?*

▼

As the closing date approached, I began to receive mail— much of it supportive, but a lot of it negative. A percentage of it dripped with vitriol and threatened violence.

I'd always followed Dick Flamson's example and tried to steer clear of the limelight. Recently, all that had changed— but not in any glamorous sense. Some individuals—disgruntled employees, miscellaneous psychotics, and customers whose disappointment in the merger surpassed what one would consider normal irritation—issued phone and mail threats that gave me reason to fear for my personal safety and the safety of my family. I went to John Stier, my assigned security person and driver, to discuss fortifying our security measures.

John Stier was a soft, gentle man by nature. But as a former LAPD officer, he'd had his moments. He had been involved in the notorious shootout with the Symbionese Liberation Army. And when he offered advice, I listened: "Bob, if I were you I would watch my back all the time now. And I would advise your family to do the same."

That evening I sat down with Loretta and my daughter Sarah. "We have to be a little careful now." I passed along John's wisdom. "From now on, for God's sake, use the alarm systems." I reminded Loretta to use the car phone if she thought she was being followed, and told both of them to be on the lookout for strange cars trolling the neighborhood.

During particularly "hot" periods—breaking news stories related to the merger, and in the weeks approaching the closure of the deal—Stier stationed an armed detective in an undercover vehicle across the street from our house around the clock.

I was frightened by the ferocity of several letters I received. Someone who was on our Christmas card list returned the card with *Xs* through my children and wife and "burned" part of the house with a kitchen match.

But there was one letter I saved. I'd received a semi-literate handwritten note stamped to a T-shirt, upon which was depicted one bank vault "mounting" a second bank vault from behind, in the manner of copulating dogs. The aggressor vault bore the Bank of America logo; the aggressee wears the Security Pacific logo.

Dear Smitty (a.k.a. the Benedict Arnold of Banking),

Hope you enjoy this t-shirt–I'm going to wear mine when I go to file for my unemployment!! Hopefully you'll "take it in the rear end" one of these days like thousands of we SPNB employees are going to.

For many years Security Pacific was *the prestige* bank until
you and your cronies ran it into the ground–then we became
vulnerable to the likes of Bank of America. Maybe you can
learn to shave by braille [sic] so you won't have to look in the
mirror every morning.

By the way, be sure to note on the t-shirt cartoon just who
is the FUCKEE and who is the FUCKOR!!!!

▼

March 31, 1992—Black Tuesday, as I would come to think
of it, and less than one month before the merger was set to
close—was the day of our semiannual review by the Office
of the Comptroller of the Currency. The report was to entail
findings and criticisms pertaining to the last half of 1991 and
the first thirty-one days of 1992.

Vaez and his three assistants met us as scheduled in a conference room on the top floor of the Security Pacific headquarters. Also present was Don Chapman from the Federal
Reserve and Wayne Hall from the FDIC. I arrived with my
key staff, including Nick Binkley, George Benter, Jerry
Grundhofer, John Kooken, and Dick Heilman. We'd choreo-
graphed an elaborate and optimistic presentation describing
how we'd striven to mitigate our problem assets prior to becoming part of Bank of America, and how the merger would
effectively end any questions regarding our capital levels and
financial stability.

I joked to Benter that I felt confident Vaez would congratulate us on the merger and tell us we had done a good job to
stifle the hemorrhage. George just laughed.

Hearty congratulations were not what Vaez had on the
agenda. After rather tepid salutations, he started in with de-
tectable delight. "There are a number of serious matters to
discuss. As you know, the financial situation of the company
is not exactly robust. Many areas are bad but let us focus on
the worst: Asset Quality continues to deteriorate to near his-

toric levels and threatens to topple the bank. As of December 31, you have $1.5 billion of nonperformers in real estate alone and another billion six in OREO."

We sat frozen in our seats as Vaez, adopting the harsh syntax of a Marine Corps drill instructor, railed against every aspect of our corporation. "Too much real estate underwriting. Inadequate credit administration. Too much emphasis on marketing and asset generation. Asset deterioration is at historic levels, threatening your company's very viability. More and more loss exposure. The assistance of the regulators was necessary. You were, however, generally *unresponsive*."

I scoffed at the last comment.

Vaez continued: "Poor, poor forecasting. Earning prospects are feeble. Liquidity could be a disaster. Limp credit culture. Employees are under strain."

Of course they are under strain, I thought.

"Poor morale."

No shit, I almost blurted.

"While your capital is just at the required minimum, it is inadequate to support your magnitude of risk."

"We know," I said. "That is, of course, the basic reason we want the merger."

"And a judicious decision it is indeed to merge."

I thanked him for that; it was the kindest sentiment I'd yet heard from Vaez.

Vaez seemed to eschew any further discussion of the merger, or of what we had done to fix our situation, and rapidly moved onto his real focus . "Let's talk about personal responsibility, accountability. I do not believe Mr. Grundhofer, having come into Security Pacific so late, was responsible for any of these major problems. But as to Heilman—"

"Wait a second," I said. "Joe, where are we going here? Why are we discussing blame at this point? Last week you heard the results of the special study you requested. And they said this entire issue of accountability is a straw man, a red herring. Why won't you listen to the results of your own study?"

Vaez scoffed. "These are consultants, and I can get consultants to say anything I want them to say."

"Then what was the purpose?"

"To explain what happened. Cause and effect." Vaez continued. "Dick Heilman we have no problem with. Benter we have no problem with. Mr. Binkley, however, is an enigma to us, a real character, and he will be watched closely at Bank of America. We will *hawk* him closely over the coming months."

"*Nick Binkley?*" I gasped, incredulous. "You've got to be kidding. You'll 'hawk' Nick Binkley?"

Binkley looked up, speechless.

"Now we turn to you, Mr. Smith, chief executive officer." My staff's ears perked in amazement; Vaez was going to dress down their boss. "Mr. Smith, it would seem you are largely accountable for this convulsion of falling dominos. In light of that conclusion it would seem that you should not be considered the heir-apparent for Mr. Rosenberg at Bank of America. That would seem to be out of the question."

Good God, I thought. Vaez was giving me a performance evaluation right in front of my management team. What an asshole.

"Mr. Vaez," I said, "hold on a second. I had no idea the purpose of an OCC review was to assign personal blame and provide career counseling. Even so, I never said I wanted to run Bank of America or that the new board would even want me to do so, notwithstanding its discussion in our agreement. That decision is three or four years away. And frankly, you're jumping to a lot of conclusions that I don't believe are substantiated by the facts.

"Furthermore, I remind you again that we chartered a special study committee, augmented by outside experts, to determine what exactly caused our problems and to find what if any personal fault current management bore for the decline of Security Pacific. You specifically asked for this study, and its findings are unambiguous. You and I both know that while the committee indicated a number of problem areas, the report falls far, far short of a lynch mob conclusion about current management." In fact, it had *absolved* management of direct blame.

"Finally, Mr. Vaez, while I am always ultimately responsible for the institution, your conclusions cover an awfully long period of time, far exceeding the six-month parameters of your exam. And your conclusions fail to recognize the significant accomplishments of the past two years. You are holding current management, and me in particular, responsible for all the errors made and excluding us from the achievements."

"Achievements?"

"Well, I think we've done a pretty good job. Mr. Vaez, to refresh your memory, we just sold our company to a large company up north; we've solved the problem of capital."

"Yes, to be sure, the merger is the deal of the century."

"I mean, please be fair about this. We take responsibility for our problems, but we have also prevented an economic catastrophe and saved your regulatory body from a huge amount of grief."

"Be that as it may, your institution's serious deterioration continues unabated. The quality of the asset portfolio is deteriorating. The capital level is deteriorating."

What was his point of this vituperation? I wondered. We'd solved the problem.

"Now let's specifically discuss management," Vaez continued. This was getting grim. "Individually, while you may be entrepreneurs, collectively you are an inferior bunch. As for you, Mr. Smith, your leadership is lacking. There appears to be no disciplined credit culture. Your directors have not held management appropriately accountable. You have ignored repeated regulatory warnings, as if they are of little apparent consequence, and this has contributed to a malaise of arrogance."

"Whoa, Joe, wait. Hold on a second. I agree that in the 1980s there were instances of arrogance on the part of many bankers in the way they treated regulators, but I don't think that has been true in recent years. You say that current management is, and I specifically, am unsatisfactory? Why is management unsatisfactory?"

Vaez reserved his harshest castigation for me. "Ultimately, you are accountable, and bear the responsibility, for this incipient decay."

I groped for words. "I accept that. I'm chairman and CEO. But I think we've faced our problems head on, we've taken your advice seriously, and we've behaved professionally and civilly, even when we felt the treatment was unreasonably harsh. We have not been reactive; we've been proactive wherever it makes sense to do so. We've drastically increased our oversight of criticized loans, we've set aside greater and greater levels of reserves, and we work constantly to develop better and more thorough safeguards and procedures to improve credit quality. We are doing everything humanly possible within the limits of the law to stabilize the health of our institution. We are even going to merge with a larger, healthier institution. I mean, what more can we possibly do? And *why* is management unsatisfactory? Give me one example."

"Take your fellow Mr. David Lovejoy's vituperation, in the presence of you, Mr. Smith, against a female regulator whom he called a 'bitch.' This is the type of thing. And you were there, heard it, and did nothing about it."

Was that the best he could come up with—a three-year-old indiscretion by an employee who'd subsequently been fired?

"That *was* unfortunate, Joe, and it should indicate to you why Lovejoy was considered somewhat lacking in certain areas and eventually let go. But you still haven't told me why *management* is unsatisfactory, or why *I'm* unsatisfactory."

"Well," he said, "you are a very arrogant group, and you are a very arrogant person."

I absolutely couldn't believe my ears. "Now Joe, I can neither refute nor attest to the institution's arrogance in the 1980s, but I've never thought of myself as being an arrogant person such that it was abusive of others."

"Well, you, you. . . . " His eyes skimmed the faces across the conference table. "You've *all* been very arrogant toward the regulators over the past many years. In one particularly egregious circumstance you went so far as to have a regulator removed because you disputed his findings."

A-ha, there it was: Flamson's abuse of the regulators a half-decade ago was being revisited upon us now. It was payback time.

"Mr. Vaez, we don't need to personalize this. For the past two years we've worked day and night like professionals to fix the problems, not to fix the blame. The origin of many of these problems goes back quite a ways, and—"

"But Mr. Smith, with all due respect, you may not have been the chairman and CEO at the time, but you were certainly in the room when the decisions were made to grant these very pitiful real estate loans."

"First of all, when the decisions were made to originate these loans, we didn't think they were bad; otherwise we wouldn't have granted them in the first place. Second, these loans weren't bad until you passed a provision in FIRREA that cratered their values and mandated that we liquidate them at a fraction of what we imagined they might ultimately be worth. When we made these loans, how were we to know that the government was going to change the valuation process a few years down the line and force the short-term liquidation of long-term credits? Third, while yes, I was in attendance at many of the meetings from the mid- to late 1980s with Dick Flamson and others, I must tell you I agreed entirely with the strategy of making these loans. And finally, I can tell you with certainty that had I disagreed with those strategies, I wouldn't be sitting here so enjoyably in this room, because Dick Flamson would have *fired* me."

Vaez snickered.

"Joe, yes, I was in the room, and I'm proud I was in the room—it is my job to be in the room. And, for the most part,

I thought we made the right decisions at the time. And the last time I checked, Security Pacific Corporation—our holding company—was still rated as a satisfactory organization."

"Not anymore. The Federal Reserve now considers the holding company unsatisfactory." Vaez shot a glance at Don Chapman, who nodded in concurrence. "Your board will soon be made aware of this. Accordingly, the overall condition of Security Pacific is now 'unsatisfactory.'"

It was a humiliating moment for me, and the end for Security Pacific. I was kidding myself to think there would be some regulatory flicker of appreciation or acknowledgment; there would be no warm phone calls, thank-you notes, or bouquets. They would continue to pummel the shit out of us, right to the bitter end.

▼

On April 3, Rosenberg and I officially set April 22 as the ambitious target date to close the merger. We still had many details to resolve, in addition to completing the divestiture of 211 branches holding more than $8.8 billion in deposits. Incredibly, I still had no idea how the ERISA decision would come down; I'd received no update on the progress of the stealthy Gibbs.

The next thing I knew, Nick and I found ourselves in an executive conference room, about to discuss the future of the Nick's FSS operation with Mike Rossi.

Rossi entered, loudly. "Good morning!"

Binkley turned his head and whispered to the desk, "The Ego has landed."

We updated Rossi on late-breaking developments in our loan portfolio, the ramifications of reclassification, and the intensification of OCC criticism in spite of the merger.

"Joe Vaez has to understand what the merger means relative to our reserve and capital levels," I said.

My ears perked when Rossi announced, "Vaez is a good

guy. I can talk to Vaez. He may not listen to you, but he'll listen to me."

I was envious, almost suspicious. The Vaez he described was not the Vaez I had seen—not my Pal Joey. Furthermore, I could count the number of times I'd heard a bank executive express adoration for a regulator on the fingers of one hand. The exaggerated sentiments expressed by Rossi now, coupled with the sparkle in his eyes and affected machismo, went beyond the pale. "It sounds like you've got a special relationship with Joe."

Rossi snarled in a macho way, grinned, and mentioned that he had recently played basketball with him. "He's a good guy, a sports aficionado like me. We sometimes go to ball games together."

We now focused on Rossi's predominant concern. "I've taken great pains to send my credit people down to your FSS and try to inject new methods and standards and now it has gotten back to me that your people, Nick, are upset with that. They do nothing but whine and complain."

Binkley appealed to Rossi's common sense. "Mike, finance company credit standards are very different than bank methodologies."

"Not different enough to justify a bunch of crybabies. They either stop bellyaching or I'm going to shut them down."

I cleared my throat. "May I remind you, it's not yet your business to shut our FSS down."

Binkley motioned for calm. "Michael, I do want to hear what you're saying. What exactly are you telling my people?"

Bank of America didn't have an FSS, and it soon became obvious, as Rossi set forth the areas of contention, that he had no idea what he was talking about. "All I asked was that your guys stop restructuring these damned consumer loans. Too many of these loans have been restructured more than once! And that's a crazy damned way to do business, to restructure these loans over and over again and pretend that these are not classified loans. Nick, you're an extremely bright guy, but that is the dumbest goddamn thing I've ever heard."

With praiseworthy understatement, Binkley said, "I think I now understand why there is no meeting of minds."

"Yeah, it's because—no offense—your FSS people are a bunch of lunkheads."

Binkley remained calm. "No, Mike, I think it has a less pernicious explanation. You're telling our people that if we have to restructure a loan more than once, that becomes a classified loan?"

"Absolutely damn right."

"There's only one problem: you don't know how a finance company works. The restructure of loans is how a finance company makes money."

"What do you mean it's 'how you make your money'?"

"Mike, if the customer can't make a payment, we recalibrate the loan and charge the customer a fee—a premium—for that service. And we keep refinancing that loan. That's how a finance company works, and that's why it's no surprise to me that you are encountering resistance."

Rossi looked at me. For a moment, it looked like his mouth might stop moving. "Is that how a finance company works?"

"Yes, Michael. Nick's telling you the truth."

▼

At my afternoon session with Rosenberg, I told him about Rossi's gratuitous "shake up" of Nick's finance company. I was almost embarrassed to have to relay details of the meeting. "This merger is difficult enough without sideshows. Rossi is complicating our task immeasurably, and this latest development is outrageous. It cannot go on. Mike Rossi doesn't own these businesses, he obviously doesn't understand these businesses, and he's going to ruin these businesses."

"Yeah, I'll take care of it."

I lowered my voice. "Dick, this goes deeper than FSS. We are less than three weeks away from bringing our two organizations together—not a simple procedure—and yet Rossi continues to perpetuate the belief that Security Pacific people are stupid. Well, everybody at Security Pacific isn't stupid. And if this mythology is allowed to saturate the transition, it's going to poison the bank. It promotes the division between Us and Them. It erodes personal confidence. Rossi shouldn't be permitted to tar and feather people. If there has to be somebody who is stupid in this transition, let it be me, let me be the butt of the jokes, but not *everybody* at Security Pacific."

"Nobody's stupid. Your people are extremely talented. They're entrepreneurial."

I pleaded with Rosenberg. "Can you get Rossi off their backs so that we can cultivate some degree of teamwork?"

"I hear what you're saying. I'll speak to Mike."

In the end nothing, no one—not even Richard Rosenberg— could shut Rossi down.

▼

I held my breath as three thousand miles East an attorney I'd never met in my life represented Security Pacific and its dilemma to a bureaucracy that held Security Pacific's future as well as my own in the palm of its hand. Most likely, everything would be decided in one brief conversation—worth $1 billion.

When Amelia told me that Russ Freeman was calling from D.C. to report on the Gibbs meeting at the IRS, I spun around in my chair and accidentally pulled the phone off the desk.

"Yes, Russ."

"Thumbs up. Gibbs marched in there, shook hands, smiled, renewed acquaintances, and showed them the facts. The IRS staff agreed with our interpretation of the transactions and, well, the rest should be history."

"Thank God. Tell me more."

"Well, it's that simple. Gibbs persuaded the IRS staff that the transactions were the innocuous oversight of a busy and well-intended Sequor. He convinced them that the overnight use of funds was just that—a wise and proper deployment of money that Security Pacific put to use to the benefit of its customers. The IRS staff accepted his view and is expected to impose an eminently reasonable penalty, probably about $300,000. It will still require their formal approval, but everyone feels that it ain't going to be no billion with a capital B. We're going to get it settled within the next two weeks."

"This is a great day, a great day," I gushed.

I was not an overly sentimental man, but joy sang in my heart like a Hallelujah chorus of angels as I called Rosenberg to report this news.

He was relieved and perhaps a little stunned. "You mean it's over?"

"It's over."

"I . . . I . . . *Good!*"

When Freeman returned he came straight to my office. "Oh, by the way, Bob, what I didn't tell you is that I agreed to pay Gibbs $1 million if the deal got settled in time for the April 22 close date. Also, I never did tell Bank of America."

"Good. It's really none of their fucking business. To me this is worth $10, maybe $100, million. Just tell Halloran that's the way it is." For the first time in months my chest puffed with pride.

The next day Russ told me that Halloran thought the million dollars was far too much to pay one attorney for a meeting with the IRS and would try to settle it for much less.

"Screw that. Send Gibbs the check," I said. "He earned every cent, and I'll write the check myself if necessary."

▼

On April 13 we received a closing report from Jimmy Barton regarding the ERISA violation. "Although the OCC is authorized by statute to assess a much higher civil money penalty for these violations, the OCC has determined that a $50,000 civil penalty is appropriate based upon information currently available." He lauded us for our cooperation and asked that we forward a check.

"I hope we have the sufficient funds," I wisecracked.

Following the meeting, Rosenberg and I met privately. The merger would officially close at 12:01 A.M., Pacific Standard Time, on April 22.

▼

On Tuesday, April 14, the OCC—in the person of Joe Vaez— delivered a formal presentation to the Security Pacific board. This was a regurgitation of the pelting he'd given us on March 31. There were no surprises, but it was decidedly unpleasant to sit through a litany of pejoratives: "Inadequate," "Unsatisfactory," "Poor," "Lacking" "Insufficient," and "Arrogant."

The special study committee's report had made no impression whatsoever.

▼

One week before the merger was set to close, the ERISA issue was finally settled in a formal agreement. The Internal Revenue Service had leveled a penalty of $238,349, a fraction of the number we'd feared.

After verification of the settlement, Binkley, Grundhofer, and I flew to San Francisco for a joint management meeting with executives at Bank of America. As expected, the ERISA violation was one of the topics that arose. Rossi took pains to remind us of our oversight and chastised us for the trouble, expense, and anxiety it had caused. "Nearly $300,000 in fines," he said. He repeated it like a mantra. He wouldn't let us forget.

The focus of the meeting then abruptly shifted to Bank of America's own legal exigencies. Having received a copy of Bank of America's briefing book, I was aware that the organization had legal troubles of its own. Among other suits,

Bank of America faced the prospect of losses abroad—in the United Kingdom—over murky securities transfers surrounding the mysterious drowning, said to be a suicide, of a millionaire publishing mogul named Robert Maxwell.

Binkley, Grundhofer, and I sat without comment as Lew Coleman made somber note of the fact they'd settled the Maxwell issue for $40 million.

In legal terminology there is something known as the *Unclean Hands Doctrine*: to accuse the other side of having dirty hands when your own hands are filthy is bad faith. We had been scolded for our $238,349 ERISA penalty and the accompanying $50,000 OCC fine, as well as for paying Gibbs a million-dollar fee.

I couldn't resist tearing a piece of paper off my yellow legal pad. I divided the paper into two vertical columns, headed one column BofA, the other Security Pacific, and wrote SCORECARD at the top:

Security Pacific   Bank of America

ERISA: $300,000   *MAXWELL: $40,000,000*

I wrote across the bottom in banner capitals, *WHO IS STUPID NOW?* Then, like a kid in school, I passed the note secretly to Binkley. He read it and chuckled out loud.

On April 16 we released our 1992 first-quarter results. We reported a loss of $496 million, or $3.93 per common share.

I said in an attached statement, "This is the last time that we expect to report operating results as our merger with Bank of America is expected to close on or about April 22nd." It was the end of a one-hundred-year tradition of quarterly reporting by Security Pacific. I was relieved. No longer would I have to proffer excuses for feeble earnings, apologize to shareholders for suspended dividends, or recount like a broken record the toll a prolonged economic downturn had taken on our real estate portfolio. That was all finished, over, kaput. I would put the past year and a half behind me and turn an eye toward greener pastures and new challenges.

▼

It happened: At 12:01 A.M. on April 22 Security Pacific Corporation became part of BankAmerica Corporation, with assets of nearly $200 billion, shareholders' equity of $13 billion, branches in eleven Western states, and thirty-six foreign countries. Our ticker symbol, SPC, was deleted from stock lists, from the New York Stock Exchange, and from the banking trades.

▼

That dawn I emerged from the shower and—in sheer relief—lifted my hands to the sky in homage to Martin Luther King, and cried to my wife, "I'm free, free, free at last!" I felt as if ten thousand pounds had been lifted off the tip of my spine. I couldn't have felt better or more free. I was so thankful the deal had closed. Then I added, "Well, we ain't broke yet, baby."

It felt very strange. It had taken us eight months to get this far, and we still had a very long way to go.

Dick Flamson's wife, Arden, called with very mixed emotions. She congratulated us on the closure of the deal but, like many, felt that in some ineffable way that despite our PR department's protestations the merger's completion was effectively the end of Security Pacific.

In a way, Joseph Sartori had predicted not only our ultimate merger with Bank of America, but virtually its timing. What historians call the high point of his career was achieved in 1929, when Sartori was seventy years old. Seizing an opportunity to convert Security Trust and Savings Bank into what was for its time one of the largest branch systems in the nation, he merged Security with Los Angeles First National Trust and Savings, creating Security–First National Bank and the eighth largest bank in the country. The merger served another function: it saved Security–First National Bank from the nation's worst financial catastrophe. The Great Depression began in 1929, causing many banks to suffer. Sartori's masterful consolidation was critical to the survival of both merged institutions in averting serious operating losses by immediately reducing its combined annual operating costs by more than $2 million.

He issued a press release in defense of the merger and used that opportunity to reflect on what his bank might look like sixty years hence: "Some people are still doubtful about the wisdom of the large consolidations of business in this country, but this tendency of our times is, in my judgment, economically sound. We might as well reject the airplane and the radio and all the other marvels of our age as to condemn big business just because it is big. Banking must keep pace with the growth of business, and combination of banks is the order of the day."

Those sixty years had elapsed. The Security Pacific name was history, and the cause was the very consolidation he had prophesized. Appearing dead-center on the DEATH NOTICES/ FUNERAL ANNOUNCEMENTS page of the *Los Angeles Times*.

SECURITY PACIFIC BANK

In loving memory, age 121 years.
Passed away in April 1992 at home
in Los Angeles, Ca. She is survived
by 39,999 loyal family members.
Friends and family are invited to
attend a curbside service with wake
to follow, Tuesday, April 22, 1992,
4:00 P.M. Flowers are encouraged.

20

Scrimmage
for Survival

With the closing began the difficult one-year process of consolidating offices and operations, coordinating products, converting accounts, and synchronizing two bank systems.

My focus shifted from the deal back to the employees and customers; it was my highest priority to make the transition as painless as possible.

It wasn't long before I discovered how superfluous I'd become. Only days after the merger, despite my impressive title at the New Bank of America—president and chief operating officer—my duties were inchoate; I had no accountability, no agenda, and no list of responsibilities. No one reported to me; all senior executives reported directly to Rosenberg, who controlled everything centrally and fastidiously.

My job, as it were, was to deliver tedious community reports in which I spoke about the sponsorship of charities, networking at the Chamber of Commerce, and the reaction of southern California citizen groups to the merger.

Initially, my community reports were relevant, but following the merger they ceased to be important and I began to think of it as a joke that I was actually expected to issue these reports. I should probably have seen this coming, but here it was.

I struggled to keep a straight face as I fielded questions:

"Bob, to what degree should we participate in the Red Cross Blood Drive?"

Don't get me wrong: These were important issues, to someone, but not to me as my principal responsibility.

For Rosenberg, it was never. "Bob, tell me what you think about financing multi-family dwellings" or "Give me your opinion on the future of banking in Arizona."

I began to feel like a fifth wheel, the odd man out, a *chump*. The contrast between what I'd been and who I was now ignited memories and evoked in me the unabashed sentimentality of a Tony Orlando song.

Following one particular management meeting, I approached Rosenberg. "Sorry, Dick, you've heard the last community report from me."

He looked shocked. "What do you mean?"

"Dick, these reports are bullshit. I have nothing of substance to talk about because I am responsible for nothing."

"I like your reports," Rosenberg purported. "I look forward to them, I anticipate them, I expect them, and I hope you keep presenting them. They are thoroughly enjoyable."

"Dick, this is nonsense. It's embarrassing to sit there and talk about the upcoming Christians and Jews dinner. Either play me or pay me. I want to stay around because I feel obligated to see this transition through, but I have to have something to do."

"You represent the bank in southern California."

"What does that mean?" Did Rosenberg expect me to cut yellow ribbons at new ATM machines? "Dick, I'd rather record the minutes of these meetings than sit there with my thumb up my ass."

"Bob, your role is important."

"The way this corporation is designed, everything lands on your desk. I am out of the loop. Now, this is your company, and you have the right to run it any way you want, but I want to have input, I want personal accountability."

Rosenberg shrugged. He was in charge and knew he was in charge. He did not want my input. "Let's discuss it sometime."

He was blowing me off. Rosenberg, who prior to April 22 had courted me like the only uninfected female in a colony of lepers, promptly dropped all pretenses and celebrated the consummation of the merger by unrolling the *Get Lost* mat at the foot of his office door. As always, he was smart, cordial, and polite—but he was also cool, distant, and indifferent. Perhaps he was trying to avoid the confrontation he knew was imminent.

Down deep, I desperately wanted to stay—this was my deal and I felt an obligation to Security Pacific, its constituents, employees, and *ideal*—but I couldn't for the life of me understand what I was expected to contribute in this environment. Culturally, I felt Bank of America was nothing like Security Pacific; it was rigid and unfriendly. It was a corporation of committees, edicts, axioms, doctrines, ordinances, and universal assent. I'd brought Security Pacific to the table, and the deal was done and my role was finished. I was obsolete. I was an emblem, an unwanted reminder of a bank Rosenberg wanted in corporeality but not in spirit. I was to be shoved in a corner with an important title but nothing to do, no decisions to make, no line responsibility, no department, and no staff.

A well-compensated but irrelevant position might have been acceptable to some people, but I couldn't be a part of it.

▼

On the morning of Monday, May 4, I met with Dick Rosenberg to discuss the OCC report on Security Pacific for the last half of 1991 and the upcoming board review scheduled by the OCC and the Federal Reserve for our climacteric June 23 meeting.

Copies of the OCC report had been issued to all directors of the New Bank of America and was, as we'd heard it would be, highly critical of Security Pacific's management. This made us look terrible. Discarding the conclusions of the special study committee, the OCC apportioned blame like a pamphleteer plastering windshields with leaflets. The report dripped with the inference of negligent management.

"I have read the report," Dick sighed. "It's nasty."

"Not only is it nasty; it's inaccurate as hell. And the regulators know that. Vaez ordered us to undertake an independent study and, as you know, the results of that report exonerated us of any negligence or wrongdoing. But the regulators have ignored that report precisely because it found no fault, and the regulators *want* fault. Don't you see what's going on here?"

"I know. But the fact that the OCC report exists at all is damaging. The new regulatory view is harsh, admittedly, but it is their view."

Now I was upset. "I really question the timing and convenience of this report, as well as the urgency attached to it." The report gave Rosenberg just the ammunition he needed to wheel me off to a corner and hang an *Out Of Order* sign around my neck.

"You know what they say: perception is the editor of reality."

"So I've learned. Dick, I think you see what's going on here. The regulators are rewriting Security Pacific's history to make us look like a bunch of cretins. I only ask that you personally review the results of the special committee."

I was not asking Rosenberg for the Lost City of Atlantis; I just wanted him to stand up and be counted. I wanted his psychological and emblematic support. I wanted him to stand by me and stand by Security Pacific. I wanted him to oppose the description of management set down in a report that had been sent out to Bank of America directors, because it was a damning indictment that totally ignored the results of the very study Vaez ordered us to commission.

Rosenberg said he was pleased that the independent study had been conducted and wanted to know more about it, but not right now. Out of the blue he volunteered that he had recently conversed with Joe Vaez. "The subject was your future management intentions in the New Bank of America. They need to be resolved."

"My future intentions?"

"I feel comfortable that if we can resolve your future intentions in this organization, a significant management issue will not become a major board issue at the June regulatory review."

"Dick, why would my future intentions become a major issue?"

"Specifically, it's the provision that you will succeed me after I retire."

"It's not a provision; it's a suggestion." Nowhere in the contract did it mandate that I, without my own and the board's concurrence, succeed Rosenberg.

"The regulators wish to clarify the agreement in such a way that it makes absolutely clear that you will not succeed me and have no legal recourse to challenge that in a court of law."

But that was not the point. I couldn't stand to hear Rosenberg toss responsibility for this into the lap of the regulators. I reminded him that succession had not been a condition of mine, but a generous incentive he had thrown in unsolicited. "Dick, I don't have a problem with modifying the agreement, but I have to say I don't like the spirit in which it has now become 'an issue.' It doesn't have to be this way; it doesn't have to be an issue. I honestly feel this matter is between you, me, and the board. And this decision is perhaps three years down the line. Why is it an issue now?"

"The regulators, largely, have made it an issue."

"Dick, you know I don't *want* it to be a major issue, and I wasn't aware it was a major issue. This is a red herring. I don't want *anything* to divide the board or cause superfluous embarrassment or conflict. I'd rather resign than see that happen. It's obvious to me that the regulators want a head to roll, and it's my head. I accepted accountability for the problems, but also for the resolution of the problems. And I want to do something important at this company. That's all I want."

"Yes, that's fair."

"Dick, I think it's right that you seek an unbiased opinion. Please review the independent study. I'm sure it will clear the air, and it will give you ammunition to stand up for me, because it's my intention to remain here. I want your belief, your support, and your *trust*."

Rosenberg made a gesture indicating disinterest. "I've already reached a conclusion on this entire matter."

"Which is?"

"We should probably modify your employment agreement."

"How so?"

"I think you should be free to leave at any time within one year."

Here it comes, I thought, the beginning of my *squeeze* out of the organization. He didn't give a shit about the facts; he wanted my expulsion and would use the regulators as a pretext.

This conversation put me in a painful and difficult position. Did the phrase "freedom to leave within one year" really mean *obligation to leave within a year?* I didn't know. I was determined to approach this as optimistically as possible. My goal and intent was to remain. I didn't want to abandon Security Pacific after this ordeal, this merger. Rosenberg wanted me out. While I should have said, *Fuck you—I'm outta here*, it was not my style to jump ship. But I'd been demoted from captain to deck hand and, frankly, had very little incentive to remain.

I told Dick I wanted to make this work. "Let me come back to the table in a week with some ideas."

"Well, all right."

For my own sanity I had to stake out fresh territory for myself, if necessary creating a position of import and opportunity. I began to conceive of a way to make my role at this company challenging and hopefully reassert a few decibels of Security Pacific's former voice in the process. I owed it our history and our employees.

On Monday, May 18—and with a child's excitement—I approached Rosenberg with my plan. And with more naïveté than realism, I expected him to jump at the idea. Incredibly, I never was given a chance to get it out of my mouth.

Rosenberg immediately seized the upper hand. "Bob, I think the regulators would frown on you being in a more responsible position, or even being in management here for any length of time."

Bullshit, I thought. "Dick, I know the regulators don't want me to run a multinational corporation, but they never said I couldn't have a meaningful job at Bank of America."

"I know. But their thinking is that you are, in spite of the contract, my most likely successor based on who you are and your long career in banking. And the regulators appear to be very uncomfortable with the fact that you are even around."

Hungry for the truth, I pinned him down. "You want me to resign?"

"The regulators want it. They're pushing me hard. What can I do?"

I felt Rosenberg had personal and political reasons to want me out, and I distrusted his use of the regulators as the excuse. *Pitiful*, I thought. *This man's got no guts.*

"The regulators want it, Dick, but you don't want it?"

He would not be pinned. "Bob, you'll be happy to know I did review the special committee's report and it is impressive. It absolves everyone at Security Pacific of negligence, wrongdoing, everything. And I even received phone calls from former Security Pacific directors who clarified the difficulties Richard Flamson had with the regulators. He clearly set into motion some animosity. I think I understand what's going on here. You should be proud of what you've done for your shareholders. You negotiated a hell of a deal, you held it together, and you've taken a lot of flack in the process."

The meeting had taken a grim turn.

"Bob, I respect your willingness and desire to stay with the new organization until the dust has settled, but the bulk of that work has been accomplished. Layoffs have been set into motion and your people have adapted nicely. There isn't one guy in a hundred who would have done what you did. You ought to be proud."

I appreciated the kind epitaph, but Rosenberg need not have sugar-coated it; I could have respected Rosenberg more had he slapped me on the knee, leaned closer and put it like this: "Bob, there just ain't room at the top for both of us. I've gotten what I wanted out of you—deal's done, shareholders are overjoyed. You are threatening to my ability to run this company. There's nothing for you to do here, because I do everything myself. Mike Rossi hates your guts, and Lew Coleman trembles at the sight of you because he has deluded himself into believing he is going to run this company after I retire. In light of those harsh truths, you ought to resign. Besides, Bob, you won't physically be able to stand what I'm going to do to your beloved subsidiaries in Security Pacific. It will be like watching your children raped and hacked to pieces in a Nicaraguan village."

I capitulated. "All right, I'll leave within a year, as we agreed. What's the next step?"

"With the revised agreement the regulators will not be tough on us in the June board meeting. I've confirmed this."

What he was telling me was that the regulators agreed not to be tough on the board so long as I withdrew my interest in the CEO position and agreed to leave within a year.

"I've agreed. You have my word."

"Let's convert that to a formal agreement. I want to complete the revisions before the May board meeting if possible and to review it with the executive compensation committee."

Before the May board meeting, I pondered. It was May 18. I had to laugh. "All right. If I'm not to stay, anytime within a year is all right. Just modify the agreement accordingly."

"That's right," Dick said. "And with the revised agreement, the regulators won't question the parachute."

This was ridiculous. The regulators had no legal basis to question, let alone rescind, the parachute, which was contingent upon the closure of the deal. I could have strolled out of the office on April 23 and still received a parachute. But the notion it had been discussed behind my back made me irate.

Rosenberg: harsh words, strung together with a smile. Always friendly, always congenial, every courtesy extended. He shakes your hand. He leans back far in his chair, engaged and at ease. He slams words together in a stutter of conviction. I tried to imagine him hiding behind a potted plant. Impossible. He was like a phantom; ephemeral, fleeting, depthless, unreadable. Vacant mask in a fine tweed suit. He doesn't want to *know* you, he wants to get the mission accomplished. His dark side was made manifest only by the absence of any light side.

Lightheaded with disappointment, I stood up and locked my eyes on the door.

"Bob, I want to assure you—and I've confirmed this with Vaez—that you are okay in the banking industry. Just steer clear of multinationals. Regionals are fine. And Vaez said that his people in Washington said you're fine."

"This is not right, and it's not fair, but I guess this is life at the top of a major company."

"You're right," Rosenberg said. "The top guy always takes the fall."

I returned to my office and memorialized the discussion in a memo. At the bottom of the note I added in parenthesis: *Real feelings of Richard Rosenberg never expressed. Wants problem out of the way.*

▼

On Wednesday, May 20, Mike Halloran and I met.

Halloran showed me drafts of the letters. "The agreement provides for a September 1 departure date."

"September, of this year?"

"September 1992."

September 1? Now they wanted to Fed-Ex me out of the building.

Not only had he restructured my employment contract, but he had provided for a fixed departure date. Maybe in the recesses of my mind, I feared this could be the outcome—but I never, never believed it could happen so quickly.

The soothing tenor of Halloran's voice made it sound like we had planned for this all along.

"Mike," I said, "a September 1 departure is not in line with my discussion with Dick." I almost had to laugh at how delicately we talked to one another. This was the same man who called me at midnight to relay his exhilaration at how well our presentation of the ERISA issue to the Federal Reserve had gone. "Dick and I set no date. We talked about a revised option for me to leave within one year."

"Right, right. As I understand it, I believe the regulators suggested that date."

What crap. The regulators were the excuse, the OCC report was the excuse, my CEO provision was the excuse, Joe Vaez was the excuse. I knew Joe Vaez was in no position to stipulate dates for my departure. It began to smack of a conspiracy, with each side blaming the other and Rosenberg playing both sides of the street like an underemployed hooker looking to drum up business. This petty and pitiful executive soap opera had now turned into *The Gang That Couldn't Shoot Straight.*

I told Halloran not to do me any more favors until I'd spoken to Rosenberg.

I returned to my office, thought for a moment, and dialed his number. Things being what they were, I was surprised he even took my call.

"Bob, I can't talk for long; I'm just about to meet with Joe Vaez."

"I'll make this fast. You know as well as I do that a fixed date for my departure was not our understanding. The point of contention was me becoming CEO, and that's fine. I may leave before the year's out or I may not, but I have a contractual right to employment through April 1993. Dick, you're aware of all this. Now what the hell's going on? Why was the date fixed and moved forward without even talking to me?"

"Sorry, Bob. It's what Joe Vaez wants."

Oh brother, I thought, *here we go again*. "Why? What is Joe's reasoning?"

"In case I die."

"What?" *Say again?*

"In case I *die*." He was completely serious. "If I should perish, you'd automatically become CEO."

I laughed out loud. "That makes no sense. Dick, if you perish, the board will decide who will become the CEO. And as for Vaez, Vaez can voice his objections at that time."

"Joe feels that you're being well compensated, with gross-ups and what not. You'll do fine."

I replayed in my mind what he'd just said. "Dick, I fail to see what my gross-ups have to do with the subject at hand. What on earth does my compensation have to do with fixing a resignation date for me?"

"You know regulators; they don't make much money."

"Dick, regulators don't make as much money as we do because regulators don't run giant corporations, and I'm beginning to see why."

"Joe feels—"

"Dick, this is wrong. I'm surprised at you. This is embarrassing. This is *feeble*."

"Well, Joe just arrived; let me discuss it with him again." Rosenberg popped off the line with a precipitous click.

▼

The next day I met with Rosenberg and after a brief discussion we concluded that I would leave on October 1. Apparently, Vaez had agreed to this one-month concession in his meeting with Rosenberg the prior day.

I believe my credibility had suffered severely in Rosenberg's eyes as he grew more familiar with the state of our credit. The process whereby Bank of America recalibrated our loan portfolio by their rigorous methodology revealed that our classifications were worse than we thought they were. They realized they would be paying more than they'd intended and, in their minds, the transaction had become less a merger than an acquisition.

▼

On Thursday, May 28, Nick Binkley stopped by my office to show me a late-breaking analysis of the merger. A name from the recent past appeared on the front page. "George Salem, Trombone of Despair, has anted up with his tardy opinion of the merger."

"I can't wait," I said.

I started to read: "Worsening loan problems are a threat to the bank's financial health. . . . There is a loan quality disease . . . a merger and cost-savings are not likely to provide an offset . . . " More gloom and doom. Perhaps remembering his last meeting with me, he wrote " . . . denial was a common behavior among California bankers and some economists when they were confronted with the poor economic data. . . . "

" . . . Security Pacific proved to be more trouble than BofA initially believed. We should emphasize, Security Pacific had one of the worst credit cultures of any major bank and thus was more vulnerable to the disappointing economy."

His final words: "Thus, our advice to BofA shareholders is to sell the stock before the coming rush."

I reread the last sentence aloud to Nick. "We've got to frame this gem. I have a feeling George is going to live to regret these words." And he did.

Agitated by the implications of Rosenberg's Star Chamber proceedings with Vaez concerning my status in the banking industry, I flew to San Francisco on Friday, June 5 to meet with Bob Parry, a former Security Pacific economist and now president of the San Francisco Fed. Anxiety caused me to walk twice my usual pace. It was hot and I broke out in a sweat. I was a block away from the Fed when I heard a familiar voice and felt a hand on my shoulder.

"Bob! I thought that was you!"

Damned if it wasn't Sam Zuckerman again. The *American Banker* journalist had an incredible knack for catching me at the worst possible time, always when my immediate future hung in the balance and I was in a mad dash to get somewhere with as little fanfare as possible. Here I was, in a mortal struggle for my very credibility, and he'd caught me again.

I whirled around. I was so locked up in my mind that it was jarring to have to communicate with anyone; I could feel that my eyes were flying like pinwheels.

"Congratulations on the merger."

"Oh, yeah, thanks, Sam."

"You must be pretty happy."

"Pretty happy." All I could think of was my not-yet-public resignation.

"How are things going at Bank of America?"

"Super. Stupendous." With a little too much gusto, I added, "You can't imagine what an adventure it's been."

"You get along well with Rosenberg, Newman, Coleman, and Rossi?"

"Newman is first-rate, a class act." I stammered for a compliment to pay Rosenberg that I honestly believed. "And Dick is no dummy."

Sensing I was in an unusual state, he probed and poked.

His face grew vital and pink with curiosity as he paid closer attention to my demeanor and shattered concentration. I watched his hands for a pad and pen—nothing, but I knew he was looking for a story. "Can you talk?"

"I wish I could, Sam."

"Will you grant me an interview when this thing is over?"

"Count on it!"

▼

I caught my breath in the lobby of the Federal Reserve and found my way up to Robert Parry's office. We shook hands and I sat down.

"Coffee?" Parry offered.

I shook my head and dove right in. I told Parry I'd decided to leave Bank of America by the end of the third quarter.

"What I want to follow up on is where I stand with the regulators."

"You mean have you been tagged?" Parry put it. "I don't think so. I spoke to my people as well as top level in Washington and their view is that you are viable; you're clean."

Whew, I thought. "Good."

"Neither the Fed in San Francisco nor Washington sees any reason why you shouldn't be acceptable in any banking position, with the possible exception of a major multi-national."

"I have no desire to run a multinational; I'm not even that interested in running a bank. But I need to know what the feeling is on the street."

Parry told me to relax. "I haven't heard anybody badmouth the merger, except for George Salem. Everybody knows it was the wise course of action. It took guts. You're well respected, you're well liked, and my sense is that most people understand the complications you ran into. You were the right man for the worst possible time."

▼

Over the next few weeks I met with other regulators. I felt these meetings allowed us to bury the hatchet. It did not appear I would be *red-tagged* from the industry, and that the success of the merger, in combination with the findings of the special study committee, effectively counterbalanced any doubts about my character that lingered as a result of Security Pacific's near disaster. I was free to work in banking—just not at the Bank of America.

▼

The June 23 board meeting had created within me enormous apprehension, because Rosenberg had used the threat that regulators would embarrass Security Pacific at the board meeting as leverage to pressure me to modify my agreement. Although I had done so, I was still nervous that the meeting might grow ugly with accusation.

This meeting had more participants than a game of Dungeons and Dragons on the Internet. Bob Parry was in attendance, as were Don Chapman, and OCC employees Vaez, Ken Muscat, Bill Redman, Jimmy Barton. Representing the FDIC was Mark Rappier. The entire board of directors was present. Rosenberg, Rossi, Coleman, Newman, Binkley, and Grundhofer were all there.

Parry praised the merger and reminded Bank of America that not so long ago they too had wrestled with asset problems.

I shivered as Vaez began to speak. I was sure he would take this opportunity to rip me to pieces and take us blow-by-blow through Security Pacific's final year. But I was surprised. Incredibly, Vaez came off sounding like the Avatar of Reconciliation.

"Security Pacific, sadly, had a rough year. But these problems happen. And we are all working as a team, for a greater purpose. Let us not dwell on the past; let us look to the bright future and prepare ourselves to meet the challenges ahead. Let us absorb the hardships and move onward and upward. Everyone in this room should feel proud of this corporation's high level of productive assets; you are keenly poised to take advantage of what we hope will soon be a recovering economy in a great state. Of immense importance is the effective assimilation of the combined management and boards." He addressed the board. "Your duty is to assure competent management, maintain appropriate plans, and implement appropriate policies. Be sure to monitor compliance control. Be aware, be diligent, use your independent judgment, be loyal to the bank's interest."

Vaez spilled lofty platitudes and familial pieties with the cozy demeanor of a father welcoming his only son home after a week away at camp. As the kinder, gentler Vaez wished us well and gazed convivially at Security Pacific management, I marveled at his duality.

▼

News of my resignation crossed the wires on June 24, and provoked a large number of faxes, telegrams, and letters that ran a continuum from angry and disappointed to laudatory and outright bizarre. People who cherished Security Pacific interpreted my departure as ineluctable evidence that Security Pacific had perished, not only in name and fact but in spirit.

One such letter read, "The news came to me as a shock, but I understand it. When I look back on the rigorous test of fire that you have gone through in the last two or three years, I am most grateful to you for what you have done to serve the interest of the stockholders."

"I admire you," began another. "Your decision was unselfishly realistic and very professional. Your shareholders should be grateful."

And how about this one, scrawled in capital letters:

"DEAR BOB: I HOPE TO GOD THAT YOU ARE NOT THINKING OF JOINING MY NEW BANK, WELLS FARGO. AFTER BEING TREATED LIKE A SECOND CLASS ASSHOLE AT SPNB AFTER A 29 YEAR RELATIONSHIP I WANT NO PART

OF YOU. I SHOULD HAVE CONFIDENCE WITH THE NEW BANK OF AMERICA WHEN YOU DON'T? WHAT A BUNCH OF HORSESHIT. I DO NOT WANT A REPLY BECAUSE IT WILL BE NO MORE THAN BUREACRATIC BULLSHIT."

I also received job offers and investment opportunities. One young entrepreneur invited me to contribute financing to a militia group, and to the production of a major motion picture tentatively titled *King Dick* which, he excitedly explained, "traces the combat actions of an Egyptian admiral's educated freed black slave who became a Republican Revolutionary leader in Haiti; the general who conquered Tripoli in the name of the United States and North Africa; a mate aboard an American privateer; the defender of Americans during the massacre at England's Dartmoor Prison; and the campaigner with Simon Bolivar's revolts for the United States of South America."

I also received an enormous and intricate wall chart from Visonary Enterprises outlining an "Integrated Space Plan" to launch bank branches into outer space sometime between A.D. 2010, when mankind would achieve "Bi-planetary Civilization" and A.D. 2030, when "Humanity Begins the Transition from a Terrestrial to a Solar Species." Hundreds or thousands of hours had gone into this effort and it could not possibly have been a joke. The author wanted me to fill in particular blanks on his chart, based on when I thought such an endeavor would be technologically feasible. It wasn't clear from the prospectus whether I was to be an investor, a consultant, or the first interstellar CEO.

▼

One year to the day after pounding out an exchange ratio with Richard Rosenberg, I stood before the combined board of directors. Monday, August 3 represented my final opportunity to address a board whose directors had any relationship with

Security Pacific; I wanted to say goodbye, but I also wanted to try to say something important.

I was warmly received, but everyone in the room knew why I was leaving, and that it had not been my hope or intention to do so.

"I would have preferred to remain here and finish my career with Bank of America, but it wasn't meant to be." I said I understood the reasons my departure was necessary. "I'm extremely proud of what we accomplished by the merger, and I'm happy I was a significant part of this great event. Directors of both companies should be very proud also. I feel that we've met our obligations to the Security Pacific shareholders during what was a very difficult period, not only for us but for banks in general. Security Pacific lasted for over one hundred years." As I spoke that last sentence, I paused in contemplation.

"I would like to thank you all, particularly the Security Pacific directors, for your trust, guidance, support, and confidence this past year. I want to assure you that the New Bank of America is and will be a great company. I have little doubt that the New Bank of America will be a leader in this next decade under the capable stewardship of Dick Rosenberg."

Reflecting on Security Pacific in the latter half of the 1980s, I added, "One bit of advice: don't get arrogant. This corporation is a success and most likely will be a success. But it's easy to begin to think, *Bank of America knows it all*. It's easy to reach for the stars. Just remember your customers. Treat each and every one of them like gold. Make sure the system works to serve their needs, in good times and bad. And be sure they all know how important they are to you.

"Lastly, whatever you do, for god's sake don't allow the bureaucracy of Bank of America to overwhelm the independent spirit of its employees. I feel this is so important. In my experience, people need to make decisions and be active participants in the business where they work and, when you grace them with that trust, respect, and autonomy, they will leap to the challenge and take responsibility for what they do."

My departure was the end of an emotional journey. The past decade, in particular, had screamed by, steeped in drama. I planned to take some time off.

▼

Our merger—like those that followed—occupies a gray area in business, evoking strong opinions, defenders and critics, and provokes emotions ranging from disappointment and disgust to gratitude and euphoria.

While I received my fair share of praise, it was a Pyrrhic victory. Unless you were a shareholder, there was really nothing to celebrate.

As bizarre as it sounds for me to say: perhaps Security Pacific served a greater purpose by dwindling into myth—one of the last of a breed of banks—than by succeeding as "just another bank." Security Pacific made its mark in this peculiar way. Like Ernest Shackleton's quest to reach the South Pole, it ended in failure, but spectacular failure.

Security Pacific wasn't a flawless operation. Like the people who ran it, it was ambitious, quirky, prideful, recalcitrant, and sometimes spellbound by its own potential. Among its staff were supernovas, shooting stars, sputtering comets, and black holes. The corporation was structurally complex and diversified. Our reach exceeded our grasp. Leadership valued growth, reputation, and innovation more than stability. Employees valued sovereignty, independence, autonomy, and the right to question, argue, say no or say yes. We thought long-term when sometimes it was more prudent to think short-term. Too often we were focused on the dream instead of the numbers. Strategy was propelled by vision and legacy as well as the bottom line, and in this respect Security Pacific was the last of a breed. For Sartori, for Flamson, for me— and everyone else involved—it wasn't *enough* just to take deposits and make loans. There had to be something more.

Epilogue:
Anatomy of a Merger

What did this mega-merger mean to shareholders on both sides of the table? What were the financial ramifications of this momentous transaction? What, in fact, had Bank of America purchased?

An analysis of the deal revealed that numbers had changed dramatically in the months after the agreement was signed. Methodologies had been corroborated and revised. The loan portfolio had been recalibrated. Regulatory fees had ballooned. Reserves had been bolstered and capital had been chewed up.

What we were left with now were the nuts and bolts, the engine specifications, the metal beneath the hood. A comparison of our key balance sheet numbers, between 1989 and the closing, not only told the story of Security Pacific's wild roller coast ride to incapacitation, but were the most honest representation of what Bank of America really ended up paying for Security Pacific. These sobering statistics illustrated, as no narrative could, the escalating drama of what had occurred at Security Pacific.

In 1989 we put $547 million into reserves. In 1990 we put $1.166 billion. In 1991 we put in $2.617 billion. In the first four months of 1992 alone we put $1.368 billion into reserves. This adds up to approximately $5 billion—the worst-case scenario number we'd imagined could potentially be the impact of FIRREA on our real estate portfolio. What sounded inconceivable at the time was now reality. Every penny of the nightmare had come true.

Look at the accelerating cost of regulatory and FDIC fees during the same three-year period: 1989: $39 million. 1990: $63 million. 1991: $112 million.

Expenses related to the management of OREO, or real estate that we had assumed ownership of following the default of borrowers. This number is important because it illustrates the legal and administrative costs associated with the write-off of real estate. 1989: $40 million. 1990: $119 million. 1991: $251 million. First four months of 1992: $295 million.

These were dramatic numbers. When I looked at them, I could hardly believe them myself.

Nonperforming loans don't collect interest. We kept track of the interest *not* accumulated by our troubled loans under the heading of *Interest Foregone*. 1989: $169 million. 1990: $236 million. 1991: $300 million.

Those factors—reserves, expenses related to managing OREO, costs of regulatory supervision, and foregone interest on nonperforming loans—directly impacted earnings, or net profit before tax: 1989: $1.165 billion. 1990: $287 million. In 1991 we reported a pre-tax *loss* of $1.92 billion. In the first four months of 1992 we lost another $1.43 billion, pre-tax.

On an after-tax basis in 1989 we made $740 million in earnings. 1990: $161 million. In 1991 we *lost* $775 million. In 1992 we *lost* $1.45 billion.

Pre-tax, pre-reserve cash flow. In 1989 we had a pre-tax, pre-reserve cash flow of about $1.70 billion. In 1990 that number was $1.50 billion and in 1991 it was $1.53 billion. This number is so critical because it revealed the continued strength of our retail business. This was our earnings stream, and in spite of everything it had remained vibrant, vigorous, and steady.

Asset quality. Classified and criticized assets (loans classified as especially mentioned, substandard, doubtful, and loss) for 1989 were $7.70 billion, or 12% of our total credit portfolio. 1990: $12.40 billion, or 19%. 1991: $16.40 billion, or *28%* of our portfolio.

Non-performing assets, including nonperforming loans and OREO, had proliferated into exponential eyesores. 1989: $1.99 billion. 1990: $2.79 billion. 1991: $4.38 billion at year-end 1991. As a percentage of our loans outstanding, our non-performing loans and OREO represented 7.5% of our port-folio—that is to say, 7.5% of our loans were not earning a nickel of interest. A regulatory rule of thumb stated that any bank whose nonperformers exceeded 10% of its total portfo-lio was dead, which relegated us firmly on life support.

Credit losses. In 1989 Security Pacific wrote off $658 mil-lion in loans, or 0.87%—slightly over what is considered normal. In 1990 that number escalated to $1.10 billion, or 1.36%. 1991: $1.58 billion or 2.32%.

Stock price. The highest stock price Security Pacific ever had was $54 1/2, achieved in 1989. By the end of 1990, it was $20 5/8. By the fourth quarter of 1990, it had dropped to as low as $17 3/4. In 1991, it opened the year at $17 5/8 and surged to $29 7/8 following the announcement of our inten-tion to merge. Had there been no merger, I feel there was no question it would have slid to the $4 range.

Book value is the net equity of a company divided by the number of shares. Our book value in 1989 was $35.5. At the end of 1990 it was $32.75. At the end of 1991 it was $24.73.

Finally, one of the most dramatic statistics: Our capital at the end of 1989 was $4.64 billion. At the end of 1990 it was $4.71 billion. By the end of 1991 it had declined to $3.47 bil-lion. And at the time the deal was closed, our capital had dwindled to $1.60 billion.

▼

These numbers told an incredible story—these were the clos-ing pages in the autobiography of our bank. What they said about the past few years of Security Pacific was self-evident, but what was their pertinence to the merger? Did they reflect the corporation that Rosenberg wanted to buy, thought he was getting, and strove to absorb? At the close of the deal—April 22, 1992—Bank of America stock was $47 per share. Because Security Pacific received 0.88 share of Bank of America stock for each share of Security Pacific, we received 111.6 million shares of Bank of America stock. This meant that the deal value was $5.24 billion. That is how much Bank of America paid Security Pacific for the consolidation. In exchange for that amount, they received $1.61 billion in capital; this means they paid 325% of capital, or 3.25 X our book value, for Security Pacific.

This is not to say that the merger was not a good deal; it *was* a good deal. It created a powerful institution, a world-class bank. Security Pacific needed the deal and its shareholders benefited enormously. Bank of America got what it wanted, and some trouble it hadn't expected. But these final numbers, had they been known in August 1991, would have represented a potentially insurmountable psychological obstacle. Rosenberg, a shrewd and intelligent businessman, probably would not have signed on the dotted line.

But Security Pacific had paid a price as well—not in dollars, but in terms of the things that mattered to me personally, and mattered to everyone who loved Security Pacific or had a stake in its name, independence, and history.

Where Are They Now?

Bank of America. Under the capable leadership of David Coulter, Bank of America turned its attention to customer service and continues its legacy of stable, name-brand banking. Bank of America agreed to merge with Nations Bank in April 1998. In October of that same year, David Coulter became a casualty of that merger.

Nick Binkley. Nick resigned from Bank of America under the terms of his employment contract in May 1993 to form an investment and venture capital firm. He formed a band, and recorded a CD called "Pin Stripe Brain."

Kathy Burke. Kathy Burke brought her enormous professionalism and skill to the New Bank of America as their vice chairperson of human resources. She outlasted every other Security Pacific senior executive who survived the transition. She recently announced her resignation as part of the Bank of America–Nations Bank merger.

Don Chapman. Chapman reportedly continued to explore a theory that our ERISA violations were the result of a brilliantly orchestrated scheme to increase the amount of our own bonuses. Chapman's interest lasted several years but went nowhere.

Lew Coleman. Considered a shoo-in to succeed Rosenberg, he was mysteriously passed over by the board of directors in favor of David Coulter. Coleman is now the CEO and managing partner at Montgomery Securities, a company acquired by Nations Bank in 1997—a bank that subsequently agreed to merge with the Bank of America in April 1998.

Bob Corteway. Bob retired following the merger but remains active on several boards, including that of Sanwa Bank.

Maurice DeWolff. Maurice continued to practice law until he died in the mid 1990s.

Richard Flamson. Dick is survived by his wife, Arden, who remains active in community causes in Orange County.

Russ Freeman. Russ went to work at O'Melveny & Meyers for a short time and then retired to live in the northern San Diego area.

Jerry Grundhofer. Jerry resigned from Bank of America under his employment contract around the same time as Nick Binkley. He is now the chairman of the board and chief executive officer of Star Bank in Cincinnati, Ohio.

John Kooken. John Kooken retired from Security Pacific at the time of the merger and continues to serve on several boards.

David Lovejoy. Following his departure, David went to work for Frank Cahouet as vice chairman of Mellon Bank. Lovejoy was considered to be one of Cahouet's possible successors. On January 1, 1999, Frank Cahouet announced his retirement. Four days later, Lovejoy left Mellon.

George Moody. Following his retirement from Security Pacific prior to the merger, George settled down for some well-earned rest. Despite a number of ailments, he continues to play golf about three times a week with the elegance of a U.S. ambassador.

Frank Newman. After Bill Clinton took office, Newman was selected to work as Under Secretary of the U.S. Treasury. He later became the chairman of the board and chief executive officer of Bankers Trust.

Robert Parry. Bob Parry remains president of the San Francisco Federal Reserve.

Richard Rosenberg. Rosenberg retired in 1995. He currently serves on the Nations Bank board.

Mike Rossi. Retired from Bank of America in 1997, he lives near Carmel and works for a long-time real estate customer of Bank of America's.

George Salem. George retired in early 1998.

John Singleton. One day in 1997 our former human resources director Irv Margol, then an outplacement consultant, received a phone call from John Singleton. "You know, Irv, I think I could run Apple." "Pippin or Granny Smith?" Irv replied with impeccable wit.

Bob Smith. Your author has spent the years since his departure from the Bank of America with a company he formed with Don Crowley, aptly called Smith & Crowley, Inc. The company provides boutique investment banking and advisory services to small bank and financially-related firms primarily in California, with nominal success. In addition, he has ventured into new concepts in banking and finance without yet finding the right strategic and financially viable project. But he continues to search. To quench his strong interest in the financial events and the banking transitions of the

1980s and 1990s, he has also dedicated much of his time to researching this period and the specific environment and events that involved Security Pacific. Thanks to the writing skills of and his association with Mike Crowley (Don's son), the story can now be told so that others can understand and learn.

Donald Trump. Trump has been on a roller-coaster ride for the past decade. He approached financial ruin before effecting a miraculous recovery with new supermodels at his side.

Peter Ueberroth. Ueberroth currently runs an investment firm out of his Orange County office. During the summer of 1999, Bank of America Securities acted as the sole financial advisor and arranger to Pebble Beach Sports Group, LLC. The $820 million deal was headed by a group of investors including Clint Eastwood, Arnold Palmer, and Peter Ueberroth.

Joe Vaez. A little over a year after the merger closed, Vaez was made an executive vice president of the New Bank of America. He's still there.

Sam Zuckerman. Sam finally got his *American Banker* interview with me in the Spring of 1993. He left the *Banker* a year or two later and is now a reporter for the *San Francisco Chronicle*.

Index

A

B

S